Mind and Embodiment in Late Victorian Literature

Nineteenth-Century and Neo-Victorian Cultures

Series editors: Ruth Heholt and Joanne Ella Parsons

Recent books in the series

Domestic Architecture, Literature and the Sexual Imaginary in Europe, 1850–1930
Aina Martí-Balcells

Assessing Intelligence: The Bildungsroman and the Politics of Human Potential in England, 1860–1910
Sara Lyons

The Idler's Club: Humour and Mass Readership from Jerome K. Jerome to P. G. Wodehouse
Laura Fiss

Michael Field's Revisionary Poetics
Jill Ehnenn

Narrative, Affect and Victorian Sensation: Wilful Bodies
Tara MacDonald

The Provincial Fiction of Mitford, Gaskell and Eliot
Kevin A. Morrison

Women's Activism in the Transatlantic Consumers' Leagues, 1885–1920
Flore Janssen

Queer Books of Late-Victorian Print Culture
Frederick D. King

British Writers, Popular Literature and New Media Innovation, 1820–45
Alexis Easley

Philanthropy in Children's Periodicals, 1840–1930: The Charitable Child
Kristine Moruzi

Temporality and Progress in Victorian Literature
Ruth M. McAdams

Life Writing and the Nineteenth-Century Literary Market
Sean Grass

Literary Illusions: Performance Magic and Victorian Literature
Christopher Pittard

Mind and Embodiment in Late Victorian Literature
Marion Thain and Atti Viragh

http://www.edinburghuniversitypress.com/series-nineteenth-century-and-neo-victorian-cultures

Mind and Embodiment in Late Victorian Literature

Edited by Marion Thain and Atti Viragh

EDINBURGH
University Press

Edinburgh University Press is one of the leading university presses in the UK. We publish academic books and journals in our selected subject areas across the humanities and social sciences, combining cutting-edge scholarship with high editorial and production values to produce academic works of lasting importance. For more information visit our website: edinburghuniversitypress.com

Edinburgh University Press Ltd
13 Infirmary Street
Edinburgh EH1 1LT

First published in hardback by Edinburgh University Press 2025

Typeset in 11/13pt Sabon LT Pro
by Cheshire Typesetting Ltd, Cuddington, Cheshire, and
printed and bound by CPI Group (UK) Ltd,
Croydon, CR0 4YY

A CIP record for this book is available from the British Library

ISBN 978 1 3995 2127 7 (hardback)
ISBN 978 1 3995 2128 4 (paperback)
ISBN 978 1 3995 2129 1 (webready PDF)
ISBN 978 1 3995 2130 7 (epub)

Contents

Series Preface

Nineteenth-Century and Neo-Victorian Cultures
Series Editors: Ruth Heholt and Joanne Ella Parsons

This interdisciplinary series provides space for full and detailed scholarly discussions on nineteenth-century and Neo-Victorian cultures. Drawing on radical and cutting-edge research, volumes explore and challenge existing discourses, as well as providing an engaging reassessment of the time period. The series encourages debates about decolonising nineteenth-century cultures, histories, and scholarship, as well as raising questions about diversities. Encompassing art, literature, history, performance, theatre studies, film and TV studies, medical and the wider humanities, *Nineteenth Century and Neo-Victorian Cultures* is dedicated to publishing pioneering research that focuses on the Victorian era in its broadest and most diverse sense.

Notes on Contributors

David Sweeney Coombs is an Associate Professor in the Department of English at Clemson University, where he is Faculty Director of the Pathways in the Humanities and Social Sciences Initiative. He is the author of *Reading with the Senses in Victorian Literature and Science* (2019), which traces the history of perceptual theories of reading in nineteenth-century science, aesthetics, and literature. He is currently working on a conceptual history of crisis as it evolves in the nineteenth-century historical novel after Walter Scott.

Bénédicte Coste is Professor of Victorian Studies at the Université de Bourgogne, France. She mainly works on Aestheticist writers. With Catherine Delyfer and Christine Reynier, she co-edited the collection of essays *Reconnecting Aestheticism and Modernism* (2016). Her latest monograph, *Walter Pater, du portrait littéraire à l'étude de cas* was published in 2022. She is currently working with Laurel Brake on a biography of Walter and Clara Pater.

Pamela K. Gilbert is Albert Brick Professor at the University of Florida. She is the author and editor of several books on Victorian literature, the body and the history of medicine and science. Her most recent book, *Victorian Skin: Surface, Self, History*, focuses on the history of the body, medicine and realism in the nineteenth century, with special attention to skin and surface. Her most recent edited collection is *Nineteenth-Century Literature in Transition: The 1860s* (2024). She is currently editing a collection on nineteenth-century literature and science and working on a book on the history of psychology and emotion.

Rachel Kravetz is an independent scholar who studies nineteenth-century literature and the history of aesthetic thought. She has published articles on George Eliot and Thomas Hardy, and is working on a book about how Victorian writers look to the fine arts as they navigate what they see as the limitations of the empiricist and idealist philosophical traditions. She teaches at Bard's Microcolleges in New York City.

Amanda Paxton is Assistant Professor in the Department of English Literature at Trent University Durham. Her research focuses on Victorian literature and culture, with particular emphasis on religious discourse and sexuality, mathematics and aesthetics, and theories of language from the nineteenth century to the present. She is the author of the book *Willful Submission: Sado-Erotics and Heavenly Marriage in Victorian Religious Poetry* (2018), as well as essays on Elizabeth Siddal, Gerard Manley Hopkins, Samuel Taylor Coleridge, and J. Sheridan Le Fanu, among others. Her current project examines non-Euclidean geometries and representation in the nineteenth century.

Anne Stiles is Professor of English and Coordinator of Medical Humanities at Saint Louis University. She is the author of *Children's Literature and the Rise of "Mind Cure": Positive Thinking and Pseudo-Science at the* Fin de Siècle (2020) and *Popular Fiction and Brain Science in the Late Nineteenth Century* (2012). She has held long-term grants from the Institute for Research in the Humanities at the University of Wisconsin, Madison (AY 2016–2017); the Huntington Library (AY 2009–2010); and the American Academy of Arts and Sciences (AY 2006–2007).

Gregory Tate is a Senior Lecturer in Victorian literature at the University of St Andrews. He has published two monographs – *The Poet's Mind: The Psychology of Victorian Poetry* (2012) and *Nineteenth-Century Poetry and the Physical Sciences: Poetical Matter* (2020) – and has edited a volume of the poetry and prose of Arthur Hugh Clough (2020). He is currently working on "Victorian Literary Languages", a collaborative project on multilingualism in nineteenth-century literature, the first findings of which have been published in *19: Interdisciplinary Studies in the Long Nineteenth Century* (2025). He is also writing a monograph, *The Grammar of Style in Victorian Literature*, about the connections between Victorian prescriptive grammar and literary style.

Marion Thain is Professor of Culture and Technology at King's College London, and Executive Dean of the Faculty of Arts and Humanities. She is Chair-Director of the Digital Futures Institute at King's, where she founded the Centre for Attention Studies (attentionstudies.org). She publishes particularly on the relationship between culture and technology (considering 'technology' in the broadest sense). Further details can be found at https://www.marionthain.org/

Colton Valentine is Junior Fellow at the Harvard Society of Fellows. He works broadly on literary and book history in the long nineteenth century, with a focus on translation and queer studies. His first book project – *Between Languages: Queer Multilingualism in the British Belle Époque* – studies how late-Victorian queer authors read, wrote, and loved across multiple languages. His essays have recently appeared in *Representations*, *English Literary History*, *Modern Language Quarterly*, *Victorian Studies* and *The New Yorker*, and his critical translation, *Vernon Lee's Cosmopolitan Prose*, is forthcoming with MHRA.

Atti Viragh is Assistant Professor in the Department of English Language and Literature at Bilkent University. His work has appeared in such journals as *New Literary History*, *English Literary History* and *English Literature in Transition, 1880–1920*. His work sets forth a new account of the birth of phenomenology by tracing its origins to Victorian literature and thought.

Introduction: Mind, Body, Literature and Psychology in the Later Nineteenth Century

Marion Thain and Atti Viragh

Bridging the divide: an interconnected psychological landscape

Between 1850 and 1880, Rick Rylance observes, Victorian psychology was an 'open discourse . . . spaciously framed in its address to common issues', and with a wide audience including 'economists, imaginative writers, philosophers, clerics, literary critics'. It was an 'emergent, energetic discipline, filled with dispute and without settled lines of theory or protocols for investigation'. However, by the closing decades of the century, with the establishment of the first psychology laboratories by Wilhelm Wundt, G. Stanley Hall, and George Trumbull Ladd, it became a closed and professionalised discipline modelled on the natural sciences.[1] In Victorian studies, this narrative has supported an explosion of interest in the relationships between literature and psychology up to the late 1870s. At the same time, it has had the effect of cordoning off the seemingly 'modernist' innovations of the psychological developments of the 1890s, by such figures as William James, Sigmund Freud, and Henri Bergson, from their immediate predecessors.

Our collection aims to revise this narrative and reframe our understanding of the relations between psychology, literature, and critical thought in the later Victorian period (c. 1860 to the end of the century). The bifurcation of an interconnected discourse into two periods – one broadly open, the other closed to all but professionals – makes it difficult to understand the growth of psychol-

1 Rick Rylance, *Victorian Psychology and British Culture, 1850–1880* (Oxford: Oxford University Press, 2000), pp. 6–7.

ogy and its place in Victorian culture. The works of psychology appearing at the end of the century show a fundamental continuity with the intellectual questions and problems of their predecessors. Indeed, many of the basic models of the mind articulated during the period, such as the double aspect theory of consciousness, remain central even today, and it was from the research and theories of their immediate predecessors that psychologists at the end of the century and early twentieth century developed their concepts. For instance, Alexander Bain, George Henry Lewes and Shadworth Hodgson set forth early accounts of the 'stream of consciousness' that would be popularised by William James in his *The Principles of Psychology* (1890). Sigmund Freud's model of the unconscious had precedents not only in early nineteenth-century romantic philosophy and Eduard von Hartmann's *The Philosophy of the Unconscious*, but in William Carpenter's 'unconscious cerebration', the 'double consciousness' explored by Robert Macnish and Henry Holland, and the analysis of dreams by John Abercrombie, Macnish, and James Sully.[2] In addition, his model of thinking, based on inhibited motor discharge, was inherited from David Ferrier and Bain.[3] The latter's 1873 *Mind and Body: The Theories of Their Relation* developed a model of neural networks that anticipated twentieth-century theories of connectionism.[4] Central features of Henri Bergson's philosophical-psychological treatises in the 1890s – on the nature of memory, time consciousness, and the qualitative character of experience – had been explored by such figures as Victor Egger in France and Hodgson in Great Britain.[5] More crucially for the essays in this book, however, such continuities extended beyond particular theoretical concepts into the moral, social, aesthetic and metaphysical dimensions of psy-

[2] See, for example, Henri F. Ellenberger, *The Discovery of the Unconscious: The History and Evolution of Dynamic Psychiatry* (New York: Basic Books, 1970). Jenny Bourne Taylor and Sally Shuttleworth provide an excellent sample of texts (of this as well as other topics in Victorian psychology) in *Embodied Selves: An Anthology of Psychological Texts, 1830–1890* (Oxford: Clarendon Press, 1998).

[3] Malcolm Macmillan, 'Nineteenth-century inhibitory theories of thinking: Bain, Ferrier, Freud (and Phineas Gage)', *History of Psychology* 3.3 (2000): 187–217.

[4] See Alan L. Wilkes and Nicholas J. Wade, 'Bain on Neural Networks', *Brain and Cognition* 33.3 (1997): 295–305.

[5] For the former, see Riccardo Roni, *Victor Egger e Henri Bergson. Alle origini del flusso di coscienza* (Pisa: Edizioni ETS, 2016).

chological experience attached to them. At this level, continuities between early and late Victorian discourse on the mind are especially strong. In particular, critiques of the materialist reductionism of early psychophysiology were absorbed into the growth of the discipline and helped furnish a rationale for how literature could raise and respond to core questions about the mind.

These continuities reveal a unified epistemic turn to problems of mind and embodiment in the second half of the Victorian period. From around 1860 to the end of the century, literature can, in this way, be understood as an opening up of a new set of theoretical problems. Despite their considerable diversity and disagreement, models of mind appearing during these years tended to share certain broader features. They rejected the simplistic and mechanistic models of association inherited from David Hume. They recognised that acts of perception were far more complex – materially, socially and philosophically – than traditional empiricist accounts of sense experience could capture.[6] They debated the possibility of a scientific exploration of psychological experience from a first-person point of view, rather than third-person observation. They increasingly recognised that the 'data' of first-person experience cannot merely be tabulated like other natural phenomena, since they pose fundamental questions about the nature of the subject recording this data. They argued over whether it was possible to perceive one's own perception, thought or feeling, or whether such an act would be a contradiction in terms or require a separate act of the mind. They raised the question of whether one conscious experience could ever be repeated in the same form – and, equally important, whether another person's experience could be empathetically shared, or only imagined.

In addition, works of psychology seeking the imprimatur of 'science' carried a special theoretical burden at a time when prevalent accounts of science, as Lorraine Daston notes, tended to be reductionist and mechanistic.[7] Psychologists of the later Victorian period faced the challenge of setting forth empirically-grounded accounts of experience that avoided not only idealism and the armchair philosophy of the earlier nineteenth century, but also the reductive materialism that had characterised mid-century British

[6] See David Sweeney Coombs, *Reading with the Senses in Victorian Literature and Science* (Charlottesville: University of Virginia Press, 2019).

[7] Lorraine J. Daston, 'British Responses to Psycho-Physiology, 1860–1900', *Isis* 69.2 (1978): 192–208.

scientific thought. Thus, in a book bearing the title of *The Physical Basis of Mind*, Lewes actively opposes narrow physicalism. As L.S. Hearnshaw observes, 'the main burden of his physiological psychology was to *dispute* the adequacy of the purely mechanistic view of the reflexes . . . he produced experimental evidence to disprove the idea of fixed reflex pathways . . . and protested against the correlation of mind and brain' (emphasis added).[8] This burden was characteristic of the challenges facing the new discourse. Psychologists would have to explore and describe the physical basis of mental phenomena without suggesting that their moral, social, developmental and metaphysical features could be resolved into anatomy and physiology. Victorian psychology, even as it became more professionalised and as it advanced in its models and findings, still remained an interdisciplinary field through to the end of the nineteenth century.

With the founding of the journals *Mind* in 1876 and *Brain* in 1878, the polyglot and interdisciplinary nature of this discourse became especially visible. In the pages of these journals – together with their counterparts abroad such as *Revue philosophique de la France et de l'étranger* – a transnational debate emerged about the fundamental nature of psychology, with leading figures including Bain, Herbert Spencer, G.F. Stout, James Sully and James Ward in England; John Dewey, G. Stanley Hall, George Trumbull Ladd and William James in the United States; Alfred Binet, Henri Bergson, Pierre Janet, Théodule Ribot and Hippolyte Taine in France; and Franz Brentano, Hermann von Helmholtz, Carl Stumpf and Wilhelm Wundt in Germany. These thinkers were reading and responding to one another's ideas, and the question of the relation between embodiment and cognition was a key axis on which these debates turned.

Our book focuses on this question rather than on the adjacent medical discourse of psychopathology (including the birth of psychiatry and psychoanalysis, whose emergence in the nineteenth century is famously documented by Michel Foucault).[9] It is our intention to return to a popular discourse on psychology conceived broadly as a study of the nature of the mind rather than a method

[8] L.S. Hearnshaw, *A Short History of British Psychology, 1840–1940* (London: Methuen, 1964), p. 49.

[9] See Michel Foucault, *Madness and Civilization: A History of Insanity in the Age of Reason*, trans. Richard Howard (London: Routledge, 2001).

of identifying, classifying and treating disorders. The great challenge of understanding how individual consciousness functions in a physical body – sensing, perceiving, remembering, thinking, understanding – tested the limits of scientific observation and verification. Not at all limited to specialists, this concern was one of the most significant theoretical problems of the Victorian era, and it increased in both urgency and popularity across the century. Bain had led the way in introducing the latest understanding of physiology into the domain of psychology. His 1855 *The Senses and the Intellect* was seen as a vanguard book for modern psychology because of its up-to-date use of the latest research in physiology.[10] The end of the 1850s and the decade of the 1860s produced a wave of British psychological works that embraced organic and physicalist explanations of mental processes. Examples include Spencer's *The Principles of Psychology* (1855), Bain's *The Emotions and the Will* (1859), Lewes's *The Physiology of Common Life* (1859), Thomas Laycock's *Mind and Brain* (1860) and Henry Maudsley's *The Physiology and Pathology of Mind* (1867). In other countries, too, this materialist direction emerged in the 1860s and 1870s: in Germany, Gustav Fechner's *Elemente der Psychophysik* (1860); in France, Pierre-Maurice Mervoyer's *Étude sur l'association des idées* (1864), Théodule Ribot's *La Psychologie anglaise contemporaine: l'école expérimentale* (1870) and Hippolyte Taine's *De L'Intelligence* (1870). Given renewed vigour by the evolutionary theory of Charles Darwin and the early neuronal theories of Santiago Ramón y Cajal, Carlo Golgi and Heinrich Waldeyer-Hartz in the 1880s, these early approaches to mental life form the backstory to today's studies in embodied cognition, neurology, evolutionary psychology and psychophysiology.

It would be wrong to claim, however, that physiological approaches came to dominate psychology, rather than becoming one side of a generative, ongoing debate. Critiques of the limitations of materialist reductionism for an understanding of consciousness emerged almost immediately and from all sides – literary, psychological, philosophical, theological. Even in the materialist moment of the mid-1860s, John Grote's *Exploratio Philosophica*, J.H. Stirling's *The Secret of Hegel*, Paul Janet's *The Materialism of the Present Day. A Critique of Dr. Büchner's System*, Friedrich Albert Lange's *History of Materialism* (the latter

[10] See Rylance, *Victorian Psychology and British Culture*, p. 174.

two soon appearing in English translation), not to mention the founding of the American *Journal of Speculative Philosophy* and new studies and edited collections of Sir William Hamilton's philosophy, all attest to a larger discourse on the mind which took a critical approach to psychology's claim to be a natural science. These discourses expanded in the following decades; resistance to naturalism informs Gestalt psychology, phenomenology, process philosophy, and psychoanalysis at the turn of the century. These developments emerged from within Victorian psychology rather than in response to it. The critique of physical and biological reductionism is continuous with the field of psychology from its emergence in the nineteenth century to recent developments in attachment theory, social psychology, narrative psychology and self and identity psychology.

We contend, therefore, that the triumphal march-of-science narrative, in which only conservative or reactionary theologians criticised the attempt to reduce psychology to a natural science (fearing its implications for the soul), obscures the true complexity of this discourse. In what is otherwise the most comprehensive historical treatment of British psychology in Victorian studies, Rylance claims that 'virtually all nineteenth-century commentators agree [that] just two schools of thought dominated debate' in philosophy of mind: faculty psychology and associationism. This simplifies a discursive field that witnessed the rise of the back-to-Kant movement, neo-Hegelianism, early pragmatism, phenomenology, the revival of logic, neo-scholasticism and speculative metaphysics – and culminated in the founding of *Mind*, the first philosophy journal in England. These discourses centred, in various ways, on the nature of the mind and of experience, and a glance at the early volumes of *Mind* dispels the notion that the main debates focused on faculty psychology and associationism. In the first eight numbers, for instance, we find articles on comparative psychology, physiological psychology, evolution, logic, sensation, ethics, geometrical axioms, Schopenhauer, introspection, the unconscious, aesthetics, childhood development, and many articles about the scientific standing of psychology.[11] The

[11] For discussion of the founding and intellectual concerns of *Mind* in its early years, see Kathleen McCormack, 'Journalists at George Eliot's Priory: Busy Editors, Writing Women, and the Founding of "Mind"', *Victorian Periodicals Review* 46.4 (2013): 539–53; Thomas W. Staley, 'The Journal Mind in Its

true breadth and sophistication of the period's inquiry into the most fundamental questions of psychology has yet to be charted in Victorian scholarship.

Unfortunately, this association of resistance to naturalism in psychology with religious or political conservatism has influenced discussions of psychology in Victorian studies.[12] It becomes difficult to understand the theoretical problems explored within fiction, poetry and criticism – including the aesthetic, ethical, existential and metaphysical debates of the period – when any approach but natural science is labelled conservative or retrograde. Readers familiar with the notion of the social construction of identity might be surprised at this insistent association between biological reductionism and progressivism. New concepts in psychology and philosophy of mind cannot be reduced to the cultural politics of their originators. Doing so diminishes our understanding of the history of psychology and the intellectual culture out of which this discipline arose.

Criticism of biological and physical reductionism emerged from every side of intellectual life throughout the period, just as the question of the relationship between matter and consciousness continues to be debated today. It was often remarked that the reduction of consciousness to biological processes was as an a priori step as arbitrary as its reduction by earlier German idealists to transcendental categories of understanding (by Kant) or to shapes of

Early Years, 1876–1920: An Introduction', *Journal of the History of Ideas* 70.2 (2009): 259–63; Atti Viragh, 'The Grammar of Instress: Gerard Manley Hopkins and the Victorian Philosophers of Mind', *New Literary History* 51.3 (2020): 501–22.

[12] See, for example, Benjamin Morgan, *The Outward Mind: Materialist Aesthetics in Victorian Science and Literature* (Chicago: University of Chicago Press, 2017). As Rylance writes in *Victorian Psychology*, 'The language of psychological polemic is soaked in indignation at the purported science's obtrusive meddling and desecration. In recoil, many fell back on the familiar phrases and concepts of the faculty psychology. Educated people asked themselves what purchase the language of psychophysiology could have on interior mental events. What rights did it have when many felt it a distorting invasion, and what obligations did it have to protect the sanctity of individual feelings and beliefs? . . . it could be considered an impertinence at best; at worst, it was a gross falsification, and the outraged, somewhat blimpish tone of some of the responses . . . should be read in this light. One must remember that even liberal opinion was confronting the scientific way of looking at the mind pretty much for the first time . . . even on the progressive, pro-science, "physicalist" side there were anxieties' (43).

consciousness (by Hegel). Such critiques gain momentum through the late Victorian period. 'What does the volume, the absolute and specific weight, the abundance of wrinkles and fat content of a human brain contribute to the development of the thoughts in it?' Wilhelm Dilthey asked.[13] 'It is all to no purpose showing an organ for each faculty and a nerve vibrating for each idea', Gerard Manley Hopkins wrote.[14] The reduction of the mind to another organ of the body, in which the act of thinking was comparable to a 'secretion' like that of the liver, was unpersuasive to many Victorians, then as today.[15] By no means was the critique purely theological, and the arguments of theologians were often the same as those of secular writers, as they shared an array of arguments drawn from the history of philosophy. Dilthey and Hopkins articulate the same logical problem irrespective of their backgrounds or beliefs. It is therefore also a mistake to assume, because of the liberal politics of Bain, John Stuart Mill, and Spencer, that the battle between reductionist and non-reductionist accounts of the mind was one between liberals and conservatives; there is nothing inherently progressive about believing that mental life can be reduced to physical processes. This epistemological and phenomenological question was debated independently of political concerns in the journals of philosophy and psychology, then as now.

In these debates, the question of the relations between mind and body stands out as unquestionably one of the dominant problems of the Victorian period. Britain was a leading site for this philosophical and scientific debate because the decline of German idealism and the rise of positivism placed the British empiricist tradition in the forefront. This tradition, however, was now confronted with a range of questions which it had not had to deal with, including questions about the fundamental nature of memory, thought,

[13] Wilhelm Dilthey, in Guy van Kerckhoven and Hans-Ulrich Lessing (eds), *Psychologie als Erfahrungswissenschaft: Manuskripte zur Genese der deskriptiven Psychologie (ca. 1860–1895)*: vol. 22, *Gesammelte Schriften* (Göttingen: Vandenhoeck & Ruprecht, 2005), 2:140.

[14] Gerard Manley Hopkins, in Lesley Higgins, ed., *The Collected Works of Gerard Manley Hopkins*: vol. 4, *Oxford Essays and Notes* (Oxford: Oxford University Press, 2006), p. 288.

[15] The notorious statement by Carl Vogt, as translated in Henry Lonsdale, ed., *The Anatomical Memoirs of John Goodsir*, vol. 1 (Edinburgh: Adam and Charles Black, 1868), p. 290: 'As the kidney secretes urine, and the liver bile, in like manner the brain produces thoughts, determinations, and feelings'.

empathy, perception, emotion and self-experience. Indeed, as the contributions in this book demonstrate, the more closely one examined any particular concept in traditional accounts of the mind – from taste to sympathy, from digestion to belief, from movement to observation – the more one finds a complexity and wealth of features and problems demanding articulation. The question of the fundamental nature of the mind and its relationship to the body is a central problem haunting these efforts at explanation of particular facets of individual experience.

Narrative and organisation of the book

The contributions in this volume show the range of literary responses to this overarching problematic in Victorian psychology. Alice Meynell and George Gissing, for example, come upon the problem of mind and embodiment by examining the nature of reading and writing as cognitive acts. Both find a much larger bodily participation in the supposedly abstract process of intellectual cogitation than had previously been acknowledged, creating a feedback loop in which bodily processes can affect the nature of the text, its writing and its incorporation by a reader. Gerard Manley Hopkins and Walter Pater tackle philosophical questions about experience and subjectivity that would be set forward systematically only in the 1890s and early 1900s. Pater recognises that the unexplored role of memory in the formation and collection of sense-experience troubles notions of the self that were derived from psychophysiology, to which his work otherwise seems amenable. Hopkins's exploration of the nature of sense experience uncovers a similar problem of continuity, this time in the very acts of taste and hearing. While Oscar Wilde may have found the theory of the neuron cell conducive to a materialist approach to the mind (as one would expect), Marie Corelli recruits the neuron cell in support of a *rejection* of materialism – the communication between neuron cells figuring for larger, intersubjective and even spiritual connections between minds.

Taken together, these chapters reveal that sophisticated literary responses to new psychological theories were not peripheral components of Victorian literature. On the contrary, Victorian literature was transformed by a wholly new set of questions, challenges, and problems. The responses offered by these writers show British literature engaged in a wider, transnational and transdisciplinary discourse about science and subjectivity. We organise the chapters in this book roughly in relation to a chronology of the psychological concepts with which they engage (rather than in relation to the publication dates of the key literary texts explored) to bring out the range of thinking reflected in, and advanced by, a group of literary authors who were all more or less contemporaneous. The first three chapters (on George Gissing, Thomas Hardy and Alice Meynell) are shown engaging broadly with the conceptualisations of psychology anchored in the earlier group of thinkers outlined above: Bain, Spencer, Lewes and contemporaries.

Colton Valentine takes the digestive system as the locus of debates around mind and body in his analysis of George Gissing's interrelationship of nutrition and cognition. Bringing a new twist to food studies, Valentine does not treat food as a material commodity, but instead turns attention to the cognitive effects of eating in Gissing's work. In so doing, he demonstrates literature's place alongside dietary and medical texts in the archive of late-Victorian psychology. Establishing the concept of 'brainworking' through an interdisciplinary field of texts from science, health and literature, and particularly the work of Lewes, the chapter goes on to place these models in dialogue with the journals and fiction of Gissing. Drawing on Gissing's avid documentation of the connections between his own purchase and ingestion of food and his literary output, Valentine argues for the significance of similar economies of digestion in Gissing's fiction, noting that *New Grub Street* famously begins with a breakfast. Gissing, he argues, 'points up the reductionist tendency of existing physiological frameworks', complicating earlier notions of the relationship between thought and digestion which saw excess in the latter impeding the former: 'By recentring the issue of scarcity, he [Gissing] plots a less reductive relationship between the streams of nutrition and consciousness'. Ultimately, Valentine argues, Gissing's attention to cognitive eating takes him toward an increasingly dualist psychology. A comparative contextualization with the work of Émile Zola – whose novels also devote considerable attention to diet and who explicitly connects his aesthetics with those of the French physiologist Claude Bernard – broadens this new perspective on Gissing. As Valentine concludes, Gissing's fiction enables us to see the connections and continuities in a late-nineteenth-century history of psychology and literature between the mid-century science of mind and Freudian psychoanalysis or Bergsonian phenomenology:

> Gissing's minor place in literary history is emblematic of our tendency to skip over late-nineteenth-century realists, and to proceed straight from Dickens to Joyce. The same, of course, can be said of histories of psychology that read the *fin de siècle* as a highway to Freudian psychoanalysis or Bergsonian phenomenology. Attending to a novel's prandial features can help us bridge those gaps, adding courses between Dickens's puddings and Proust's madeleine.

In Chapter 2, Rachel Kravetz focuses on Thomas Hardy's *The Woodlanders*, which was published in 1887 but set in the years 1856–8: a moment at which the mental sciences began to advance rapidly, setting the stage for the discourse explored in this book. She finds the historical tension between materialism and idealism in the 1870s and 1880s dramatised in the central character of the doctor, Edred Fitzpiers. Her analysis explores the implication of the doctor's interest in idealist thinking (and his own idealist mindset) for his medical work that 'requires attention to the human body as seen as part of the natural order'. Kravetz concludes that Hardy's novel ultimately offers 'an assumption that another's mind can only be read through the living body's surface'. The novel recurs to the process of 'noticing' as the method it is primarily concerned with. This method is one that combines mind and body, as mind interferes with observation; and one which combines medical and literary arts, because patient observation is itself analogous to the type of noticing ('appreciative judgment') that the writer of fiction engages in. Reading Hardy's novel as bringing to life and dramatising that historically-formative tension between empiricism and idealism, Kravetz ultimately suggests that Hardy offers a commentary on the issue from the perspective of one who, although not involved in medical science, was deeply involved in thinking through the issues from a different perspective; novel-writing becomes a practice that can confront a central issue of art and science alike.

Alice Meynell forms another crucial node in our narrative of literature's response to changing but connected debates about the relationship between mind and body in the later decades of the nineteenth century. In Chapter 3, Gregory Tate argues that Meynell's notion of poetic rhythm responds to theories of physiological psychology, and that engaging with her work enables us to recognise interrelations between the discourse of literature, science, and religion that are characteristic of late-Victorian culture. Meynell's configuration of thought and feeling as rhythmic processes underpins her model of intersubjectivity, Tate argues; these rhythms of embodiment 'enable a communicative exchange between self and other that is simultaneously material, sympathetic, and spiritual'. This connection between personality and intersubjectivity fascinates Meynell throughout her career and she draws from scientific and spiritual discourses in her poetry in order to explore it. Tate traces a developing body of theory on rhythm and waves across the later nineteenth century in relation to Meynell's work, including works by James Knowles, Balfour Stewart and Peter Guthrie Tait from the 1860s and 1870s, and on into work by Joseph Adalbert Dewe and others in the 1890s. What emerges here is a theorisation of waves as the fundamental unit of processes natural, physiological and psychological. Such waves or vibrations connect processes across vastly different scales: from internal individual physiology and psychology to the flow of energy across the universe and, crucially, to poetic expression. For Meynell, rhythm not only connects the mind ('secluded' within the body) to other minds and bodies, it also, ultimately, connects us to the divine. Metaphors of rhythm, wave and vibrations harmonise Meynell's commitment to Catholic orthodoxy with the new theories of physiological psychology circulating in her lifetime.

The next three chapters together form a 'hinge' in the book, explicitly drawing out connections and conflicts between earlier and later theoretical moments in the second half of the nineteenth century. Two chapters with distinct readings of Walter Pater's thought demonstrate his centrality as a figure whose thought straddles both theoretical contexts. Bénédicte Coste's analysis of Pater explicitly takes as her point of reference the moment of inflection which saw the 'redistribution of scientific authority, the development of scientific education, the creation of numerous learned societies, and the professionalization and disciplinarization of the fields of investigation that were to form the sciences of the mind of the twentieth century including psychology'. Coste sees Pater drawing on the discourses of British psychology in the 1860s and early 1870s, including Henry Maudsley and Spencer, to develop his own psychology of aesthetics worked out in the relationship between subject and object in *The Renaissance*. Amidst the plurality of conceptions of subjectivity emerging from diverse fields such as psychophysiology, psychology, psychopathology and philosophy, Coste argues that Pater does not choose one, but identifies literary prose as the best field to formulate and express the operations of the psyche. In doing so he both contributes to the formation of the discipline of literary studies and to the formation of ideas about the operation of the embodied psyche. While grounded in the psychophysiological and evolutionary theories of the mid-century, Pater's aesthetic criticism becomes a discipline that can work out theories of the psyche and subjectivity that are distinctive and at times 'more accurate' than existing ones. His literary approach to the questions of mind-body interaction that constitute the subject affords him, Coste argues, an important place in late-nineteenth-century psychological conceptions because of the new perspective his concern with the aesthetic enabled him to bring to these questions.

Juxtaposed with Coste's chapter, David Coombs's analysis situates Pater's thought alongside William James and the 1890s rather than with the earlier community of psychological thinkers Coste invokes. Taken together, these two chapters display the central rationale of this book by showing the fundamental continuity between them. Coombs compares Pater's 1885 *Marius the Epicurean* with William James's 1902 *The Varieties of Religious Experience*. *The Varieties* draws on recent ideas of the unconscious by Sigmund Freud, Josef Breuer, Pierre Janet, Alfred Binet and Frederic Myers. Arguing that 'mystical experiences result when energies hitherto kept to margins of consciousness become its center and focal point', James theorises spiritual conversion as the return of the repressed. For James, religious conversion is understood in terms familiar from the natural sciences, but which also leave open the door to forces beyond the natural. More importantly for Coombs, however, the conversion moment in James is one that integrates individual experience with 'deep history and deep time', in a way closely comparable with Lukaćs's description of the formal demands of the Victorian historical novel. Coombs uses the comparison with *Marius* to work through and exemplify this late-century understanding of conversion not as a dramatic, instantaneous moment of transformation, but a psychological process that unites individual experience with broader historical forces.

Amanda Paxton provides the third point to this theoretical hinge in her analysis of Gerard Manley Hopkins's innovative theory of 'self-taste'. Taste was understood in nineteenth-century psychology to offer a unique combination of continuity and complexity.

It therefore offers Hopkins a rich model for the formulation of the self: 'on a metaphorical level, it denotes the individual perceiving her own interiority in a way that is inaccessible to any other being'. Paxton argues that he uses this model to theorise 'consciousness as continuous, qualitative, and irreducible, in contrast to the "discontinuous" and quantitative models posited by materialist accounts of the mind that were becoming dominant in the later nineteenth century'. Finding in Hopkins's work a reaction against the thinking of Bain and other Victorian theorists from the 1860s and 1870s, she notes a similarity with the challenges to Victorian science posed by Bergson and James. Paxton demonstrates how Hopkins's poetic language becomes a tool for expressing this continuity of experience. Hopkins's use of 'the middle voice' addresses the failure of language to represent fully the continuities of experience, well before these issues were taken up by Bergson and phenomenology. By positioning Hopkins conceptually between Bain and Bergson, this chapter foregrounds the need to see continuities and differences not only between major psychological works but immanently within the works of individual writers. In line with the Paterian experiments analysed in the previous two chapters, Paxton understands Hopkins to be foregrounding the capacity for literary text to be a distinctive tool and method for working out the relationship between mind and body – highlighting the ways in which literary text actively contributes to the theoretical debate rather than simply reflecting it.

The final two chapters in the book move to a late-century context of psychological thought. Anne Stiles explores how Marie Corelli and Oscar Wilde thought through the possibility of the new theory of the neuronal cell in their works. Stiles describes the emergence of this cornerstone in modern neuroscience from the 1870s to the early 1900s and its stake in broader debates about cerebral localisation and the possibility of a fully material mind. The neuron doctrine held, contrary to the notion that the human nervous system is composed of a web of interconnected fibres, that the nervous system is composed of discrete cells that communicate with one another through synapses. The debate about these two versions of the nervous system is explored in the fiction of Wilde and Corelli who, however, develop distinct perspectives on it. While both were early adopters of theory of the neuron cell (or 'brain cell'), Wilde aestheticises it, seeing it as 'an isolated, impermeable, and unknowable entity, as mysterious as the soul itself', and shows less interest in its interaction with other cells. Corelli, by contrast, imbues it with 'spiritual overtones befitting her fascination with the new religious movements of the period'. She resists the materialist approach to the mind to which Wilde was drawn. While Wilde's engagement with neuron theory has been relatively well explored in criticism, Corelli's work, Stiles argues, offers fascinating new possibilities that go beyond anything that Wilde conceived: the communication between brain cells is imagined to link 'not just cells, but also other human brains, angels and spirits, and even God himself'. From *The Romance of Two Worlds* (1886) to *The Life Everlasting* (1911), the neuron cell is incorporated into her Electric Creed of Christianity. Corelli's work shows how, even in this foundational moment of the birth of a 'neuroscience' from the supposedly less rigorous psychology that preceded it, the neuron cell need not entail a commitment to materialist reductionism.

In the last chapter, Pamela Gilbert focuses on the psychological theories of Vernon Lee, who published both works on physiological aesthetics *and* works of fiction. Opening with an illuminating outline of Lee's still-underestimated contribution to, and engagement with, psychology, Gilbert sets up Lee's understanding of the relationship of music and writing to ethics, emotion and memory via the body in works spanning from the late nineteenth to the early twentieth century. Gilbert disentangles Lee's understanding of sympathy and empathy, noting that both depend on the activation of 'memory-engrams', and gives an overview of some of the key shifts Lee makes in her theorisation of psychological aesthetics over the course of her career. Gilbert goes on to read Lee's 1915 pacifist 'closet ballet', *The Ballet of Nations* (expanded and republished in 1920 as *Satan the Waster*), showing how this ballet creates a psychological amphitheatre in which the reader can recognise the capacity of art (particularly music and literature) to elicit moral emotions and empathy in ways that risk becoming 'tools in the arsenal of Satan' – leading populations into jingoistic war-mongering. In so doing, Gilbert argues, Lee wants her readers to understand how their proper perception of war is clouded by a tendency to aestheticise and oversimplify it. Expertly disentangling Lee's formulation of sympathy and empathy, Gilbert ultimately emphasises the author's awareness of the dangers and opportunities afforded by both. Though the war challenged Lee's earlier desire to 'see beauty as intrinsically good, and aesthesis as inherently pro-social', Gilbert maintains that Lee never entirely gave up on her desire to link physiological aesthetics with a moral purpose. We end the book with Lee to provide a bridge between the Victorian and modernist.

Thinking together: literature and the sciences

It is particularly important to the overall narrative of this book that the chapters reflect on the *nature* of the relationship between literature and the early science of psychology as well as its *content*. We know that artists and novelists inspire science just as much as scientists inspire art and fiction. While some notable cases are fully acknowledged, most of this mutual influence exists in an un-documentable soup of quotidian experience. Making the case for specific causal relationships between particular literary texts and particular scientific developments is not, for the most part, possible or necessary. Nonetheless, the connections our authors draw out in the following chapters mostly go beyond simply noting the significance of scientific discourse as part of the writer's historical context, understood as the wealth of influence in which they operate. It is clear that literature has its own role to play in the circulation, consideration and elaboration of ideas about mind and embodiment. This role – as it is articulated in the following chapters – might be summarised in a few key points.

First, and perhaps most loosely, there is a broad point to be made about the cultural circulation of ideas. Especially before the twentieth-century formalisation and reification of individual disciplines, ideas circulated and concepts developed across different modalities and forms that all took part in the same broad cultural current. Scholarship has long emphasized 'two-way' traffic, as Gillian Beer describes it, between literary and scientific work in the period: 'because of the shared discourse not only *ideas* but metaphors, myths, and narrative patterns could move rapidly and freely to and fro between scientists and non-scientists'.[16] We see this in Coombs's comparison of Pater's novel with James's psychological writings. Valentine identifies this type of approach more explicitly:

[16] Gillian Beer, *Darwin's Plots: Evolutionary Narrative in Darwin, George Eliot and Nineteenth-Century Fiction* (Cambridge: Cambridge University Press, 2000), p. 5. See Morgan, *The Outward Mind*, p. 275, n.40.

> One way to configure the relationship between scientific and literary discourses is to identify which texts a given author is known to have read, and then relate those frameworks to their own compositions. Here, I take a different approach, looking not for documented patterns of influence, but for thematic resonance between the figure of the embodied brainworker and its manifestation in Gissing's life-writings and novels.

This theory of influence suggests these writers and thinkers caught the same cold because they were sitting in the same draft, as it were. 'Resonances' are important when we deal with the formation of ideas at this time of mass print and mass communication technologies, and before disciplines had become specialised. As Rachel Kravetz shows, Hardy's narrator employs a methodology of observation not dissimilar to that of the doctor, and the analysis of the classic realist narrator and the case study of the medical scientist might come together particularly around considerations of the relationship between mind and body – between the internal psychological workings of a character or person, and their physical manifestation.

Secondly, there are the instances where direct influence between scientific thought and fiction can be observed and documented. Tate's chapter on Meynell is a great case study for such an approach. As Tate notes, Meynell and her husband Wilfrid edited the periodical *Merry England* from 1883 to 1895, publishing articles on the 'wave paradigm' that Tate uncovers in Meynell's own poetic theory and practice. Meynell's circle of friends and acquaintances was large, and letters attest to the direct influence of ideas of spiritualism from W.B. Yeats, for example, and the science of the biologist and Catholic convert St George Mivart (whom, as Tate notes, she knew from the 1870s). Tate observes that 'Mivart is one the few writers whom Meynell quotes directly rather than paraphrasing (although without attribution) in her essays', thus establishing an explicit connection with scientific discourse of her time. However, it would be strange to believe that there was not also influence in the other direction, as her poetry and poetic theory were read and commented on by her interlocutors. As Tate notes, when Meynell published the poem 'The English Metres' (in 1921) she was a participant in this discourse rather than simply an observer: 'The poem's closing stanzas demonstrate how, in Meynell's hands, poetic form acts as a fractal expression both of the rhythmic waves that organise the embodied mind and the physical universe, and of the reciprocal interaction between them'.

Thirdly, and most crucially for this book, as Coste notes, quoting Sally Shuttleworth: '[l]iterary texts did not simply supply material for medical case studies, [but] also helped frame the questions and categories of an emerging scientific field'.[17] Pater's indebtedness to writings discussing aesthetic cognition in the periodicals of his day has been well documented,[18] and he was certainly influenced by Bain's definition of consciousness, for example.[19] Yet, as Coste argues, Pater was an influential participant in the debates that raged across the major monthly periodicals in the 'lively multi-polar and multi-disciplinary debate whence modern psychology was forged'. Pater was particularly notable for the redefinition of the subject his aesthetic perspective enabled; he challenged and complicated contemporary understandings of mind – 'including' says Coste, 'its functional understanding'. Pater 'gave the term [mind] a new meaning, turning it into a site for processing linguistic activity'. There is no question that Pater is a 'legitimate participant' in the late-century work of theorising mind, body and their inter-relations.

Fourthly, and finally, we can identify in writers such as Vernon Lee a fully-fledged integration: a writer who published both works on psychology and physiological aesthetics *and* works of fiction. It thus becomes clear that properly understanding the formation of concepts and the histories that led up to our current understanding requires interdisciplinary study, and an approach that attends to the multifaceted, difficult-to-categorise intellectual practices and genres that preceded our own siloed academic endeavours. To sidestep these deep connections between the literature and science

[17] Sally Shuttleworth, *The Mind of the Child: Child Development in Literature, Science, and Medicine, 1840–1900* (Oxford: Oxford University Press, 2010), p. 362.

[18] To quote Coste: 'Evolutionary theory and physiology provided tools for rescaling aesthetic response: for Herbert Spencer and Grant Allen, the experience of beauty was a reflex that had evolved slowly in evolutionary time; while for Alexander Bain, it was an immediate neurophysiological response to stimuli of form, color, or sound'.

[19] In *The Emotions and The Will* (West Strand: John W Parker & Son, 1855, second edition London: Longmans, Green and Co, 1865), Bain defined consciousness in terms of its discontinuous impressions, themselves invested by language, which alone is capable of endowing them with a certain permanence, a view shared by Pater.

of the period is to risk leaving out some of the most creative, flexible and influential minds of the historical record, resulting in siloed accounts of the formation of a discourse that actually operated fluidly across fields.

One of the key motivations for this project is to reframe the existing scholarly field in order to correct an accident of our own disciplinary periodisation that that has tended to bifurcate, on the one hand, Victorian literature and the scientific discourses on mind and body of Spencer, Bain, Lewes and others from the 1860s and 1870s, and, on the other, modernist literature and the psychological discourse on mind and body of William James, Henri Bergson and others from the 1890s. We hope to have revealed something of the multiplicity and complexity of the types of conversations that were taking place between late-nineteenth-century literature and broadly contemporaneous scientific/psychological understandings of the relationship between mind and body. More than this, though, our volume strongly advocates for the necessity of an interdisciplinary approach to understanding the history and cultural formation of ideas at a time that pre-dates disciplinary segregation. Literature was in itself a tool, method and arena for analysing and theorising the relationship between mind and body. This is perhaps most explicit in the work of authors such as Pater and Hopkins, where literary language is itself a way of configuring the relationship between mind and body, but it is apparent across the rest of the volume too – in Kravetz's persuasive insistence that the empirical observations of Hardy's narrator are a form of psychological study, Meynell's embodied rhythmical poetics, and Vernon Lee's deliberate deployment of the alienating symbolism of the closet ballet genre. Ultimately, it might be that one of the most important lessons we can learn from the Victorians is to think more fluidly across the science–humanities boundary. There is much to be said today for a return to a more flexible and multifaceted conceptual approach – one that can combine insights of the human and natural sciences to frame more effectively our academic response to both the individual and planetary challenges we face today.

1

Cognitive Eating: George Gissing and the Victorian Brainworker

Colton Valentine

'Generally speaking, the man who thinks least, digests best; and he who thinks most, usually digests worst', declares Samuel Smiles in *Life and Labour* (1887): 'The hard-working man has the digestion of an ostrich, and scarcely knows where his stomach lies; while the brain-worker has to watch every mouthful that he eats, and is scarcely ever allowed to forget that he has a stomach'.[1] Best known for his primer on upward mobility, *Self-Help* (1859), Smiles went on to publish a series of manuals that crystallised the Victorian period's concern with the corporeal nature of thinking. As this quote indicates, nutrition offered a compelling site to interrogate mind–body dynamics. An event as quotidian as digestion posed the question of a relationship between physical and mental labour. If these species of exertion were distinct yet convertible, did they point toward dualism? Or could they be reduced to a monism of the stomach?

Only recently have scholars begun to take such questions seriously. In the past few decades, food studies has emerged as a new interdisciplinary field drawing on literary, historical and sociological methods, to name a few. Nineteenth-century novels have proved generative resources for critics such as Michael Parish Lee, Annette Cozzi, Gwen Hymen and Joseph Litvak who excavate the many ideological underpinnings of fictional diners and victuals.[2]

[1] Samuel Smiles, *Life and Labour* (London: John Murray, 1887), pp. 251–2.

[2] See Annette Cozzi, *The Discourses of Food in Nineteenth-Century British Fiction* (Basingstoke: Palgrave Macmillan, 2010); Gwen Hyman, *Making a Man: Gentlemanly Appetites in the Nineteenth-Century British Novel* (Athens, OH: Ohio University Press, 2009); Michael Parrish Lee, *The Food Plot in the Nineteenth-Century British Novel* (Basingstoke: Palgrave Macmillan, 2016);

While these scholars have largely treated food as a material commodity, my chapter turns to cases that register the *cognitive* effects of diegetic eating. Focusing on representations of what Smiles calls the 'brainworker', I contend that not only dietary and medical texts, but also prandial novels offer promising archives of late-Victorian psychology. These texts do more than describe a drift in the scientific episteme; they narrate forms of monism and dualism in their rendering of minds and meals.

The first section of this chapter explores the mind–body relationship inherent to 'brainworking'. It draws on scientific, health, and literary works and gives special attention to the presentation of cognitive eating in George Henry Lewes's *The Physiology of Common Life* (1859) and *Problems of Life and Mind* (1874–9). I then place these models in dialogue with the writings of George Gissing, showing first how his diary and his novel *New Grub Street* (1891) transform the clichéd metaphors of writing as cooking and reading as eating into metonymies. In this novel, each unit of brainwork generates a cash flow equivalent to a unit of purchasable food, and an abundance of thought does not impede digestion; a scarcity of digestion impedes thought. While Gissing thus draws on contemporary analogies of mental and physical labour, his fiction points up the reductionist tendency of existing physiological frameworks.

To contextualise this point, I place the psychological affordances of Gissing's realism in dialogue with those of his French predecessor Émile Zola, whose novels also devote significant attention to their subjects' diets. While Gissing draws implicitly on physiological frameworks, Zola's treatise *Le Roman expérimental* (1880) explicitly aligns his aesthetic protocol with those of the French physiologist Claude Bernard. Since Zola never applied the method to his own literary milieu, however, we can read *New Grub Street* as turning the naturalist experiment upon the scientist: as an inquiry into whether a materialist monism can account for a writer's own mental acts. Indeed, in Gissing's last published novel, *The Private Papers of Henry Ryecroft* (1903), we find the author's self-reflexive attention to cognitive eating taking him toward an increasingly dualist psychology.

Joseph Litvak, *Strange Gourmets: Sophistication, Theory, and the Novel* (Durham, NC: Duke University Press, 1997).

The brainworker

The first recorded use of the term 'brainwork' predates Gissing by nearly three centuries: John Marston's Jacobean drama *Parasitaster* (1606). Amid a scene where Princess Dulcimel and her friend Philocalia discuss the former's plan to seduce Tiberio, Dulcimel cries: 'Oh *Philocalia*, in heauy sadnes and vnwanton phrase, there lies all the braine worke, by what meanes I could fal into a miserable blanke verse presently'.[3] Here signifying the mental exertion involved in romantic scheming, 'brainwork' enters the English language in a dramatic context and in a literary rather than scientific text. By the century's end, however, the concept had become associated with paid labour. In his satirical polemic *New News from Tory-land and Tantivy-shire* (1682), John Phillips rails against the poet Thomas Flatman (the 'Devil, *Heraclitus*') who 'does not deserve the weekly *Wages* of a *Peny-post-man*, for a Months *Brain-Work*', while the translation of Louis Lahontan's influential travelogue *New Voyages to North America* (1703) has mouthpiece Adario observe that 'it must be only the Learned Men that fall into such Disorders . . . for I am fully convinc'd that *Brain-Work* infeebles the Body extreamly'.[4] These early appearances anticipate the major questions that 'brainwork' as a social and scientific category will pose to Victorian writers. Is it enervating or enlivening? How do its physiological demands and effects differ from those of manual labour? What sort of mind–body relationship does it index?

The nineteenth century sees a significant uptick in the term's usage, and a shift from 'brainwork' signifying local instances of mental exertion to the daily labour involved in the professions of industrialisation and urbanisation.[5] As before, the term circulates across a range of genres and discourses, appearing in novels and medical treatises alike, and taking on diverse connotations. Compare for instance, the mock-romantic image provided in an

[3] John Marston, *Parasitaster, or, The Fawne* (London: Printed for Thomas Purfoot, 1606), Act III, Scene I.

[4] John Phillips, *New News from Tory-land and Tantivy-shire* (London: Printed for S. Norman, 1682), p. 7; Louis Lahontan, *New Voyages to North-America* (London: Printed for H. Bonwicke, 1703), 2:165.

[5] On these shifts, see Marcus Waithe, *The Work of Words: Literature Craft, and the Labour of Mind in Britain, 1830–1940* (Edinburgh: Edinburgh University Press, 2023), esp. pp. 39–62.

1831 *Athenaeum* review, with the infernal imagery Dinah Craik uses to render the British Museum Reading Room in her novel *The Ogilvies* (1849):

> A floor near the sky in Grub Street is no pen-spot now, but down fifty fathoms deep in Portland Place, or Portman Square, or some far-retired old country house, you shall find the author: his red cuffs turned up over his light blue jacket sleeves, the pen in his hand, and his inspired eye looking out upon the area. There doth he correct the brain-work which is to carry his name up above the earth, and keep it there, bright as cleaned plate.[6]

> You see ranged at various tables scores of mute readers, who sometimes lift up a glance as you pass, and then, like Dante's ghosts in purgatory, relapse into their penance. Indeed, the whole scene, with the spectral attendants flitting to and fro, and the dim vista beyond the man who takes the checks (alas for poetic diction!), might easily be imagined some Hades of literature, where all pen-guiders and brain-workers were doomed to expiate their evil deeds by an eternity of reading.[7]

These quotations point both to the codification of brainwork as a vocational category and to the term's ongoing flexibility as a signifier. It applies to the processes of both production and reception, accommodating outputs and inputs of all categories and quantities. Indeed, this elasticity poses a problem of definition: given the different embodied experiences in the country house and purgatorial reading-room, is all brainwork created equal?

The physician Benjamin Ward Richardson believed some discriminations were in order. In his highly influential *Diseases of Modern Life* (1876), Richardson argues that 'when the labour of the brain is carried on with evenness and order and generalization, brain work is healthy work', but also warns that authors are endangered by their particular mental demands.[8] Richardson highlights three types of perils: the strains of 'concentration' on a single subject over an extended time, the 'impulse to chronicle

[6] Review of *Attempts in Verse* by John Jones in *The Athenaeum* (February 26, 1831), pp. 130–2, 130.

[7] Dinah Craik, *The Ogilvies* (London: Chapman and Hall, 1849), 2:104–5.

[8] Benjamin Ward Richardson, *Diseases of Modern Life* (London: Macmillan, 1876), p. 399.

instantly' when inspiration strikes, and 'writing against time' for immediate publication (401, 402). He then maps these risks onto certain metiers, suggesting, 'Our philosophical and historical writers feel most acutely the first of these dangers; our poets and novelists the second; our journalists the third' (402). Literary genres, by this account, have corresponding genres of mental exertion, and a given text's composition elicits a specific mental and physical effect. A work of philosophy and history demands overlong absorption in arguments and sources, whereas a poem or novel requires that we forsake well-being to seize inspiration, and journalism that we ignore all else till the deadline is made. In Richardson's writing, brainwork invites us to plot a physiology of literary genres – one based not in their reception by readers but in their production by authors.

Nutrition was a crucial feature of this emergent brainworker discourse. The brainworker's dietary needs were broadly understood to differ from those of the manual labourer, yet opinions varied on how they diverged. For Richardson, the brainworker's poor working conditions, 'coupled now and then with a little too much negligence in eating, drinking, and avoiding, make them dyspeptic and nervous, so that without being actually ill, they are led to feel their life a dismal burthen' (400). In his much-reprinted pamphlet *On Overwork and Premature Mental Decay* (1873), the physician Charles Henry Felix recommended 'phosphorised foods' – namely seafood – for those who had overexerted.[9] '[P]opular experience has gone before science', he added drolly: 'Young ladies and gentlemen who have exhausted themselves by dancing and excitement, fly as if by intuition to the lobster salad. The rake finds nothing so calculated to excite his fading sexual power as oysters and shell fish' – a juxtaposition that cast phosphorous as an equal resource for the work of brain and body alike (14). Other writers were more fixated on prandial timing, especially given the combined temporal exigencies of sleep and work. As Sally Shuttleworth has shown, early sleep experiments performed by Arthur Durham and William Hammond in the 1860s paved the way for the widely circulated belief that brainworkers were at particular risk for insomnia, such that 'books on sleep often offered lists of food stuffs and

[9] C.H.F. Routh, *On Overwork and Premature Mental Decay: Its Treatment* (London: Baillière, Tindall, and Cox, 1873), p. 14. The pamphlet was repeatedly revised and expanded in the following decade.

the times they took to digest, so that readers could adjust their diet accordingly'.[10] Popular manuals and specialist publications alike contributed to the nineteenth-century emergence of nutrition science, which centred the stomach as the privileged organ of both physical and mental well-being.[11]

The very category of 'brainwork', then, elicited newfound attention to the embodied nature of cognition, and especially to the influence of diet. Food was of especial import to George Henry Lewes, whose *The Physiology of Common Life* (1859) opens by defining hunger as 'the very fire of life . . . the motive power which sets the vast array of human machinery in action', and whose management is essential for those pursuing both physical and manual labour.[12] The crux of Lewes's model is a belief that the nervous system operates as a 'fountain of influence' from which 'three streams' flow: the nutritive, locomotive and sensitive (1:22). Organs, he believes, should not draw on multiple streams at once, but nor should they allow any stream to go dormant for extended periods of time. Timing thus becomes key to Lewes's dietary recommendations for brainworkers. At one extreme, starvation could lead the nutritive and then locomotive stream to shut off, causing an overabundance of brain activity, leading to madness. On the other, he warns against 'the vicious habit of studying at, or shortly after, meals, or of tasking the brain when the stomach is also tasked' (1:290). George Eliot's *Middlemarch* (1871–2) invokes the later plight when the narrator observes of Casaubon: 'digestion was made difficult by the interference of citations, or by the rivalry of dialectical phrases ringing against each other in his brain'.[13] A subtle model of cognitive eating lurks in the droll image, one placing intellectual and digestive activity in a simultaneously combative and co-dependent relationship.

[10] Sally Shuttleworth, 'Fagged Out: Overwork and Sleeplessness in Victorian Professional Life', *Interface Focus* 10 (2020): 1–10, 7.

[11] See Ian Miller, *A Modern History of the Stomach: Gastric Illness, Medicine and British Society, 1800–1950* (London: Pickering & Chatto, 2011); Manon Mathias and Alison M. Moore, eds, *Gut Feeling and Digestive Health in Nineteenth-Century Literature, History, and Culture* (Basingstoke: Palgrave Macmillan, 2018).

[12] George Henry Lewes, *The Physiology of Common Life* (Edinburgh: William Blackwood and Sons, 1859), 1:1.

[13] George Eliot, *Middlemarch*, ed. Rosemary Ashton (London: Penguin, 1994), p. 281.

In his important recovery of Lewes for the history of psychology, Rick Rylance highlights how Lewes's coinage of 'stream of Consciousness' long predates that of William James, and indeed 'suggests something both richer and more complicated' through its connection to the 'stream of Sensation'; namely a 'rich, physical, ontological grounding in that activity'.[14] Yet Rylance himself only highlights one of the three streams that Lewes identifies – that of Sensation. In his *Problems of Life and Mind* (1874–9), Lewes develops the image and framework to sketch a psychology that, in Peter Garratt's words, 'treads a subtle path between a theory of mental autonomy and its dread opposite, materialism, which would explain mind literally through neural mechanics'.[15] Central to Lewes's project is his assertion of the mind's 'twofold root, man being not only an animal organism but an unit in the social organism'; even the mind's 'Physical Basis' detailed in the third volume of *The Problems* is thus understood as the product and producer of a broader social milieu.[16]

As Lewes makes clear, this framework draws on but departs from that of the French physiologist Claude Bernard. Bernard's influential theory of the 'milieu intérieur' (internal environment) explained how organisms self-regulate in response to external stimuli to maintain what would later be called homeostasis. '[*L*]*a nutrition n'est que la génération continuée*', he asserted, '*vivre* et *se nourrir* sont deux expressions synonymes'.[17] For Lewes, the nutritive stream was certainly essential, but not singular. While citing the Frenchman's internal/external distinction, he made sure to qualify that 'Bernard only includes the nutritive fluid; but inasmuch as each organism possesses a temperature and electrical state of its own, . . . I include them with the plasma among the constituents of the Physiological Medium' (*The Physical Basis*, 43–4). This amendment was part of a broader project to nuance

[14] Rick Rylance, *Victorian Psychology and British Culture, 1850–1880* (Oxford: Oxford University Press, 2000), p. 11.

[15] Peter Garratt, *Victorian Empiricism: Self, Knowledge, and Reality in Ruskin, Bain, Lewes, Spencer, and George Eliot* (Madison: Fairleigh Dickinson University Press, 2010), p. 152.

[16] George Henry Lewes, *The Physical Basis of Mind. Being the Second Series of Problems of Life and Mind* (London: Trübner & Co., 1877), pp. v, vi.

[17] Claude Bernard, *Rapport sur les progrès et la marche de la physiologie générale en France* (Paris: Imprimerie impériale, 1867), p. 92: '*Nutrition is but continued generation. . . . to live* and *to be nourished* are synonymous expressions'.

materialist accounts. 'Vital facts, especially facts of sensibility, have factors neither discernible in machines nor expressible in mechanical terms', Lewes asserts. 'We cannot ignore them, although for analytical purposes we may provisionally set them aside' (321). Brainwork is the sort of qualia that troubles that analytic bracketing; it is at once a mechanical and a 'vital' fact.

We will return to both Lewes and Bernard shortly, but for the moment we might register how the dialectical phrases impeding Casaubon's digestion point to the way the mind eludes reduction to either an animal or a social foundation. As Garratt puts it: 'Casaubon may imagine himself as all mind, but like the psychological theories emerging in the period, the novel questions his dualistic propensity to separate mind from matter' (*Victorian Empiricism*, 141). Indeed, *Middlemarch* poses that query not only by plotting and describing Casaubon's physical decline, but also by attending to the way his stream of consciousness depends on, yet conflicts with, the stream of nutrition.

Cash for cognition

One way to configure the relationship between scientific and literary discourses is to identify which texts a given author is known to have read, and then relate those frameworks to their own compositions. Here, I take a different approach, looking not for documented patterns of influence, but for thematic resonance between the figure of the embodied brainworker and its manifestation in Gissing's life-writings and novels. Consider, first, what might appear the most banal feature of his – or anyone's – diary: the fixation on what, when, and for what price one eats. That Gissing perceives these factors to structure his literary output reveals his markedly cognitive approach to eating. For instance, he declares 23 January 1888 'A wasted day', blaming tea for his 'sluggish digestion, constipation, etc.' and noting his being 'Made bilious also by having Irish stew for dinner'.[18] A few months later he records:

> *Thursd. Ap. 12.* Some home-made cakes from Broadway. Foresee indigestions. Wrote my 4pp.

[18] George Gissing, *London and the Life of Literature in Late Victorian England: The Diary of George Gissing, Novelist*, ed. Pierre Coustillas (Hassocks: Harvester Press, 1978), p. 20.

> *Frid. Ap. 13*. Four pages.
> *Sat. Ap. 14*. In doubt about last pages. Tried to alter, but only ended in doing nothing. Perhaps the Broadway cakes to blame. (26)

Whereas the tea and stew impede brainwork outright, the cakes threaten its quality. Rarely when working does Gissing ever record any positive or gustatory response to eating; victuals are noted largely for their negative cognitive effects. Timing is treated in a similar fashion. Gissing's normal routine was to dine at an eating-house midday, take a post-prandial walk, and then complete his daily page quota in the afternoon and evening. A shorter work session sometimes preceded the midday meal, but Gissing was not a morning writer. On May 20, he records having 'beheld an idiotic experiment', explaining: 'I rose at 5.30 (glorious sunshine), made a cup of cocoa, at 6 o'clock and sat down—to write! The result was that by 7 o'clock I had written five words, and had fretted myself into a headache. This has solved decisively the question of Walter Scottian work in my case; it is wholly out of the question' (29). The term 'experiment' is worth keeping in mind. The mere act of recording these quotidian details attributes value to the imbricated patterns of eating and brainwork – value both as private knowledge and as fodder for future fictions.

During the composition of *New Grub Street*, Gissing was increasingly attentive to the financial factors subtending cognitive eating. Returning to England from a trip to the continent in 1890, he observes, 'Have £77 left in bank. Will support me till end of September' and settles into a routine: 'Have resumed my afternoon walk right round Regent's Park. Breakfast at 8; dinner (Edgware Rd) at 12.30; cup of coffee alone at 4; supper (bread and butter with cold tea) at 7.30. Do not really have enough to eat, but no help for it' (210, 211). Deviations from the ritual elicit dismay. On Good Friday, for instance, Gissing spends the morning travelling to Victoria and records: 'Had dinner before 12 at a restaurant there, paying more than I can afford 1/6. Afternoon read at Heine. Evening did not quite a page. Feeling out of the right mood; always the result upon me of these public holidays' (213). Here, it is not specific victuals – stew or cakes – that are to blame for the lack of cognitive output, but rather the psychophysical fallout of a holiday treat one cannot 'afford'. Gissing's diary thereby points out how embodied cognition cannot be divorced from economics;

the 'fountain of influence' from which flow Lewes's three streams depends on cash.

Reading Gissing's life-writing alongside his novels does not require that we take a biographical approach to fiction; rather it allows us to see both sources' prandial fixations as archives of late-Victorian embodied cognition. This approach diverges from the tendency to read Gissing's novels in relation to power and ideology, a rich tradition indebted to Raymond Williams, and crystallised in Fredric Jameson's declaration that Gissing was the writer for whom the 'ideologeme' of *ressentiment* was 'extended to a universal principle and absolutized as the very motor force' of his fictions.[19] 'One of Gissing's trademarks as a novelist is indeed to give programmatic expression to the processes of contemporary ideology', observes William Greenslade, 'and to enact the drama of the individual's subjection to it'.[20] While recognising the benefits of this approach and critical idiom, might we take Gissing's insights into the social and material conditions for 'thought' in a different, more psychological direction?[21]

New Grub Street famously begins with a morbid breakfast. Poised to crack an egg, the writer Jasper Milvain 'remark[s] with cheerfulness: "There's a man being hanged in London at this moment"'.[22] 'There's a certain satisfaction in reflecting that it is not oneself', he continues. 'Things are bad with me, but not so bad as *that*. I might be going out between Jack Ketch and the Chaplain to be hanged; instead of that, I am eating a really fresh egg, and very excellent buttered toast, with coffee as good as can be reasonably expected in this part of the world.—(Do try boiling the milk, mother.)' (5). At first glance, the prandial setting seems only to mark Jasper's blithe disinterest toward his gallows-bound

19 Fredric Jameson, *The Political Unconscious: Narrative as a Socially Symbolic Act* (Ithaca: Cornell University Press, 1981), p. 205.

20 William Greenslade, *Degeneration, Culture and the Novel, 1880–1940* (Cambridge: Cambridge University Press, 1994), p. 149. See also Adrian Poole, *Gissing in Context* (New York: Macmillan, 1975); John Goode, *George Gissing: Ideology and Fiction* (London: Vision Press, 1978).

21 See, by contrast, Nicholas Dames's discussion of speed reading in *The Physiology of the Novel* (Oxford: Oxford University Press, 2007), pp. 207–46. Dames highlights 'Gissing's reliance upon psychological, rather than purely sociological, reasoning' but focuses on that reasoning's application to these novels' imagined readers and their physiology of vision (p. 243).

22 George Gissing, *New Grub Street*, ed. Katherine Mullin (Oxford: Oxford University Press, 2016), p. 5.

compatriot. But it also sets up a thorny connection between nourishment, print culture, and mortality that structures the lives of every character in the novel.

The specifically psychological insight of the scene emerges when compared to a moving passage in *Problems of Life and Mind*, in which Lewes presents the breakfast table as a microcosm for how presentist myopia propagates error-ridden thinking. 'On the bleached damask stand the silver teapot and electro-plated toast-rack, the china service and glass butter-cooler, the bronzed urn and the morning's *Times*', Lewes observes; 'but they call up no image of the plantations of China, the factories of Sheffield, the potteries of Staffordshire, or the epitomised nation of Printing-House Square. The very bread and milk, accepted as if they were the free gifts of Nature'.[23] Against this narrow frame, Lewes urges us to see the teapot, *Times*, and milk alike as 'representants of man's struggle' with material, social, and spiritual 'existence' (2:136). What is striking about Lewes's image, however, is that its critique of commodification and turn to deep history – in which milk is traced to 'nomadic existence' and 'the domestication of animals' – transforms the victuals into symbols (2:136). This rhetoric thus elides the nutritive function to which his work is otherwise so attentive. Jasper, by contrast, is all too aware that bread and milk drive an ongoing 'struggle' for existence, as well as a historic one.

Where Gissing's novel departs from Lewes's study, then, is on the timescale at which *New Grub Street* relates cognition to nutrition – what Nicholas Dames calls a 'narrative procedure that rarely fails to cite, and wonder at, the bewildering rapidity of experience' (*Physiology*, 232). Consider, this later, oft-cited episode in which Jasper recounts a working day that 'deserves to be chronicled for the encouragement of aspiring youth':

> I got up at 7.30, and whilst I breakfasted I read through a volume I had to review. By 10.30 the review was written—three-quarters of a column of the *Evening Budget* . . . from 10.30 to 11, I smoked a cigar and reflected, feeling that the day wasn't badly begun. At eleven I was ready to write my Saturday *causerie* for the *Will o' the Wisp*; it took me till close upon one o'clock, which was rather too long. I can't

[23] George Henry Lewes, *Problems of Life and Mind. First Series. The Foundations of a Creed* (London: Trübner & Co., 1875), 2:135–6. See Rylance's discussion of this passage in *Victorian Psychology*, pp. 326–7.

> afford more than an hour and a half for that job. At one, I rushed out to a dirty little eating-house in Hampstead Road. Was back again by a quarter to two, having in the meantime sketched a paper for *The West End*. Pipe in mouth, I sat down to leisurely artistic work; by five, half the paper was done; the other half remains for to-morrow. From five to half-past I read four newspapers and two magazines, and from half-past to a quarter to six I jotted down several ideas that had come to me whilst reading. At six I was again in the dirty eating-house, satisfying a ferocious hunger. Home once more at 6.45, and for two hours wrote steadily at a long affair I have in hand for *The Current*. Then I came here, thinking hard all the way. (*New Grub Street*, 160–1).

The passage reads less like 'encouragement' than an Edenic version of Gissing's diary. Here, we find prandial input and literary output optimised to a tee. The first volume is read by breakfast, the paper sketched over lunch, and the pace of processing newspapers and magazines builds to a 'ferocious hunger', which can be satisfied promptly at six. Refuelled and undulled, Jasper races back to another 'long affair' – with evident brain capacity to spare since he's still 'thinking hard all the way' home. Met with this report, his sister Maud inquires as to the 'value of it all' (161). 'Probably from ten to twelve guineas', Jasper reckons, and when she qualifies, smiling, that she meant the 'literary value', he responds: 'Equal to that of the contents of a mouldy nut' (161). That image itself has scant literary value, relying on the hackneyed trope that likens books to food, and reading to eating, but the prior speech turns those trite metaphors into searing metonymies. Jasper's writings may be symbolically equal to a mouldy nut, but they are economically convertible to ten-to-twelve guineas – more than enough for the three full meals that produce his work.

The brainwork cycle is less smooth for the novelist Edwin Reardon and his wife Amy. When Amy's acquaintance Edith invites the couple over to dinner, she declines, observing: 'Edwin can't possibly leave his work' (121). Like Gissing, Amy extrapolates from one refusal to total abnegation, continuing: 'I'm very sorry. I don't think we shall ever be able to accept invitations in the future. . . . We find that social engagements consume too much time' (122). Yet unlike the diary, the novel's dialogism probes the decision further. Hoping to convince her friend, Edith suggests that Edwin's creative process might benefit: 'You know what you once told me, about how necessary it was for a novelist to study all sorts of people. How can Mr Reardon do this if he shuts himself up in the house?' (122). 'For the present, Edwin has quite enough "material"', Amy responds, selecting a term, like Maud's 'value', whose fungibility allows us to think about writing as both a physiological and a psychological process (122). Indeed, the subtext of the exchange is the question of misplaced material: there may be plenty of intellectual material, but there is not enough of the prandial and economic sort – certainly not enough to dine out.

In her reading of the novel's consumerism, Rachel Bowlby notes that Jasper's 'economy of daily management succeeds in getting the maximum output from the mind and its supporting physical body', which she too compares with Gissing's diary and with Reardon's suboptimal day.[24] Dames likewise suggests the report 'represents a perfect adaptation of bodily and mental rhythms to the demands of a certain kind of routinized craft labour' (*Physiology*, 236). But whereas Bowlby glosses the scene as Gissing's pessimistic response to the capitalist restraints on artistic liberty, and Dames sees it posing a narratological problem of acceleration, we can also read it for a kind of psychological insight. For *New Grub Street* does not simply render 'the mind and its supporting physical body' as a single composite entity; rather it narrates their dynamic exchanges (*Just Looking*, 109).

The metonymic structure of cognitive eating is rendered sharpest in the novel's portrayal of its most ostensibly immaterial character: Edwin's friend Harold Biffen. While Biffen's 'excessive meagreness would all but have qualified him to enter an exhibition in the capacity of living skeleton', he is also judged 'superior to these accidents of flesh' (*New Grub Street*, 125). Indeed, the novel treats us to a scene of idealised and disembodied intellectual exchange, the pair 'talk[ing] Greek metres as if they lived in a world where the only hunger known could be satisfied by grand or sweet cadences' (126). Just a few pages later, however, that hypothetical 'as if' becomes a material reality, when Reardon interrupts their conversation on contemporary fiction to suggest: 'suppose we eat a morsel of something. I'm rather hungry' (129). In a less prandial novel, the line would introduce a scene change, but here it elicits a narratorial gloss:

[24] Rachel Bowlby, *Just Looking: Consumer Culture in Dreiser, Gissing and Zola* (New York: Methuen, 1985), p. 109.

> In the early days of his marriage Reardon was wont to offer the friends who looked in on Sunday evening a substantial supper; by degrees the meal had grown simpler, until now, in the depth of his poverty, he made no pretence of hospitable entertainment. It was only because he knew that Biffen as often as not had nothing whatever to eat that he did not hesitate to offer him a slice of bread and butter and a cup of tea. They went into the back room, and over the Spartan fare continued to discuss aspects of fiction. (129)

Rather than allow the characters to live in a world where hunger can indeed be 'satisfied by grand or sweet cadences', Gissing summons that Arnoldian option as a counterfactual only to reassert the constraint of sustenance: To keep talking, you need to keep eating.

While this scene stages the embodied nature of reader reception, a later one concerns that of the production of writing. As Biffen draws to the end of writing his novel, *Mr Bailey, Grocer*, we are told:

> It was very weak of Harold Biffen to come so near perishing of hunger as he did in the days when he was completing his novel. But he would have vastly preferred to eat and be satisfied had any method of obtaining food presented itself to him. He did not starve for the pleasure of the thing, I assure you. Pupils were difficult to get just now, and writing that he had sent to magazines had returned upon his hands. He pawned such of his possessions as he could spare, and he reduced his meals to the minimum. Nor was he uncheerful in his cold garret and with his empty stomach, for 'Mr Bailey, Grocer', drew steadily to an end. (378)

Once more, the novel toys with the possibility of severing mind from body, before reminding us that the distinction is fallacious. First there is the caution against any idealised conception of the starving artist, the notion that malnourishment would give Biffen a masochistic or romantic sort of 'pleasure'. Then, we track his pursuit of different options – each itself an expenditure of the sensitive and locomotive streams – and the resulting reduction to bare existence. And while the gesture to his not being 'uncheerful' entertains an affect-driven escape from material conditions, Gissing plots it so that, on Biffen's final day of writing, his stomach's exigencies become simply impossible to ignore. Again, timescales are the key:

> At eight o'clock in the evening there remained half a page to be written. Biffen had already worked about nine hours, and on breaking off to appease his hunger he doubted whether to finish to-night or to postpone the last lines till tomorrow. The discovery that only a small crust of bread lay in the cupboard decided him to write no more; he would have to go out to purchase a loaf, and that was disturbance.
>
> But stay; had he enough money? He searched his pockets. Two pence and two farthings; no more.
>
> You are probably not aware that at bakers' shops in the poor quarters the price of the half-quartern loaf varies sometimes from week to week. At present, as Biffen knew, it was twopence three-farthings, a common figure. But Harold did not possess three farthings, only two. Reflecting, he remembered to have passed yesterday a shop where the bread was marked twopence halfpenny; it was a shop in a very obscure little street off Hampstead Road, some distance from Clipstone Street. Thither he must repair. (378–9)

As in the characters' discussion of contemporary literature, the act of its composition is invaded by hunger, and once more the narrator takes the opportunity to detail eating's economics – first through free indirect style, then reader apostrophe. While Jameson contrasts Gissing's 'privileged yet placeless observer' with the 'systematic mapping' of urban space we find in other naturalist novels, here there is a clear attention to how characters are both placed and physically incarnate (*Political Unconscious*, 191, 190). Biffen's mapping is not systematic but personal, his perceptions informed by the stomach as well as the eye. Luckily for this brain-worker, the 'twopence halfpenny' sale is still on offer, and, newly nourished, he returns to the garret where: 'He sat down, wrought with unusual speed, and at half-past ten wrote with magnificent flourish "The End"' (*New Grub Street*, 379). The scene is the mirror image of Jasper's 'encouragement'. It is similarly attentive to the rhythms of nutritive input and cognitive output, and our narrator attends to them with real numerical precision. It reminds us that even the writer ostensibly indifferent to his skeleton state cannot live on aesthetic 'value' alone; eventually, the stream of consciousness will run dry.

The scholarly tendency to treat Gissing's novels symptomatically has a close corollary in food studies readings writ large, which tend to excavate the many ideological underpinnings of fictional diners and victuals. *New Grub Street*, however, seems one step ahead of its critics. From its very title to that of Biffen's *Grocer*, the novel thwarts our tendency to read food as symbol or even signifier. Instead, what the work offers is a close study in food's metonymic relation to brainwork. In doing so, it challenges our critical idiom and supplements Lewes's model for physiological life. For Gissing, thought and digestion lack a clear-cut relationship where the excess of one function impedes the other. By recentring the issue of scarcity, he plots a less reductive relationship between the streams of nutrition and consciousness.

Novel experiments

Compared to *Middlemarch*, *New Grub Street* may seem to offer a flat sort of psychology, yet its portrait of Biffen is not so different from that of Casaubon: two brainworkers pursuing passion projects in ignorance of the market. The difference lies not only in their economic positions but also in the codes of their fictions – and by extension the novel's generic tools for rendering the mind. Like Eliot, Gissing was attentive to the way realism could take many forms, and Biffen overtly situates his own novel vis-à-vis prior models. *Mr Bailey, Grocer*, he explains, constitutes 'an absolute realism in the sphere of the ignobly decent', qualifying: 'Zola writes deliberate tragedies; his vilest figures become heroic from the place they fill in a strongly imagined drama. I want to deal with the essentially unheroic, with the day-to-day life of that vast majority of people who are at the mercy of paltry circumstances' (128). Though readers are never treated to Biffen's prose, Gissing makes it clear that *New Grub Street* does not itself provide an 'absolute realism' on the terms of *Mr Bailey, Grocer*. 'The first duty of a novelist is to tell a story', the narrator reminds us: 'the perpetual repetition of this phrase is a warning to all men who propose drawing from the life. Biffen only offered a slice of biography, and it was found to lack flavour' (431). Indeed, eating becomes psychologically significant in the novel precisely based on 'story': a story that trades Lewes's *longue durée* interest in 'nomadic existence' for the medium timescale of plot, as well as the short timescales of Jasper's one review per breakfast, and Biffen's half-a-page per evening loaf-of-bread. Still, Biffen's comments are a productive invitation to think of how Gissing's rendering of embodied cognition differs from those we see in Zola's 'deliberate tragedies'.

By the Frenchman's own account, naturalist novels could be considered 'deliberate' only in their commitment to research. Consider his *ars poetica*, *Le Roman expérimental* (1880), in which Zola synthesises his understanding of a 'literature governed by science', namely in the 'experimental method' of Claude Bernard.[25] For Zola, this disciplinary transfer is relatively straightforward, often requiring the mere replacement of 'the word "doctor" by the word "novelist"' (1–2). Whereas the doctor seeks knowledge of 'physical life', the novelist pursues that of 'passionate and intellectual life' (2). *Le Roman expérimental* proceeds to deliver a capsule history of science, in which vitalism cedes to mechanism such that comparable laws are, by 1880, understood to regulate human and inhuman action. 'When it has been proved that the body of man is a machine, whose machinery can be taken apart and put together again at the will of the experimenter, then we can pass to the passionate and intellectual acts of man', Zola explains. 'A like determinism will govern the stones of the roadway and the brain of man' (16–17). By this account, the limits of scientific experiments to capture affective and mental activity will be filled not by doctors or psychologists but by the naturalist novel.

Victuals are a beloved reagent of Zola's experiments in his *Rougon-Macquart* novel cycle. From the famous cheese inventory of *Le Ventre de Paris* (1873) to the searing depiction of alcohol in *L'Assommoir* (1877) to the inquiry into department store fare in *Au Bonheur de Dames* (1883), this naturalist eye casts hunger and thirst as primary mechanisms in the human 'machine'. Perhaps no novel captures these dynamics better than *Germinal* (1885), in which the miners' protest cry – '*Du pain! du pain! du pain!*' – courses through the novel, interrupting the luxe meals of company manager Hennebeau, until their strike is finally broken by hunger. Yet one of the striking lacunae in Zola's expansive oeuvre is an 'experiment' on the literary milieu, a *Nouveau Grub Street* of *fin-de-siècle* Paris, and therein lies Gissing's innovation.[26] By turning the experiment back upon the scientist, Gissing reveals that a novelist's own cognitive acts are embodied in a human

[25] Émile Zola, *The Experimental Novel, and Other Essay*, tr. Belle M. Sherman (New York: Cassell, 1893), p. 1. Though somewhat stilted, Sherman's very literal translation captures Zola's points.

[26] The closest Zola comes is the study of painterly ambition in *L'Œuvre* (1886), which features the novelist secondary character, Pierre Sandoz.

machine, their fictions written of and for the same bread they depict.

Indeed, that project calls into question Zola's naturalist teleology in which personality, and by extension human psychology, will be gradually explained on physiological grounds. For to perform experiments on oneself is to recentre consciousness, not simply as a requisite but undesirable factor, but as the very basis for analysis. Here we might think back to Gissing's use of that very term 'experiment' to describe his waking at 5.30 to try out the Walter Scott schedule for literary production. The experiment's goal here may simply be optimised word count, but it posits an embodied model for cognition and self-observation as the way to access that knowledge. From *Demos* (1886) to *The Nether World* (1889), many of Gissing's novels can look derivate of naturalism, applying Zola's naturalist method to London's different milieus. But within *New Grub Street*'s attention to brainworkers and cognitive eating, we find a less materialist psychological model.

That model comes to the fore in Gissing final completed novel: *The Private Papers of Henry Ryecroft* (1903). Like *New Grub Street*, *Henry Ryecroft* takes up the literary milieu, only it does so through the retrospective account of its deceased eponymous protagonist, whose papers we read courtesy of a fictional editor. A preface recounts Ryecroft's toils in London until the age of fifty, when a friend's will bequeaths a life annuity allowing him to retire to a rustic cottage life near Exeter – where he composes the passages comprising the remainder of the novel. As Mary Hammond points out, Ryecroft is in many ways a revised Reardon, and she suggests the novel marks a political, moral, and artistic 'retreat'.[27] Adrian Poole puts the contrast more trenchantly, asserting that 'the Utopian calm so affectionately figured here can only be considered as a deplorable but logical capitulation', one that replaces the writer's dialectic struggle against society with a 'comfortable tapestry of Self' (*Gissing in Context*, 204, 206). In truth, the 'tapestry' *Ryecroft* provides is anything but 'comfortable'; attending to its figuration of embodied cognition, we can see it as a

[27] Mary Hammond, '"Amid the Dear Old Horrors": Memory, London, and Literary Labour in *The Private Papers of Henry Ryecroft*', in John Spiers, ed., *Gissing and the City: Cultural Crisis and the Making of Books in Late Victorian England* (Basingstoke: Palgrave Macmillan, 2006), pp. 171–9, 176.

development in Gissing's portrait of psychology rather than an unscrupulous departure.

These continuities become clear in the passages that revisit the prandial topoi of *New Grub Street*. Consider a moment when Ryecroft surveys his bookshelves and reflects on the 'sacrifice' that each work represents:

> Many a time I have stood before a stall, or a bookseller's window, torn by conflict of intellectual desire and bodily need. At the very hour of dinner, when my stomach clamoured for food, I have been stopped by sight of a volume so long coveted, and marked at so advantageous a price, that I *could* not let it go; yet to buy it meant pangs of famine. My Heyne's *Tibullus* was grasped at such a moment. It lay on the stall of the old book-shop in Goodge Street—a stall where now and then one found an excellent thing among quantities of rubbish. Sixpence was the price—sixpence! At that time I used to eat my midday meal (of course my dinner) at a coffee-shop in Oxford Street, one of the real old coffee-shops, such as now, I suppose, can hardly be found. Sixpence was all I had—yes, all I had in the world; it would purchase a plate of meat and vegetables.[28]

Books and food again form metonymic chains, only now the nexus is framed through the first-person and retrospect. We track how the bookshelf elicits Ryecroft's memory, then journey into this 'conflict' between his nutritive and sensitive streams, both mediated by the material of sixpence. That number itself leads his mind from Goodge to Oxford Street, and from *Tibullus* to meat. A later scene applies the same framework to literary production, as Ryecroft wonders whether there are still hack workers living in garrets as he once did. Imagining that the industry is now dominated by well-fed men of fashion and youths paying for 'instruction in the art of fiction', Ryecroft recalls one of his own famished compositions, 'On Battersea Bridge', and concludes of the sketch: 'I wrote it because I enjoyed doing so, quite as much as because I was hungry' (129, 130). Remembrance, here, suggests a newfound uncertainty, as Ryecroft's current state of satiation elicits his and our own scepticism toward his memories of brainworks past. How, the novel asks, can one experience or

[28] George Gissing, *The Private Papers of Henry Ryecroft*, ed. Mark Storey (Oxford: Oxford University Press, 1987), pp. 29–30.

experiment of embodied cognition be reconstructed by another person?

Another chapter plays out the question through a fruity analepsis. 'Blackberries hanging thick upon the hedge bring to my memory something of long ago', Ryecroft observes, before detailing a story from his garret days, where he found himself so sated by similar brambles that upon reaching an inn he experienced 'a sort of bewilderment' at having been provided for by nature rather than toil (118). The chapter goes on to detail the specific social and psychological insight he gained by having such 'conscious joy' in secured sustenance (119). 'The average educated man has never stood alone, utterly alone, just clad and nothing more than that, with the problem before him of wresting his next meal from a world that cares not whether he live or die', Ryecroft reflects. 'There is no such school of political economy. Go through that course of lectures, and you will never again become confused as to the meaning of elementary terms in that sorry science' (119). We might add 'school of psychology' to that of political economy. The experience of watching brainwork respond to hunger reveals the nonsense of either positing mental autonomy or equating the brain to a roadway's stones. 'If my knowledge be only *subjective*, why, it only concerns myself; I preach to no one', Ryecroft continues, furnishing a model of experiment and experience quite different from Zola's (120). It is relativist but avoids descending into crippling scepticism, remaining committed to the value of subjective, embodied knowledge.

In many ways, *Henry Ryecroft* takes us toward the autofictional modernisms of Marcel Proust and James Joyce, yet it maintains a late-Victorian emphasis on physical milieu as the basis for both thinking and literary production. As Hammond, drawing on Raymond Williams's lecture 'When Was Modernism?', points out, Gissing's minor place in literary history is emblematic of our tendency to skip over late-nineteenth-century realists, and to proceed straight from Dickens to Joyce. The same, of course, can be said of histories of psychology that read the *fin de siècle* as a highway to Freudian psychoanalysis or Bergsonian phenomenology. Attending to a novel's prandial features can help us bridge those gaps, adding courses between Dickens's puddings and Proust's madeleine. In Gissing's ravenous brainworkers, we find a middle path between an idealism that would abnegate the 'nutritive stream' and a materialism that would deny the particularity of the mind.

2

Fitzpiers the Empiricist: Illness and Desire in *The Woodlanders*

Rachel Kravetz

In *The Woodlanders* (1887), the doctor Edred Fitzpiers chooses to start a practice in Little Hintock by marking the locations of four existing practices on a map of the area and using a pair of compasses to find 'the exact middle'.[1] Compasses have a long history as a symbol of virtuous intellectual pursuit and measured judgment.[2] Like the figure in Johannes Vermeer's austere *Geographer* (1668–9), Fitzpiers holds the instrument to measure distances on a map, but for him, the tool is a mechanism of random chance rather than an attribute of rationality and prudence.[3] His practice stalls in the ensuing months, and the reader sees folly in his use of a tool of precision to calculate propitious conditions for a new professional and social life.

Thomas Hardy initially called his story set in the woods *Fitzpiers at Hintock* for the country doctor, who through most of the novel defies expectations Victorian readers might have had for a character in his profession. He should have represented the 'empirical mindset', as Tabitha Sparks has written, with special access to 'truth' through habits of observation. The story is set in the

1 Thomas Hardy, *The Woodlanders*, ed. Dale Kramer (Oxford: Clarendon Press, 1981), 50. Further references appear parenthetically in the text.

2 See Anthony Blunt, 'Blake's "Ancient of Days": The Symbolism of the Compasses', *Journal of the Warburg Institute* 2 (1938): 53–63; James Hall, 'Compasses', in *Dictionary of Subjects and Symbols in Art* (Boulder: Westview Press, 2007).

3 Michael Hollington finds a pattern in fiction where 'conventional instruments of measurement become useless': 'Svevo, Joyce, and Modernist Time', in Macolm Bradbury and James MacFarlane, eds, *Modernism 1890–1930* (Middlesex, UK: Penguin, 1974), p. 431.

years 1856–8, as science began to advance rapidly but before these advances completely transformed medical practice.[4] Sparks locates an 'epistemological shift' in medicine in the mid-1870s, as it 'embraced, or at least confronted, a newly rational and empirical consciousness'.[5] Even at mid-century, a doctor character should not be an unconditional idealist; but Fitzpiers reads idealist philosophy and romance novels and performs scientific experiments with an unusual purpose. He has a mid-Victorian ambition 'to carry on simultaneously the study of physiology and transcendental philosophy, the material world and the ideal, so as to discover if possible a point of contact between them' (126–7). From the vantage of the late nineteenth century, this project reads as quaint, as though to underscore the incompatibility of the two modes of thought.

This essay proposes that a historical tension between materialism and idealism in the 1870s and 1880s is dramatised in a split in Fitzpiers's character. He speaks an assortment of German idealist dicta before running away to unspecified places on the Continent. He has empirical aptitudes when he returns. Empiricist and idealist philosophy were not incompatible in the eighteenth century, yet the nineteenth century often framed them as opposites, as Hardy's notebooks attest.[6] After rapid advances in anatomy and physiology in the late 1850s and 1860s, British empiricism had taken on a scientific form by the 1870s, and the empirical sciences increasingly

4 We can identify the time frame through allusions to the Matrimonial Causes Act of 1857.

5 See *The Doctor in the Victorian Novel* (New York: Routledge, 2009), pp. 2–7. Sparks quotes medical historian A.J. Youngson on a 'gap between scientific developments and medical practice: "Most doctors before 1850, and many as late as 1870 . . . simply did not observe or think scientifically"'. She proposes that Victorian novelists chose the doctor over other kinds of scientist to represent the empirical mindset to depict the 'usefulness, authority, and application of naturalistic knowledge'. In fact, as this knowledge grew, so did 'public distrust' (pp. 16–19). Philip Collins writes that in *The Woodlanders*' portrayal of the 'doctor-as-scientist, the assumption is that science so truncates the humanity of its professional adherents as to incline them to regard mankind merely as automata explicable in scientific terms, and thus to disregard traditional notions of feeling and morality'. See 'Physicians in Victorian Fiction', in Colin Gibson, ed., *Art and Society in the Victorian Novel: Essays on Dickens and His Contemporaries* (Springer, 1989), pp. 112–16; 123.

6 Variants of this opposition appear in press cuttings throughout the notebooks. See *The Literary Notebooks of Thomas Hardy*, ed. Lennart Björk (New York: New York University Press, 1985).

took on a reductively materialist cast, adopting the premise that nothing exists beyond what can be empirically observed. Peter Garratt notes that with regard to Victorian science, 'empiricism' denotes the 'rigorous pursuit of exactitude, descriptive purity, or a neutral and final description of reality-as-given'.[7] A British school of idealist philosophy based in British universities arose in response to scientific thought, which was nonetheless the long-term winner.[8] Looking to 'Plato, Kant, and Hegel', idealists ranged themselves 'against a set of outlooks they variously called empiricism, materialism, or dualism', writes W.J. Mander.[9] Hardy splits these late-century epistemologies across the character of Fitzpiers, as the scenes of him practicing medicine demonstrate. The doctor, hardly shown in his professional role, treats one patient at the beginning of the novel and one at the end. While both patients die, he is depicted as oblivious to his patient's condition and incompetent in the first scene, and skilful in the second – based, as would be necessary, on new empirical aptitudes.

Empiricism was for Hardy a frame of mind, rather than a stable epistemological framework. As philosophers and scientists sought physical and metaphysical truths, he described processes of 'noticing' – a recurring word in the novel – and ways the mind interferes with observation. The transcendental philosophy Fitzpiers reads is directly reflected in his dialogue, and I treat the novel's philosophical language as a shorthand for types of perception, of more interest to Hardy as a novelist than the frameworks he knew.[10] Life

7 Peter Garratt, *Victorian Empiricism: Self, Knowledge, and Reality in Ruskin, Bain, Lewes, Spencer, and George Eliot* (Vancouver, British Columbia: Fairleigh Dickinson University Press, 2010), p. 23.

8 Rick Rylance refers to an 'age-old dispute between empiricists, sceptics, and materialists, on the one hand, and the school of Kant and Reid, on the other'. Revived interest in German idealist thought 'reopened this quarrel'. *Victorian Psychology and British Culture: 1850–1880* (Oxford: Oxford University Press, 2000), pp. 235–42. Sandra Den Otter notes that the two camps, each encompassing a range of positions, were defined mainly in relation to the other. *British Idealism and Social Explanation: A Study in Late Victorian Thought* (Oxford: Oxford University Press, 1996), p. 53. See also A.M. Quinton, 'Absolute Idealism', in Anthony Kenny, ed., *Rationalism, Empiricism, and Idealism* (Oxford: Clarendon Press, 1986), pp. 124–50.

9 W.J. Mander, *British Idealism: A History* (Oxford: Oxford University Press, 2014), p. 5.

10 William Rutland has found that Hardy read J.S. Mill and others from his youth, and increasingly read philosophy after 1880. *Thomas Hardy: A Study*

may be a 'physiological fact', he would write as he contested the strictures of respectability in 'Candour in English Fiction' (1890), but he saw the mind working tirelessly to evade that fact.[11] In Hardy's novels, idealism, like empiricism, is mainly a subjective state, in which the mind projects its desires onto visible surfaces. This unphilosophical variant of idealism is the principal subject of *The Well-Beloved*, published serially in 1892 and as a three-part novel in 1897, but also appears among most major characters of *The Woodlanders*. The strongly marked shift in the doctor's character draws us to notice the others' minor vacillations. The regular contrasts between 'rustic' and 'cultivated' characters, often in class terms, may be a concession to readers expecting this theme from Hardy, or a prod to trace other configurations, based on perceptual habits, among the five romantically entangled characters – Fitzpiers, the woman he marries (Grace Melbury), his paramour (Felice Charmond), his rival for Grace (Giles Winterbourne), and that rival's admirer (Marty South).[12]

The mind's turns toward or away from the material world is especially guided in this novel by the sight of a body. In both *The Woodlanders* and *The Well-Beloved*, the beautiful body and the idealist gaze create one another, the body evoking the gaze that projects onto it. When Hardy conceives an idealist figurative sculptor in the later novel, he alludes to a history of German aesthetics that finds the ideal embodied in classical sculpture. In a novel with

of His Writings and Their Background (New York: Russell & Russell, 1962), pp. 89–90.

[11] *Thomas Hardy's Personal Writings*, ed. Harold Orel (London: Macmillan, 1966), pp. 125–33.

[12] Readers who emphasise the opposition between rustic and cultivated characters include J.B. Bullen, who sees an elegy 'for the loss of a simple, primitive mode of perception', comparing it with a 'more highly developed view . . . colored by introspection and subjectivism'. *The Expressive Eye: Fiction and Perception in the Novels of Thomas Hardy* (Oxford: Clarendon Press, 1986), pp. 175–80. Suzanne Keen contrasts the woodlanders' 'old-fashioned minds' or 'psychological backwardness' with outsiders' 'modern interiority'. *Thomas Hardy's Brains: Psychology, Neurology, and Hardy's Imagination* (Ohio State University Press, 2014), pp. 153–4. Readings that question this opposition include George Fayen, Jr, 'Hardy's *The Woodlanders*: Inwardness and Memory', *Studies in English Literature, 1500–1900* 1.4 (Autumn 1961): 81–100, 95; David Lodge, 'Introduction', in *The Woodlanders* (London: Macmillan, 1974), p. 18; and John Bayley, 'A Social Comedy? On Re-reading *The Woodlanders*', *Thomas Hardy Annual* 5 (1987): 3–21, 16–17.

a doctor protagonist, ill bodies appear and demand concentration on their physical condition. By giving an idealist mindset to the doctor, Hardy considers its implications for work that requires attention to the human body as seen as part of the natural order.

The Woodlanders depicts how the mind responds to another's body as an object of desire as well as a physical problem. David Morris has written that 'medicine tends to flee the erotic, with good reason. Eros, as an ancient representative of passion and irrational desire, is the sworn enemy of instrumental reason'.[13] The common illnesses in *The Woodlanders* relate how easily bodies slip out of health, and an eroticised body becomes a body in need of care-taking. Elaine Scarry notes a point in *Tess of the d'Urbervilles* (1891) when Angel Clare acts out of the 'twin imperatives of desire and rescue'.[14] In Hardy's preceding novel, these imperatives are always proximate and continually interfere with one another. As other characters share Fitzpiers's idealist mindset, they take on his medical role. Bodies resist interpretation because illness rarely manifests clearly, but also because desire projects and interposes an ideal image. Desire and illness imply together that there cannot be any controlling understanding of the mind, as each imperative of the body insists on and tends to eventually elicit a different type of perception.

The reclining figure is a form shared by the ideal body and the ill body in *The Woodlanders*. In what follows, I trace the novel's series of reclining figures, which form a symmetrical pattern of nested pairs. The framing scenes show Fitzpiers engaged in medical treatment, the first emphasising his empirical weakness as well as that of Giles. Each of the four intermediate scenes pairs a man and a woman who are erotically attached, and all except one involve at least a pretence of healing. Nested within the outermost scenes of treatment are two episodes in which Grace unexpectedly comes upon an unconscious man. First, she finds the doctor sleeping in his elegant home and returns his erotic interest. Later, she finds Giles fatally ill on a 'rude couch' of 'hay and sacks' in a makeshift shelter, his recumbent figure both ill and beloved. She then calls on Fitzpiers, who displays new empirical abilities. The central pair

[13] David Morris, *Eros and Illness* (Cambridge and London: Harvard University Press, 2017), pp. 22–5.

[14] Elaine Scarry, 'Work and the Body in Hardy and Other Nineteenth-Century Novelists', *Representations* 3 (Summer 1983): 90–123, 117.

of scenes portrays the mutual seduction of Fitzpiers and Felice, her feigned injury the guise for an affair that leads to his genuine injury. This pattern accentuates the ease with which erotic lure and physical vulnerability may replace each other, and the great gap between them.

When the novel's erotically reclining figures resemble types from the history of art, the allusions are not merely cues for the reader; the educated, higher-class characters seem to have internalised them. Thus, Fitzpiers's taste, and not only his scientific profession, brings the novel into relation with British empiricism in its later years.[15] His interest in 'abstract philosophy' is itself said to be a 'taste'. This phrase, like the novel's mentions of 'old association', implicitly show how the language of empiricism had for Hardy come to name everyday experiences (5; 119).[16] The empirical tradition developed philosophical aesthetics in the eighteenth century, grounding appreciation for both beauty and goodness in the instinctive experience of pleasure. As Carolyn Korsmeyer has found, this philosophy downplays the ways that 'taste preferences may be molded and altered' and 'subject to change both within a society and between cultures'.[17] David Hume's 'Of the Standard of Taste' (1757) and Alexander Gerard's *An Essay on Taste* (1759), to take two examples, acknowledge training as a factor in taste but consider it secondary. Nineteenth-century physiologically-based aesthetics continued to pursue a natural basis for consensus through pleasure.[18] Hardy refers to philosophical aesthetics in

15 For histories of the modern notion of taste, see David Summers, *The Judgment of Sense: Renaissance Naturalism and the Rise of Aesthetics* (Cambridge: Cambridge University Press, 1990); and Luc Ferry, *Homo Aestheticus: The Invention of Taste in the Democratic Age*, trans. Robert de Loazia (Chicago: University of Chicago Press, 1993).

16 David Coombs has discussed the importance of the concept of association to Hardy in 'Reading in the Dark: Sensory Obscurity in *The Return of the Native*'. See *Reading with the Senses in Victorian Literature and Science* (Charlottesville: University of Virginia Press, 2019).

17 Carolyn Korsmeyer, 'Taste as Sense and Sensibility', *Philosophical Topics* 25.1 (Spring 1997): 201–30. James Noggle emphasises that 'the prominence of immediacy in the discourse of taste has often led historians of thought to overlook or push aside . . . training in preferences, and its role in constituting various exclusive social, national, class-, and gender-identities through history'. *The Temporality of Taste in Eighteenth-Century British Writing* (Oxford: Oxford University Press, 2012), p. 10.

18 I see *The Woodlanders* as taking up 'new questions' of psychology that Rylance

the essay 'The Profitable Reading of Fiction' (1888), noting that 'volumes have been written on the development of the aesthetic sense by the study of painting and sculpture' as he attests to the value of pleasure.[19]

Victorian writers tend to bring out what is latent and unresolved in the classical empiricist tradition, and in *The Woodlanders*, learned, rather than instinctive, tastes form a basis for accord. The novel alludes to the discourse of taste when Fitzpiers forgoes professional ambition for a 'reciprocity of tastes' in his courtship of Grace (146). The narrator tells us that she is drawn to him by the possibility of 'pleasure' in a 'refined and cultivated inner life', indicating that pleasure is not prior to culture but its product (155–6). After the labourer Giles arranges for Grace to lunch at a rough tavern, she believes that it was 'her superficial and transitory taste which had been offended, and not her nature or her affection' (265). Yet she seems to misunderstand the way taste creates bonds. To unite, characters must be able to fit each other into mutually recognised ideal types. The educated characters project desire onto figures and landscapes emulating artistic genres that Europe considered ideal in their assimilation of models and themes from classical antiquity. They find the ideal in forms that philosophers and fine artists had given it, in genres that were well-known and even seen as exhausted through repetition by the late nineteenth century.

When Fitzpiers arrives to check on his patient John South, he enters as a doctor tends to when 'the room is that of a humble cottager; looking round toward the patient with a preoccupied gaze'. The narrator first explains his gaze through class difference, then revises and describes it as a more fundamental trait. Presenting the doctor in a tone of formal introduction, the narrator states, 'His eyes were dark and impressive, and beamed with the light either of energy, or susceptivity. . . . That quick, glittering, empirical eye, sharp for the surface of things if for nothing beneath, he had not'. Given this description of his eye, the reader doubts his cure for the patient, who sees a tree sway in the wind and fears it will smash his house. Fitzpiers decides that 'the tree ought to be cut

outlines: 'Is this means of transmission' of an organism's inheritance 'organic or cultural? To what extent is the mind only a phenomenon of consciousness and habit?' *Victorian Psychology*, p. 209.

19 *Personal Writings*, pp. 110–24.

down'. In this sole instance of medical treatment that is free of erotic energies, the consequence of the doctor's eye for his patient is clear. Giles brings the tree down at the doctor's direction, and South dies at sunset. Readers have suggested that Hardy would have understood his ailment as psychological, and the doctor dramatically fails to interpret how the mind and body interact in his case.[20] This scene also establishes Fitzpiers and Giles as thinking similarly, beneath a more conspicuous class difference. While Giles carries out the physical labour involved in Fitzpiers's treatment, he has devised a similar approach before Fitzpiers arrives, removing branches so the wind will affect the tree less. Each man thinks of his solution as an 'experiment', an activity more associated with the doctor (90–101).

Both men idealise Grace. In the market scene that shows her return from abroad, Marty sees Giles 'lift his eyes' and follows his gaze towards Grace 'looking glorified and refined to much above her former level'. Elevation is at once a metaphor for her cultivation and for the effect of Giles's gaze. The narrator soon introduces her in this way: 'It would have been difficult to describe Grace Melbury with precision'. He seems to be assuming an idealist perspective, continuing, 'Nay, from the highest point of view, to describe a human being, the focus of a universe – how impossible'. This helps to explain the next sentence: 'But, apart from transcendentalism, there probably never lived a person who was in herself more completely a *reductio ad absurdum* of attempts to appraise a woman even externally by items of face and figure'. Yet the narrator goes on to describe her complexion, build and expression, reading in them a character of diffidence. She is a 'shape in the gloom' only to 'Sherton eyes', as the woodlanders take a 'cursory view' of her fashionable dress and see 'very little' (38–40).

20 Anna West finds that the description of South's illness 'matches contemporary medical discourse on delirium and illusions', understood at the time as misinterpreted perceptions. She proposes that his death has a material or neural cause that Fitzpiers fails to discern: 'Two Brains and a Tree: Defining the Material Bases for Delusion and Reality in *The Woodlanders*', *Victorian Network* 7 (2016): 36–60, 47. Suzy Anger finds that Fitzpiers diagnoses South's case as one of 'aberrant psychology' in 'Naturalizing the Mind in the Victorian Novel: Consciousness in Wilkie Collins's *Poor Miss Finch* and Thomas Hardy's *Woodlanders* – Two Case Studies', in Lisa Rodensky, ed., *The Oxford Handbook of the Victorian Novel* (Oxford: Oxford University Press, 2016), p. 502.

Grace will later attribute to Giles an ability to see nature with extraordinary clarity, yet he is often in insensible states, even as he performs agricultural work. As he drives Grace home upon her return, Giles does not 'notice much with his outward eye', like Fitzpiers (43). As he and Marty plant firs together, he handles them as unconsciously as their roots grasp the earth. Absorbed in planning his Christmas party, 'he hardly was conscious of Marty's presence', and at the party, he remains in a 'half unconscious state' (63–5; 73). The competition between him and the doctor for Grace draws the idealists into closer parallel. Fitzpiers first appears during the planting scene as Giles's mirror image, watching Grace pass 'over the hedge on the opposite side of the way' (65). Fitzpiers soon offers Giles a ride, where the doctor quotes Shelley, paraphrases Spinoza, and explains love as a projection in Kant's language, saying, 'I am in love with something in my own head, and no thing-in-itself outside at all'. Giles models the reader's surprise, asking, 'Is it part of a country doctor's duties to learn that view of things?' He is 'struck by a curious parallelism between Mr. Fitzpiers's manner and Grace's' in how they blithely discuss subjects foreign to him while they are with him (114). Yet the reader sees the two men riding side by side and gazing up in unison toward her shape in her window.

After Grace approaches Fitzpiers on behalf of a servant who wishes to cancel an agreement to sell her brain, he leads her to a microscope holding a sliver of South's brain and explains his aim to learn how the material and the ideal may touch.[21] During this period, in the 1850s and 1860s, psychologists studied brain tissue to pursue the different question of the relation between the body and the mind.[22] The diffuse field of psychology came to incorporate the body, 'especially nervous structures, into the theory of subjectivity', after the body was generally 'absent in eighteenth-century discussions of the mind'.[23] Yet even as psychology moved into laboratories and its physiological discourse sought to attrib-

[21] George Levine describes this scene as a parody of philosophical thought in '*The Woodlanders* and the Darwinian Grotesque'. See Keith Wilson, ed., *Thomas Hardy Reappraised: Essays in Honor of Michael Millgate* (Toronto: University of Toronto Press, 2006), p. 191.

[22] The doctor's combination of activities was 'in opposition to the current of scientific thought' by the time Hardy conceived *The Woodlanders* in 1874, according to West. 'Two Brains and a Tree', 40.

[23] Garratt, *Victorian Empiricism*, pp. 34; 127–30.

ute mental processes to physical workings and localise the brain's functions, the mind was seen as largely inaccessible to science, as it still is. At the time Hardy wrote *The Woodlanders*, the physicist John Tyndall and the biologist T.H. Huxley had made this claim, even as they presumed a relation between the body and the mind.[24] The idealist philosopher T.H. Green had opened his *Prolegomena to Ethics* (1883) with the assertion that there cannot be a natural science of consciousness as pursued by empirical psychology.[25] In keeping with this statement, I find in Hardy's novel an assumption that another's mind can only be read through the living body's surface.

While Giles and Grace are incongruous in each other's homes, while he has one, she fits Fitzpiers into a familiar template when she finds him asleep in his sitting-room. Hardy often renders a beautiful body a Greek statue, and the narrator has already described the face of Fitzpiers as 'artistically beautiful enough to have been worth modelling by any sculptor not over busy'. His mouth has a 'classical curve' (99). Leonard Barkan notes that though reclining statues have usually been female since the Renaissance, the 'beautiful boy has at least as long a history as passive sex object'.[26] On the morning she meets her husband-to-be, Grace sees 'a handsome man snugly ensconced on the couch, like a recumbent figure within some canopied mural tomb of the fifteenth century'.[27] The

[24] Levine writes that Tyndall 'famously conceded' the impossibility of the mind-body problem in his 1868 essay 'Scientific Materialism'. See 'Darwinian Grotesque', 197. Anger writes, 'As Huxley points out, that there exists a close relationship between the physical and the mental is clear, but how to explain that relationship remains unclear. Almost every serious Victorian commentator on consciousness makes a version of the "explanatory gap" argument, admitting that we must recognize that we are unable to bridge the chasm in our understanding between brain and mind'. See 'Naturalizing the Mind', 485–6. J. Hillis Miller describes Hardy's dualism as a 'paradoxical form' that sees the human mind, having 'arisen accidentally, from the play of physical causes', as 'radically different from its source'. *Thomas Hardy: Distance and Desire* (Cambridge: Harvard University Press, 1970), pp. 12–13.

[25] Quoted in Mander, *British Idealism*, pp. 89–90.

[26] See Leonard Barkan, 'The Beholder's Tale: Ancient Sculpture, Renaissance Narratives', *Representations* 44 (Autumn 1993): 133–66, 149–50.

[27] Patricia Pulham looks at the complex ways that sculpture, including funerary sculpture, mediates 'forbidden desire' in *The Sculptural Body in Victorian Literature* (Edinburgh: Edinburgh University Press, 2020), pp. 188–9. John Addington Symonds, who corresponded with Hardy, remarks of Antonio Rossellino's tomb of the Cardinal of Portugal at San Miniato a Monte in

larger scene inserts Fitzpiers into a line of paintings of idealised sculptural figures in repose. He takes the place of Venus, who in European paintings tends to recline in erotic availability or attend to her appearance in a mirror. Hardy places the mirror on the wall, and Grace turns toward it to see Fitzpiers's reflection as part of a 'world of figment', in Isobel Armstrong's phrase.[28]

When Fitzpiers momentarily makes eye contact with Grace in the mirror, Hardy makes the reflection a site of transmission between minds. Empiricist texts figure the mind as mirrorlike, its crystalline images of the outside world eroded in memory and scrambled by errors, dreams, and imagination.[29] Hardy turns an empiricist metaphor for sensory fidelity and its violation into a surface for ideal images mutually evoked by the two beholders. Fitzpiers later recounts that in this moment, he briefly believes that 'the design is for once carried out', describing a daydream as the fulfilment of the intellectual project he explains, just after, at his microscope (125). His idealism seems to evoke hers through their exchanged look.[30] Grace previously has been selectively observant, especially noticing her own appearance, that of Fitzpiers, and that of their homes; his is visible from her bedroom window. Reflecting the houses where they hang, Hardy's mirrors situate such encounters within a world of aesthetic conventions. When Grace is invited to Hintock House, she and Felice stand before a mirror, and the reader finds a double mirror effect as they look at themselves and one another against the luxurious background (58). This image confirms the older woman as a model to the

Florence, 'The sublimity of the slumber that is death has never been more nobly and feelingly portrayed than in the supine figure and sleeping features of this most beautiful young man, who lies watched by angels beneath a heavy-curtained canopy'. *Renaissance in Italy: The Fine Arts* (London: Smith, Elder, & Co., 1880), p. 153.

28 Isobel Armstrong, *Victorian Glassworlds: Glass Culture and the Imagination 1830–1880* (Oxford: Oxford University Press, 2008), p. 8.

29 See Francis Bacon, *The Advancement of Learning: Book I*, ed. James Spedding, Robert Leslie Ellis and Douglas Denon Heath (Cambridge: Cambridge University Press, 2013), p. 6; 35; and John Locke, *An Essay Concerning Human Understanding*, ed. Peter Nidditch (Oxford: Oxford University Press, 1979), 2.1.25.

30 Penny Bouhelma writes that Grace's 'attraction to Fitzpiers seems, at their first meeting, simply to reflect back the unknowing gaze of desire which she intercepts in the mirror'. *Thomas Hardy and Women: Sexual Ideology and Narrative Form* (Sussex: Harvester Press, 1982), p. 101.

younger one; meeting her afterward, Giles notes that Grace could 'enter into the views' of Felice, 'talk like her, and dress not unlike her' (67). The women have synonymic names, if 'grace' is taken to mean 'charm', a word repeatedly associated with her (113–15; 128; 266). Felice, meanwhile, compares herself unfavourably to Grace and distances herself. The mirror at Fitzpiers's home kindles and displays the mutual ideal pull between him and Grace – each sees the other as a 'vision' – and a sense of their mutual exclusion (125).[31]

The ideal space surrounding Grace and Fitzpiers extends into the landscape. In the novel's short account of their marriage, the view she sees from the Earl of Wessex hotel in the town of Sherton-Abbas after their honeymoon resembles an ideal landscape painting, a genre that usually sets a biblical or mythological story within an Italianate landscape. Hardy's image, a bejewelled landscape fading into mist, turned into a quotation by the window frame, conveys that the ideal may be a learned type. Below, Giles supervises the crushing of fruit into cider, appearing in the place of the mythological figure he will later become to Grace (165–6). Fitzpiers has found her to range 'unerringly at his level in ideas, tastes, and habits' during their wedding tour on the Continent, the novel's realm of fantasy, which is never represented directly (169). Yet in the woods, his repeated 'distaste' for her milieu divides them. He experiences a 'profound distaste' during a dinner with neighbours on their return (172–3). The change of setting mars the picture and undoes his attachment to his wife. Fitzpiers is then drawn to Felice at Hintock House, already described as isolated in a 'spot to inspire the painter'. This description alludes to the way the British had sought and shaped picturesque, or painting-like, landscapes for more than a century. Hardy's characters have a similar habit of looking for likenesses to genres of the plastic arts in the world around them. The novel's ideal imagery is concentrated around the erotically reclining figures of Fitzpiers in his sitting-room and Felice in her manor house.

[31] Audrey Jaffe explores how Hardy 'rewrites' mirrors and windows, conventional metaphors of realism and its 'transparency', as 'blocking mechanisms'. They serve 'both as material the viewer sees through and a barrier or site for projection' that makes 'shared fantasy' conditional on shared narratives about the viewer's relation to the natural or social landscape. 'Outside the Gates of Everything: Hardy's Exclusionary Realism', *Novel: A Forum on Fiction* 43.3 (Fall 2010): 381–400, 384–91.

In a third, central scene of Fitzpiers practicing medicine, doctor and patient masquerade in their roles. Felice sends for him after her carriage overturns, and he is shown to a room where he sees 'a woman of elegant figure reclining upon a couch . . . her left arm, which was naked nearly up to the shoulder, was thrown upwards'. To seduce him, Felice seems to have knowingly assumed the pose of Venus in Renaissance paintings, modelled in turn on the classical statue of the *Sleeping Ariadne* (2 BC). Curiously unhurt, she has invented the pretence of a 'little scrape' on the arm she lifts. Alastair Smart suggests that Hardy alludes to a work of art 'in order to make a description vivid'.[32] Yet the pose is legible to Fitzpiers as well the reader. He finds that the 'sentiment and essence of the moment were indescribably familiar' (175–6). In a literal sense, the cause is their forgotten youthful encounter in Germany. Perhaps the familiarity is also there because the scene takes the recognisable format of an ideal female figure reclining. Visiting daily, Fitzpiers 'always found Felice reclining on a sofa', and they imagine themselves as figures in a painting, their memories of a few days in the past becoming a 'canvas for infinite fancies' (182–3). The doctor departs his role most fully when he becomes a patient. Felice becomes his nurse after he falls from one horse and is thrown by George Melbury from another. During this episode, Fitzpiers complains to his wife's father, as though speaking as an artwork, that except for the rich and beautiful Felice, 'people don't appreciate me here!' (237).

Grace's idealism, which becomes unfastened from her husband through his increasing absence, seeks out Giles. Atop a hill, she fits him into another ideal landscape as an allegorical figure, 'Autumn's very brother' (193). In her 'passionate desire for primitive life', she expresses the primitivism that has at times been attributed to Hardy (208).[33] Giles knows too much to be 'primitive', having

[32] Smart notes that Felice shares this pose with Lucetta Templeman, who adopts 'the pose of a well-known conception of Titian' when she seduces Donald Farfrae. He sees an allusion to Giorgione and Titian's *Sleeping Venus* (1510) or Titian's *Bacchanal of the Andrians* (152–6) or *Rape of Europa* (1560–2). 'Pictorial Imagery in the Novels of Thomas Hardy', *The Review of English Studies* 12.47 (August 1961): 262–80, 265. Fayen, Jr, sees Felice as having 'assumed the pose of a typical continental coquette' and finds in her beauty a Pre-Raphaelite type. 'Inwardness', 85–6. Yet this type gestures to a line of Renaissance prototypes, thought to begin with the *Sleeping Venus*.

[33] David DeLaura writes that 'an unexamined and simplistic primitivism' appears

understood it to be a category based on class when he reflects on the 'primitive simplicity of the subject' of varieties of apple trees, and when he worries that 'homely Christmas gatherings in the jovial Hintock style seemed so primitive' (44; 67). Grace finds that Giles's 'homeliness no longer offended her acquired tastes' (206). She now sees in the country the orchards, rustic figures, and sunsets her milieu would have found appealing.

Giles becomes the novel's final reclining figure, both beloved and patient. As the novel's purest scenes of seduction parody medicine, Hardy draws the scenes of severest illness as a parody of seduction. After Fitzpiers breaks with Felice, announces his return to England by letter, and arrives in Little Hintock, Grace flees to Giles, who gives her his hut and sleeps in a 'wretched little shelter' during a storm (281–2). The image echoes that of Fitzpiers in a canopied bed. Grace finally finds Giles with his arms 'flung over his head', now an ineffective gesture of protection rather than a pose of seduction. The blush that reddened Felice's face is replaced by a flush of 'unnatural crimson'. The 'burning brightness' of Giles's eyes expresses a 'visionary' delirium rather than a fantasy of love (290). In their resemblance to the seduction scenes, these images of illness heighten the reader's perception of the distance between the two physical states.

Grace nurses Giles in a scene the narrator compares to the tending of Fitzpiers by Felice, yet the gravely ill body requires 'a medical man, competent and near', and 'there was one such man and only one' with 'the brain' likely to save Giles. 'One speciality of Fitzpiers was respected by Grace as much as ever: his professional skill'. The narrator confirms: 'In this she was right'. On a literal level, his previous failings are explained through a lack of application. Yet we can only see Fitzpiers as changed. He has become a skilled doctor, observant and scientifically informed. When he arrives, his 'inspection was concluded in a mere glance', the illness diagnosed as a 'sequel' to another 'disorder—possibly typhoid' (296). Having determined that the patient is dying, Fitzpiers gives Grace directions for alleviating the pain and prescribes her a preventative medicine he has brought from Italy. When she falls ill, his medicine cures her 'in less than an hour', and he fulfils his medical role (305).

in the late novels in '"The Ache of Modernism" in Hardy's Later Novels', *English Literary History* (September 1967): 380–99, 397–8.

In 1886, the year serial publication of *The Woodlanders* began, Leslie Stephen, Hardy's friend, recapitulated the intractability of the mind-body problem in a lecture, writing, 'A man is a materialist for the time being so long as he has only to do with that which may be touched, handled, seen, or otherwise perceived through the senses'. Hardy seems to render in fictional form the notion that one is a materialist only 'so long as' one has 'the point of view of the physical inquirer'.[34] He does not presume that this mindset lasts beyond the acts of diagnosis and treatment. Her conscience troubled, Grace determines that the 'relief of consulting a skilled mind, the one professional man who had seen Giles at that time, would be immense' (311). This leads to her reconciliation with Fitzpiers, after which the couple continue to find beauty in conventional places, reuniting in a storybook bower of new leaves and soft moss under the moon. He buys, in her words, a 'beautiful practice' in a larger town (334). This ending is unusual in that late-century novels tend not to 'admit' doctors into marriage due to their 'clinical detachment and hyper-rationalism', expressing a 'tension between medical and romantic epistemologies'.[35] The reunification of Grace and Fitzpiers suggests that science and love proceed on separate logics of empirical observation and learned taste.

Previous to this, Grace and Marty briefly mourn Giles together and make weekly visits to his grave, a coordination that makes the difference between them plain, like the mirror that shows Felice the contrast between her and Grace. Now Grace creates a retroactive bond between Giles and Marty through an idealised account of the empirical gaze: 'The casual glimpses which the ordinary population had bestowed upon that wondrous world of sap and leaves called the Hintock woods had been with these two, Giles and Marty, a clear gaze. They had been possessed of its finer mysteries as of commonplace knowledge; had been able to read its hieroglyphs as ordinary writing'. Rather than affirming her ideas, the narrator describes them as 'mournful fancies' (306–8). In the nineteenth century, the notion of nature as a hieroglyphic language represented an effort to reconcile the material and ideal.[36]

34 Leslie Stephen, 'What Is Materialism?', in *An Agnostic's Apology and Other Essays* (London: Smith, Elder, & Co., 1893), pp. 129–35.

35 Sparks, *The Doctor in the Victorian Novel*, pp. 15; 22.

36 Metaphors of nature as hieroglyphics, related to the metaphor of nature

Grace thus seems to have absorbed Fitzpiers's ideas, though she soon asks him to concentrate on his profession and he readily agrees. Reading nature is not shown as a mystical process in the novel. Marty predicts fine weather when she sees three pheasants settle near the end of a bough, presumably because she has noticed this before (68).[37] Only she has an empirical eye throughout.

The aim to reconcile the empirical and ideal was not only a philosophical but also an aesthetic project in the Victorian period, as Hardy knew. He would rehearse this idea in 'The Science of Fiction' (1891), where he states that a contemporary scientific approach to literary realism involves the 'fallacy' that a 'widened knowledge of the universe and its forces' oblige the writer to copy 'in its entirety the phantasmagoria of experience'. He writes, 'To advance realism as complete copyism . . . is the hyperbolic flight of an admirable enthusiasm, the exaggerated cry of an honest reaction from the false, in which the truth has been impetuously approached and overleapt in fault of lighted on. Possibly, if we only wait, the third something, akin to perfection, will exhibit itself on its due pedestal.' In this image of ascent, the 'low' mode of realism flies up into the space where we expect the ideal to reside. The ideal of fully 'reproducing' experience is an 'impossibility'. Yet Hardy also portrays the intermediate approach of 'truth' as an ideal, in the place of a worshipped classical statue on a pedestal. Perhaps it will be realised, as classical statues were, but this is a question of art, not science. The writer who wishes to render character requires not a 'keen eye to the superficial', but a 'power of observation informed by a living heart'.[38] This returns us to the beginning of *The Woodlanders*, where the narrator imparts that a 'watchful loving-kindness' would be needed to see Grace's

as a book, had been common since the seventeenth century. See Liselotte Dieckmann, 'Renaissance Hieroglyphs', *Comparative Literature* 9.4 (Autumn 1957): 308–21. They came to represent 'the nexus between the tangible and intangible, the finite and the infinite' in the nineteenth century, according to Dieckmann. See 'The Metaphor of Hieroglyphics in German Romanticism', *Comparative Literature* 7.4 (Autumn 1955): 306–12.

37 As Sara Lyons writes, 'Marty's and Giles's understanding of the woods is so profound that it appears instinctual and even magical to Grace, but it is in fact the product of patiently accumulated observation and experiment'. 'Thomas Hardy and the Value of Brains', *Victorian Literature and Culture* 48. 2 (2020): 327–59, 341. Bullen classes Marty among Hardy's 'most sensitive and observant watchers': *Expressive Eye*, p. 4.

38 *Personal Writings*, pp. 134–8.

'true quality'. One of Hardy's gifts is his ability to fuse image and character; an eye or laugh expressing a temperament. He describes Grace, for example, as a 'flexible young creature' who is 'elastic in movement', and thus embodies her tendency to guide herself by the thoughts and acts of others.[39] The novel's only artistic presence, the narrator suggests that patient observation itself is a form of appreciative judgment, its medium fiction.

[39] Fred Reid relates this 'plastic' quality to Hardy's resistance to the idea, learned from Mill, that humans lack agency in a world of natural law. *Thomas Hardy and History* (Palgrave Macmillan, 2017), pp. 190–2.

3

Alice Meynell's Brain Waves

Gregory Tate

In one of her numerous essays about Coventry Patmore, Alice Meynell offers this praise of what she terms his 'classic' poetry:

> The fusion of thought and word is unmistakable, whether the fire of an impassioned thought bring it to pass, or the close coldness of fancy made perfect; for since we hear that metals pass into one another, *in vacuo*, by pressure in the cold, this latter image is possible; but even if, with Thomas à Kempis, we contemplate the metal that is one with fire and is changed into fire, it is less by the fusion of fire that a greatly classic poem is to be figured, than by a more vital union; mind and body, where tidal thought and feeling are quick with the blood and various with the breath of life, give a juster, as well as a simpler and a human, image of a vital poem.[1]

These comments bring together several important aspects of Meynell's writing, in particular her championing of Patmore, a poet with whom she had a close but at times contentious friendship; her commitment to the language and theology of the Catholic faith that she shared with Patmore; and her fashioning of elaborate and overdetermined metaphors. Meynell's reference to Thomas à Kempis's fifteenth-century *Imitation of Christ* is juxtaposed and aligned with the strikingly technical language of a scientific metaphor, but this composite 'image', integrating science with faith, is then rejected in favour of another, which according to Meynell is more 'human', but which is equally informed by science: the image

[1] Alice Meynell, 'Coventry Patmore', in *The Second Person Singular and Other Essays* (Oxford: Oxford University Press, 1922), pp. 95–6.

of the 'vital union' of 'mind and body', in which 'tidal thought and feeling' flow and pulse in time with the blood and breath and also with the rhythms of verse.

Rhythm is central to Meynell's understanding of poetry, of psychology, and of embodiment. Her most frequently quoted essay, 'The Rhythm of Life' (1889), opens with the claim that 'if life is not always poetical, it is at least metrical. Periodicity rules over the mental experience of man, according to the path of the orbit of his thoughts'. It ends by asserting that this periodicity is in turn 'ruled by the law that commands all things—a sun's revolutions and the rhythmic pangs of maternity'.[2] Throughout her poetry and her prose, Meynell insists that the human mind and body are organised by a rhythm that is at once metrical and universal, analogous to the motions of tides, planets, and stars. An essay on reading, published in 1896, is typical in its identification of mental processes as rhythmic, embodied 'action': 'the open mind has rhythm like the blood. Putting aside the labour of thought', Meynell observes, 'there is some movement even in pleasure'.[3] A number of critics have developed valuable analyses of the part played by rhythm in Meynell's innovative thinking about child psychology and gendered embodiment.[4] In this chapter I would like to build on their work, and on scholarship about Meynell's views on poetic form, to argue that her notion of rhythm responds to theories of physiological psychology, and to suggest that her writing points to new ways of thinking about the interrelations between literature, science and religion in late-Victorian culture. In 2006 Linda Austin set out a wide-ranging analysis of the 'psycho-physiology of memory' in Meynell's poetry.[5] My goal, however, is to be more exclusively historicist, tracing the various lines of debate that helped to shape Meynell's historically specific understanding of the mind.

2 Meynell, 'The Rhythm of Life', in *The Rhythm of Life and Other Essays* (London: Elkin Mathews and John Lane, 1893), pp. 1 and 6.

3 Meynell, 'Forty-Fifth Thousand', in P.M. Fraser, ed., *The Wares of Autolycus: Selected Literary Essays of Alice Meynell* (Oxford: Oxford University Press, 1965), p. 14.

4 See, for example, Cristina Richieri Griffin, 'Writing the Rhythms of the Womb: Alice Meynell's Poetics of Pregnancy', *Modern Philology* 112.1 (2014): 226–48.

5 Linda M. Austin, 'Self Against Childhood: The Contributions of Alice Meynell to a Psycho-Physiology of Memory', *Victorian Literature and Culture* 34.1 (2006): 249–68.

These lines converge, I argue, in Meynell's presentation of thought and feeling as rhythmic processes that are not restricted to the personal mind. She figures the rhythms of embodiment as enabling a communicative exchange between self and other that is simultaneously material, sympathetic and spiritual. Her interest in relationality and intersubjectivity has been widely recognised. According to Isobel Armstrong, her poetry reminds readers that 'the single lyric ego alone can't create community'.[6] Maria Frawley suggests that, 'resisting the temptation to depict thought processes as the solipsistic activity of isolated individuals, Meynell's poems more typically establish an interaction between voices, some presumed to be entirely internal and others more overtly externalized'.[7] And Meynell epitomises Emily Harrington's argument that late-Victorian women poets 'represent modes of interaction that exhibit proximity without identification, where subjects are both separate and connected, where someone can be fully aware of another's feelings without needing to try to feel them herself'.[8] In what follows, I aim to show that this aspect of Meynell's writing is informed by Victorian debates in psychology and in other sciences, and specifically by the controversial speculation that, if the rhythmic action of the embodied mind is one particular example of a general law of motion that governs physical phenomena across the universe, then thinking might constitute a means of materially connecting the mind both to other minds and to natural processes. This speculation is reshaped, for Meynell, by Catholic doctrines of Incarnation and Communion, and her writing thus highlights the period's overlapping intellectual concerns, shared between seemingly discrete modes of knowledge (poetry, religion, spiritualism, psychology, physiology and physics).

It is not easy to identify specific scientific theorists whom Meynell read and might have been influenced by, because her writing is both allusive and elusive. She frequently borrows from and quotes other writers, but only infrequently identifies her sources. In her essay on Patmore, she notes that 'we hear that metals pass into one another, *in vacuo*, by pressure in the cold', but neglects to specify

[6] Isobel Armstrong, *Victorian Poetry: Poetry, Poetics, and Politics*, 2nd edn (London: Routledge, 2019), p. 462.

[7] Maria Frawley, '"The Tides of the Mind": Alice Meynell's Poetry of Perception', *Victorian Poetry* 38.1 (2000): 62–76, 63.

[8] Emily Harrington, *Second Person Singular: Late Victorian Women Poets and the Bonds of Verse* (Charlottesville: University of Virginia Press, 2014), p. 2.

from whom. Similar constructions, often referring specifically to the sciences, abound in her other essays: 'it has been said that Tennyson, midway between the student of material science and the mystic, wrote and thought according to an age that wavered, with him, between the two minds'; 'the life of our bodies has never been defined so suggestively as by one who named it a living relation of lifeless atoms'; 'professors have written of the mental habits of women as though they accumulated generation by generation upon women, and passed over their sons'.[9] This aspect of Meynell's style poses some problems for historicist scholarship. It requires that interpretation be founded in part on an assessment of the limited evidence of her intellectual interests and personal connections available in sources such as letters and biographies, and in part on informed speculation. But it also offers a potentially illuminating analogy for the open exchange of theories about the mind between late-Victorian disciplines in general, and for Meynell's interest in the relationality of thought in particular.

As well as alluding to other writers, Meynell also borrowed from herself, reusing and revising arguments from earlier writings throughout her career. Kathleen Anderson has identified introspection rather than relation as 'the essence of Meynell's poetry: she answers to herself', while Julie Wise has similarly examined what she terms Meynell's 'self-haunting poetic voice'.[10] This habit of self-revisiting reflects another abiding concern of Meynell's work, to which an understanding of mental life as a recurring and material process is directly relevant: the development and alteration of personality across time. This concern is evident in Meynell's first volume of poetry, *Preludes*, but it was sustained and informed in her later writings by the unusual duration and pattern of her career. Born in 1847, she published *Preludes* in 1875, before spending more than a decade writing essays for and editing periodicals. In 1893 she published *Poems*, in effect a revised edition of *Preludes*, as well as her first volume of essays, *The Rhythm of Life*.

[9] Meynell, 'Some Thoughts of a Reader of Tennyson', in *Hearts of Controversy* (London: Burns and Oates, 1917), p. 15; 'The Sun', in *The Rhythm of Life*, p. 19; 'A Woman in Grey', in *The Colour of Life and Other Essays on Things Seen and Heard* (London: John Lane, 1896), p. 65.

[10] Kathleen Anderson, '"I Make the Whole World Answer to My Art": Alice Meynell's Poetic Identity', *Victorian Poetry* 41.2 (2003): 259–275, 259; Julie Wise, 'Alice Meynell's Doubled Voices', *English Literature in Transition 1880–1920* 61.3 (2018): 291–309, 291.

From then on, for the remaining thirty years of her life (she died in 1922), Meynell combined regular work for the press and frequent publication of volumes of prose with renewed poetic composition. *Later Poems* was published in 1902, *Collected Poems* in 1913, and *Last Poems* posthumously in 1923.

In this chapter I will examine Meynell's writing about the mind as it develops chronologically, arguing that, while her interest in the connection between personality and intersubjectivity remains consistent, the terms in which she examines it change across different literary forms and at different stages of her career, as she returns to and rethinks the issue. Meynell's essays consistently use scientific terminology to discuss psychology. Her early poems, in contrast, articulate her notion of the intersubjectivity of mental processes by reworking established poetic forms and metaphors. But the language of psychology in her later poems is more various, incorporating both scientific terminology and overt references to her Catholic faith, suggesting a greater willingness on her part to articulate her views on the interrelation between science, spirituality, and poetry. The first four stanzas of 'Regrets', published in *Preludes*, exemplify the style in which Meynell writes about psychology in her early poems:

As when the seaward ebbing tide doth pour
    Out by the low sand spaces,
The parting waves slip back to clasp the shore
    With lingering embraces;

So in the tide of life that carries me
    From where my true heart dwells,
Waves of my thoughts and memories turn to thee
    With lessening farewells;

Waving of hands; dreams, when the day forgets;
    A care half lost in cares;
The saddest of my verses; dim regrets;
    Thy name among my prayers.

I would the day might come, so waited for,
    So patiently besought,
When I, returning, should fill up once more
    Thy desolated thought.[11]

[11] Meynell, 'Regrets', in *Preludes* (London: Henry S. King, 1875), pp. 44–5.

The poem's structuring metaphor of the sea points to two overlapping sources of influence. Its language is to some extent conventional, indicating a young writer's effort to demonstrate her skill in a specific mode of poetic diction: the sexualised language of flowing water that was widely used to convey desire and regret. As Armstrong has shown, this language was specifically reformulated by women poets to express both 'a longing for completion' and 'a sophisticated awareness of *separation* and its discontents', through which 'the uneasy contradiction between desire and the actual becomes a critique of existing experience'. This 'oceanic' mode is bodily, gendered and political, but, as Armstrong also notes, 'its lyric movement arises from a universe of flux and frequently returns to it'.[12] In other words, it is informed in part by the notions of rhythm that shaped much Victorian thinking about physics as well as physiology and poetics.

These notions are summarised by William Stanley Jevons in his *Principles of Science* (1874), in which he observes that 'modern Science tends more and more' to the 'conclusion that all motion is alternating or rhythmical, energy flowing onwards but matter remaining comparatively fixed in position'. Energy's rhythmic motion is traceable in a range of material forms. 'The waves of the ocean are large and visible', Jevons writes, and 'from such palpable cases of rhythmical movement we pass by analogy to waves of sound', and in turn to those of light. 'Thus we pass gradually from the palpable and evident to that which is obscure, if not incomprehensible'.[13] Jevons's argument is based on theoretical and experimental work that identified analogies between different waves and vibrations, conducted by a number of physicists since the start of the nineteenth century. But, as Shelley Trower notes, the wave paradigm was not exclusive to physics: 'scientific and spiritualist writers' both 'used sound as a model for various kinds of vibrations, including those of the human nerves, frequencies of light and heat, electricity, X-rays and radio waves and spiritual energies'.[14] And Anna Henchman argues that 'undular-

[12] Armstrong, 'Msrepresentation: Codes of Affect and Politics in Nineteenth-Century Women's Poetry', in Armstrong and Virginia Blain, eds, *Women's Poetry, Late Romantic to Late Victorian: Gender and Genre, 1830–1900* (Basingstoke: Palgrave Macmillan, 1999), pp. 15–16; Armstrong's emphasis.

[13] William Stanley Jevons, *The Principles of Science: A Treatise on Logic and Scientific Method*, 2 vols (London: Macmillan, 1874), 2: 293–4.

[14] Shelley Trower, 'Vibrations', in Anna Snaith, ed., *Sound and Literature*

ity was a universal form' that also 'had longstanding associations with rhythm and poetic metre, a fact noted by poets and scientists alike'.[15]

In 'Regrets', the number of different images incorporated within Meynell's oceanic metaphor demonstrates the comprehensiveness of its scope. The waves of the sea are refigured both as 'the tide of life' and as 'waves of my thoughts', which are then embodied in a 'waving of hands', which is in turn equated, through a paratactic listing of nouns, with 'dreams', 'a care', and 'the saddest of my verses'. In its relentless iteration of its marine metaphor, the poem suggests that the sea, poetic form, mental processes, and physical actions and impulses can each be understood in equivalent terms of motion and reflux. In this way, it participates in a widespread argument that waves or vibrations were an explanatory metaphor applicable at several different scales, from the flow of energy throughout the world and the universe to the workings of the human body and the rhythms of verse.

The reach of this metaphor, and its applicability to the kind of interpersonal thinking imagined in Meynell's poem, is exemplified in the theory of 'brain-waves' set out by the journalist James Knowles in the *Spectator* in 1869. The premises of Knowles's theory are 'that whensoever any action takes place in the brain, a chemical change of its substance takes place also; or, in other words, an atomic movement occurs', and 'that there is, diffused throughout all known space, and permeating the interspaces of all bodies, solid, fluid, or gaseous, an universal, impalpable, elastic "Ether," or material medium of surpassing and inconceivable tenuity', through which light is transmitted in waves. Because 'the movement of any solid particle submerged in any such medium must create a wave', then, 'if these two assumptions be granted', Knowles argues, 'we should have as one result of brain action an undulation or wave in the circumambient, all-embracing ether,—we should have what I will call Brain-Waves proceeding from every brain'.[16] Equating the motion of his hypothetical waves

(Cambridge: Cambridge University Press, 2020), pp. 288–9.

15 Anna Henchman, 'Outer Space: Physical Science', in Matthew Bevis, ed., *The Oxford Handbook of Victorian Poetry* (Oxford: Oxford University Press, 2013), p. 695. See also Gregory Tate, *Nineteenth-Century Poetry and the Physical Sciences: Poetical Matter* (London: Palgrave Macmillan, 2020).

16 James Thomas Knowles, 'Brain-Waves: A Theory', *Spectator* 42 (30 January 1869): 135–7, 136.

with that of light and sound, he suggests that the waves might in certain circumstances resonate in other brains:

> The sound-wave passes on through myriads of bodies, and among a million makes but one thing shake, or sound to it; a sympathy of structure makes it sensitive, and it alone. A voice or tone may pass unnoticed by ten thousand ears, but strike and vibrate one into a madness of recollection.

Analogously, 'if, indeed, there be radiating from living brains' any 'streams of vibratory movements (as surely there must be), these may well have an effect, even without speech' (Knowles, 'Brain-Waves', 136–7). Knowles proposes a material 'sympathy of structure' between brains as a possible explanation of the phenomena of spiritualism, an argument that was soon enlisted in debates about personal immortality, the existence of ghosts, and the legitimacy of cases of 'thought-transference'. The hypothesis of a universal ether had been first mooted in the seventeenth century, and its involvement in the transmission of sensation and thought within the body and brain was suggested by David Hartley in his *Observations on Man* (1749). But Knowles was the first writer to speculate that the ether might act as a medium of the propagation of thought between minds. And, despite the idiosyncrasy of his theory, its terms were embraced by a number of other writers. In *The Unseen Universe* (1875), for example, the physicists Balfour Stewart and Peter Guthrie Tait deploy the ether – which they identify as a 'hypothesis' that cannot be verified by 'the direct evidence of our senses', but that has 'nevertheless been adopted as affording the best explanations of the phenomena of the visible universe' – as the foundation of their 'physical speculations' on immortality and on the transmission of thought.[17] Using language similar to Knowles's, Stewart and Tait suggest that 'every thought that we think is accompanied by a displacement and motion of the particles of the brain, and somehow', 'in all probability' through the ether, 'we may imagine that these motions are propagated throughout the universe' (*Unseen Universe*, 156).

There is no evidence that Meynell read Knowles's brief article. As I will discuss, there are other routes through which she is

[17] Balfour Stewart and Peter Guthrie Tait, *The Unseen Universe or Physical Speculations on a Future State* (London: Macmillan, 1875), pp. 46–7.

likely to have heard about similar speculations. For now, the point I would like to emphasise is that Knowles's theory is just one example of the way in which waves were identified in the late nineteenth century as the foundational impetus of natural, physiological and psychological processes. The circulation of this kind of thinking can be traced specifically through the cultural space of which Meynell formed a centre. Allusions to the wave paradigm are reflected and transmitted between and within her poems, the articles published in *Merry England* (a periodical edited by Meynell and her husband Wilfrid between 1883 and 1895), and the letters and conversations that constituted her (sizeable) networks of friendship and acquaintance. The language of the paradigm is present across her writing: in her essay 'The Young Child', one of her numerous studies of child psychology, she observes that 'the nurse has her private business, and when it does not prosper, and when the remote affairs of the governess go wrong, the child receives the ultimate vibration of the mishap'.[18] And, framed in terms of 'waves' rather than 'vibrations', a similar model of intersubjectivity is evident in 'Regrets': the wish that a mind, 'returning, should fill up once more' the 'desolated thought' of another is explicable not just through the metaphor of the sea but also through the supposition, simultaneously metaphorical and scientific, that thought itself is structured and communicated through recurring waves of motion.

'Regrets' also demonstrates the way in which poetic form was integrated with, and used to articulate, models of rhythm. The 'waves of my thoughts' and the 'waving of hands' are presented as analogous to 'the saddest of my verses', and Meynell's verse in this poem undulates and moves in a distinctive pattern: a stanza of alternating rhymes of iambic pentameter and iambic trimeter, rhyming *abab*, that she used throughout her career. Adela Pinch has pointed out that 'fin-de-siècle poets were experts at measuring short lines against long', and that their metres and rhymes typically deploy 'the conjunction of metrical brevity with reverberating sound to heighten our subjective experience of duration, and its existential pangs'.[19] In Meynell's poetry, the interplay between long and short lines can be read as expressive of a particular

[18] Meynell, 'The Young Child', in *The Children* (London: John Lane, 1896), p. 116.

[19] Adela Pinch, 'Rhyme's End', *Victorian Studies* 53.3 (2011): 485–94, 485–6.

manifestation of the experience of time: the processes of physical and physiological motion, and the corresponding cycles and returns, that for Meynell structure the relations between minds. In 'Regrets', these mental recurrences are voiced in the rhyming of opposites – 'spaces' and 'embraces'; 'me' and 'thee'; the unrealised desire of 'besought' and the union of intersubjective 'thought' – that remain isolated from each other on separate lines of verse, but that also 'clasp' and 'return to' each other in sound.

This aspect of poetic form is directly discussed by Meynell in a poem published in 1921, 'The English Metres':

> Not Common Law, but Equity, is theirs—
> Our metres; play and agile foot askance,
> And distant, beckoning, blithely rhyming pairs,
> Unknown to classic France.[20]

In this stanza, Meynell invokes two arguments that were central to her thinking about poetry and intersubjectivity. What she refers to as the agility of English verse enables it to represent, in its variable structures of metre and rhyme, the 'distant, beckoning' recurrences that characterise mental life. As Meynell suggests in 'The Rhythm of Life', the mind is always metrical, but it is not regular or predictable. Instead, thought 'flits upon an orbit elliptically or parabolically or hyperbolically curved, keeping no man knows what trysts with Time' (*Rhythm of Life*, 2–3). In 'Regrets', this variability is evident both in the structure of the stanzas and in local metrical effects, such as the line-opening trochaic inversions on 'waves' and 'waving' that articulate the surges of bodily and emotional desire. And, in 'The English Metres', Meynell implies that the irregular liberty of metre expresses a kind of natural justice and impartiality that can be understood in social as well as in psychological terms: 'not Common Law, but Equity'.

This sidelining of 'Common Law' points to another important dimension of her interlinked understandings of poetry and the mind: her response to Patmore's theories as set out in his 'Essay on English Metrical Law' (first published in 1857). Patmore's essay presents what he identifies as 'the true view of metre, as being pri-

[20] Meynell, 'The English Metres', in *Last Poems* (London: Burns, Oates, and Washbourne, 1923), p. 36.

marily based upon isochronous division by ictuses or accents'.[21] As both Yopie Prins and Irmtraud Huber have shown, Meynell 'resists' this 'artificial imposition of isochrony' or invariable regularity on metre, preferring (in Prins's words) 'a more natural variation according to a more natural measure of time'.[22] But I would like to suggest that Meynell embraces another aspect of Patmore's theory, namely its ambiguous assessment of whether metre is a physical phenomenon or an abstract ideal. Patmore asserts, seemingly unequivocally, that the '"ictus" or "beat"' of poetry '*has no material and external existence at all*, but has its place in the mind, which craves measure in everything'. Yet he also claims, following Hegel, 'that versification affords a necessary counterpoise to the great spiritualisation of language in poetry': 'art, indeed, must have a body as well as a soul; and the higher and purer the spiritual, the more powerful and unmistakeable should be the corporeal element' (Patmore, 'English Metrical Critics', 136 and 130; Patmore's emphases). Both for Patmore and for Meynell, this seeming contradiction is resolvable through the dualism of Catholic theology; as Tyson Stolte has argued, Patmore's essay 'reveals the close connections between religion and a dualist psychology' in Victorian culture.[23]

Catholicism, and specifically the doctrines of the Incarnation and of the transubstantiation or 'real presence' of Christ's blood and body in the Eucharist, offered Meynell a dualism that prioritised the soul ahead of the body, but that also traced a reciprocal relation between the two, in which the spiritual and the divine might be realised in matter. Isobel Armstrong has noted Meynell's 'poetics of transubstantiation' (or 'of spiritually charged matter') and 'its logic—the conversion of one substance into another that effects a material and a metaphysical or suprasensual change simultaneously' (*Victorian Poetry*, 465). And Tracy Seeley argues that this logic aligns with a specifically 'decadent Catholic' and

[21] Coventry Patmore, 'English Metrical Critics', *North British Review* 27 (1857): 127–61, 128.

[22] Yopie Prins, 'Patmore's Law, Meynell's Rhythm', in Joseph Bristow, ed., *The Fin-de-Siècle Poem: English Literary Culture and the 1890s* (Athens, OH: Ohio University Press, 2005), p. 269. See also Irmtraud Huber, *Time and Timelessness in Victorian Poetry* (Edinburgh: Edinburgh University Press, 2023), p. 212.

[23] Tyson Stolte, '"The Infinite Within the Finite": Victorian Prosody and Orthodox Theories of Mind', *Victorian Poetry* 54.3 (2016): 245–74, 249.

'*fin-de-siècle* insistence on body and spirit as necessarily entwined'. In Meynell's poetry, 'religiosity and sensuality are not mutually exclusive but necessarily conjoined'.[24] Similarly, Meynell did not see religion and psychology as antagonistic to each other, instead viewing the exchange of thought between embodied minds as a form of Communion, in which people are joined to each other and to God through the spiritual offices of matter. Patmore, writing in *Merry England* in 1892, argued that any disagreement between science and religion is accidental rather than essential, the result of methodological rather than spiritual error: 'psychology has come to be a science the first axiom of which is that there is no soul', but this 'seems commonly to be owing, not so much to the vicious interest of corrupt passions, as to physical impatience of the attitude of attention demanded for the contemplation of human realities.'[25]

The inseparability of Meynell's views on science from her Catholicism is evident in her sustained engagement with the work of the biologist and Catholic convert St George Mivart, whom she knew from the 1870s.[26] Mivart is one of the few writers whom Meynell quotes directly rather than paraphrases (although without attribution) in her essays.[27] For much of his life Mivart struggled to reconcile his scientific work with his faith, and the compromises he proposed led to breaches both with other scientific thinkers (most famously Charles Darwin and Thomas Henry Huxley) and, in the end, with Meynell. After his views led to him being denied the sacraments by Cardinal Herbert Vaughan, just months before his death in 1900, he wrote to Meynell to defend his position. Her reply was unforgiving: 'it seems to me wrong and lamentable that a man should be eager to write and talk about his loss when he has lost Jesus Christ'; 'only a cold and corrupt heart could fail to suffer'.[28] In the 1870s and 1880s, however, they shared similar

24 Tracy Seeley, '"The Fair Light Mystery of Images": Alice Meynell's Metaphysical Turn', *Victorian Literature and Culture* 34.2 (2006): 663–84, 671–2.

25 Coventry Patmore, 'Attention', *Merry England* 20 (1892): 4–8, 4.

26 Discussing plans for a new periodical in a letter to her husband in 1877, Meynell assured Wilfrid that 'Mivart shall write for us' on 'comparative anatomy'. Viola Meynell, *Alice Meynell: A Memoir* (London: Jonathan Cape, 1929), p. 60.

27 See Meynell, 'Some Thoughts of a Reader of Tennyson', pp. 14–15.

28 Meynell to Mivart, March 1900, in Damian Atkinson, ed., *The Selected Letters of Alice Meynell* (Newcastle: Cambridge Scholars, 2013), p. 149.

views about the relation between science and Catholicism, and Meynell championed Mivart's work in *Merry England* in 1885. The articles that Meynell wrote, and those that she edited, for this periodical represent an important and underacknowledged context for her poetry and other essays, and her article on Mivart features one of the most direct statements of her recognition of the intellectual validity of the sciences:

> he who thinks that the religious difficulties suggested by astronomy, or geology, or physiology, or those which arise from the acute sensitiveness of the modern mind before the mysteries of evil or of eternal loss, are to be disposed of by a sneer at 'so-called science' or a smile at 'so-called philosophy,' have realized little indeed of the conditions of the physical or of the mental world in the midst of which they live.

But she also sounds a note of caution about the potential materialism of science, advising that 'the pity which is akin to respect rather than to scorn is due from those who are happy enough to believe, towards those who have been mysteriously misled by a wrong reading of the records written' by God 'in the stones of His world and the bones of His creatures'.[29] At this point, Meynell does not consider Mivart to be one of those 'misled': she hails him as 'a diligent student of Nature after the manner of the latest science—the manner of experience and experiment—and a devoted believer in that Church which begins her work in the heart from the opposite point' ('For Faith and Science', 290).

In 1905, the evolutionary theorist and spiritualist Alfred Russel Wallace suggested that 'my friend Mivart' was also a believer in spiritualism. Wallace claims in his autobiography that Mivart was the author of 'A Speculation Regarding the Senses', signed 'M' and published in *Nature* in 1880.[30] This short article puts forward an argument that, like Knowles's theory of brain waves, combines physics and physiology in its explanation of psychical phenomena. 'M' claims that 'on examining the modes of action of the senses we find a series of advances in refinement', from the 'contact' of touch to the ethereal 'vibrations' registered by sight. 'Guided by

[29] Meynell, 'For Faith and Science', *Merry England* 5 (1885): 285–93, 285.

[30] Alfred Russel Wallace, *My Life: A Record of Events and Opinions*, 2 vols (London: Chapman and Hall, 1905), 2: 309–10.

the gradation' of the senses, 'M' then speculates about a mode of action 'of a still more delicate kind', which 'may be supposed to obtain when the eyes, and perhaps other avenues of sense, are closed':

> the molecular vibrations in the brain accompanying thought, may affect a surrounding medium, and through that, other brains at a distance, awaking in these corresponding vibrations and thoughts. The medium might be supposed, perhaps, one of different nature from that in which light-vibrations occur, or (not to multiply ethers) the same as the so-called luminiferous ether; and in the latter case we might suppose the vibrations such as not to be appreciated through any of the present senses of ordinary persons.[31]

Wallace's attribution of this article to Mivart suggests the possibility that Meynell might have learned of a theory of vibrations, commencing in the rhythms of the body and then communicating themselves to other brains, from a friend whose scientific work she admired. And it positions Mivart as a figure who exemplifies how scientific theorisation, Catholic belief, and spiritualist or psychical speculation might be reconciled with each other.

But there are problems with this supposition. As an advocate of spiritualism, Wallace is hardly impartial, and so his claim that 'through my conversation' Mivart 'became satisfied that the phenomena were at least partly genuine' should be taken with a pinch of salt (*My Life*, 2: 300). In his writings about evolution and about Catholicism, Mivart was a combative polemicist, not afraid to voice controversial opinions, and so, if he were the author of this 'speculation', it is perhaps surprising that he did not acknowledge it publicly. And the article's argument contradicts his stated views on physical and physiological theories of psychology, which he set out in 1889 in *On Truth* (the book which Meynell quotes in her essay 'Some Thoughts of a Reader of Tennyson'). Mivart here acknowledges that

> the functions of nerves and brain-cells, no less than heat, light, and chemical phenomena, *must* be easier to imagine as 'modes of motion'—waves, oscillations of particles, or what not—than in any other way,

31 'M', 'A Speculation Regarding the Senses', *Nature* 21 (5 February 1880): 323–4, 323.

> however unsatisfactory that representation may ultimately prove to be.[32]

But he imposes a rigid epistemological barrier between the 'practical use' of 'mechanical hypotheses' and 'their real acceptance as truths'. 'The use of mechanical conceptions, even with respect to the science of living beings, is not only blameless but natural and useful', but 'its absolute acceptance leads to downright absurdity' (Mivart, *On Truth*, 395–6). Whether or not Mivart was the author of the article in *Nature*, Meynell may have been more enthusiastic about the kind of 'speculation' which it sets out than about his position in *On Truth*, because in her writing she consistently presents both poetry and thought as 'modes of motion'.

The article in *Nature* illustrates the way in which the paradigm of rhythmic motion was both scientific and speculative in its methods, material and spiritual in its scope. Similarly, while Roger Luckhurst has shown that, for the most part, spiritualism was 'equally despised by the orthodox Churches and the scientific naturalists', and while Philip Waller, in his illuminating discussion of late-Victorian converts to Catholicism, argues that Meynell's 'faith conferred on her an immunity against radical religious chic', her thinking about the mind cuts across straightforward distinctions between science, spiritualism and religion.[33] On meeting W.B. Yeats in 1913, Meynell wrote that

> spiritualism absorbs him, it seems to me; and I cannot understand why the most important thing in the modern world should be banned by the Church, and despised by everyone else. Of course I don't practice it, but I was willing to hear his extraordinary experiences. (*Selected Letters*, 348)

As in the case of Mivart and her knowledge of science, Meynell's social networks are an important means of tracing her interest in

[32] St George Mivart, *On Truth: A Systematic Inquiry* (London: Kegan Paul, Trench, 1889), p. 443; Mivart's emphasis.

[33] Roger Luckhurst, *The Invention of Telepathy 1870–1901* (Oxford: Oxford University Press, 2002), p. 30; Philip Waller, 'Roman Candles: Catholic Converts Among Authors in Late-Victorian and Edwardian Britain', in Peter Ghosh and Lawrence Goldman, eds, *Politics and Culture in Victorian Britain* (Oxford: Oxford University Press, 2006), p. 210.

spiritualism. She knew Frederic Myers, co-founder of the Society for Psychical Research and coiner of the term 'telepathy'. In *Phantasms of the Living* (1886), his exposition of the Society's work co-written with Edmund Gurney and Frank Podmore, Myers repeatedly discusses 'undulations', 'vibration-waves', and 'ether-waves' as possible explanations of telepathy (although often with a high degree of scepticism).[34] Meynell recalled in 1918 that 'Myers thought that what was immortal in us and would survive death was the mind that dreams. If so what silly asses we must look to be!' (Viola Meynell, *Memoir*, 311–12). Dreams were an important focus of the Society for Psychical Research's investigations, and, despite her amused scepticism here, they are central to the vocabulary of Meynell's writing too. In an 1885 essay on Patmore, for instance, she writes that the 'images' of his poetry 'belong to the universe rather than to the world, like the dreams that visit a delicate brain in sleep'.[35]

Another example is 'Renouncement', a sonnet written in the 1880s. This poem shares with 'Regrets' its traditional poetic diction and its focus on thwarted love, but it uses this seeming conventionality to set out an intellectually and formally complex depiction of mental processes:

I must not think of thee; and, tired yet strong,
    I shun the thought that lurks in all delight—
    The thought of thee—and in the blue Heaven's height,
And in the sweetest passage of a song.

Oh, just beyond the fairest thoughts that throng
    This breast, the thought of thee waits, hidden yet bright;
    But it must never, never come in sight;
I must stop short of thee the whole day long.

But when sleep comes to close each difficult day,
  When night gives pause to the long watch I keep,
    And all my bonds I needs must loose apart,

34 Edmund Gurney, Frederic Myers and Frank Podmore, *Phantasms of the Living*, 2 vols (London: Trübner, 1886), 1: 1, 1: 111, and 2: 315.

35 Meynell, ''Twixt Anacreon and Plato', *Merry England* 6 (1885): 69–80, 79.

Must doff my will as raiment laid away,—
  With the first dream that comes with the first sleep
    I run, I run, I am gathered to thy heart.[36]

As in 'Regrets', the minds in this poem are in perpetual motion: 'I', 'thee', and 'thoughts' move towards and away from each other, while thought also moves through the body ('this breast'), the sky ('Heaven's height'), and the rhythms of sound ('the sweetest passage of a song'). In the octave, this motion – suggestive both of a Wordsworthian interfusion of mind with nature and of the transmission of waves through the ether – is checked by the speaker's mental exertions, as the successive stresses of self-directed imperatives ('I must not think', 'I must stop short') arrest the sonnet's iambic metre and the speaker's approach to the addressee. But the check is temporary: the recurrent motion of thought cannot be stopped, and it re-establishes itself through the structure of the Petrarchan sonnet form, as the relation between 'I' and 'thee' is reversed at the turn from octave to sestet, day to night. In the sestet, 'must' signifies the dissolution rather than the imposition of will, and the speaker's impulsive motion towards the other, figured as simultaneously emotional and physical, is resumed and consummated. Pinch has pointed out that, both in this poem and in the publications of the Society for Psychical Research, 'love thinking', mental activity directed towards another person, is equated with 'night thinking'.[37] In *Nature*, 'M' suggests that brain vibrations 'obtain' when the 'avenues of sense' are 'closed', and Knowles also attributes 'ghost and dream stories' to the activity of brain waves ('Brain-Waves', 137). The similarities between these articles and Meynell's sonnet can be explained, perhaps, by her interest in and sympathy with such speculations about the psychological conditions most conducive to intercommunication between minds.

Her writing also attends to the limitations of and barriers to such intercommunication. In her essay 'The Unready', for example, she discusses children's slow responses both to environmental stimuli and to their own thoughts:

[36] Meynell, 'Renouncement', in *Poems* (London: Elkin Mathews and John Lane, 1893), p. 71.

[37] Pinch, *Thinking About Other People in Nineteenth-Century British Writing* (Cambridge: Cambridge University Press, 2010), pp. 61 and 85.

> Their poor little slowness is so distinctively their own, and must needs be physiologically so proper to their years, so much a natural condition of the age of their brain, that of all childishnesses it is the one that the world should have the patience to attend upon, the humanity to foster, and the intelligence to understand.[38]

And in 'The Child of Tumult', published alongside 'The Unready' in *Ceres' Runaway* (1909), she extends this observation to children's thinking about other people: 'Nature takes care that her young creatures shall not be injured by sympathies. Nature encloses them in the innocent indifference that preserves their brains from the more harassing kinds of distress' (*Ceres' Runaway*, 132). In contrast to her frequent examinations of and exhortations to intersubjectivity, in these essays Meynell identifies childhood as a stage of development in which the mind is cut off from sympathy by its 'slowness' and 'innocent indifference'. And, using the language of physiology and neurology, she interprets this insularity as a bodily defence mechanism, protecting the developing brain from the violence of sudden recognition and close connection.

A number of Meynell's later poems go further, suggesting that this state of embodied isolation is not exclusive to childhood. These poems elaborate a model of psychology in general in which the mind is both diffuse – its motions continuous with those of natural processes, poetic metres and other minds – and discrete, divided from others by its bounded physical form. By using this duality to examine the mind's relation to God, they also highlight the close connection between Meynell's views on psychology and her Catholic faith. As well as demonstrating the development of a more distinctive style over the course of Meynell's poetic career, her later poems can also be seen as evidence of the wider visibility both of Catholicism and of scientific psychology in Britain at the turn of the century. 'The Unknown God', published in her 1913 *Collected Poems*, presents intersubjective sympathy as a specific and limited example of the universal relationality guaranteed by Catholic belief. After watching 'one of the crowd' in a church receive Communion, the speaker recites this prayer:

[38] Meynell, 'The Unready', in *Ceres' Runaway and Other Essays* (London: Burns and Oates, 1909), p. 124.

'O Christ, in this man's life—
This stranger who is Thine—in all his strife,
All his felicity, his good and ill,
In the assaulted stronghold of his will,

'I do confess Thee here,
Alive within this life; I know Thee near
Within this lonely conscience, closed away
Within this brother's solitary day.

'Christ in his unknown heart,
His intellect unknown—this love, this art,
This battle and this peace, this destiny
That I shall never know, look upon me!

'Christ in his numbered breath,
Christ in his beating heart and in his death,
Christ in his mystery! From that secret place
And from that separate dwelling, give me grace.'[39]

Depicting not just the transubstantiation of Christ in the Eucharist but also his ingestion, the poem locates the divine in the body as well as the soul of 'this brother'. In its first use, the word 'heart' seems conventionally abstract, synonymous with soul, but its second is unambiguously visceral: 'his beating heart'. And while the breath is 'numbered' in the sense that it is temporary and ordained to cease, it is also, along with the beating of the heart, counted in the beats of Meynell's verse: like other aspects of physical and spiritual existence, communion with the divine is structured and articulated through quantifiable rhythm.

The speaker is certain of Christ's presence within these embodied measures. F. Elizabeth Gray argues persuasively that in this poem 'Meynell discusses the breakdown of difference between humans as she discusses the breakdown of difference between human and God', and that 'through its emphasis on Christ's humanity, its re-enactment of the Incarnation, the poem creates a new kind of egalitarian interrelation, uncovering and exploring the rich layers

39 Meynell, 'The Unknown God', in *Collected Poems* (London: Burns and Oates, 1913), pp. 43–4.

of meaning in "communion."'[40] But while the poem offers the consolations of sympathy and shared belief, it also emphasises the barriers that separate one human mind from another. As its title indicates, much of the poem is concerned with the limitations of knowledge, although it is humanity, rather than God, that is first and foremost presented as 'unknown'. 'I know Thee near', the speaker says of Christ, but the language she uses to refer to the man consistently highlights their mutual isolation: 'lonely conscience', 'solitary day', 'intellect unknown', 'this destiny / That I shall never know'. This isolation is framed not just in cognitive but also in corporeal and poetic terms. As in 'Regrets', written almost forty years earlier, Meynell uses differing line lengths to measure the distances across which minds strive to connect: the foreshortened first line of each stanza, further separated from the others by punctuation, interrupts the poem's metre with pauses that, through their silence, highlight the gaps in interrelation. And something analogous happens in the poem's depiction of the body: the rhythms of breath and heartbeat are quantifiable, but they are also (both in their continuation in life and in their cessation in death) distinctive to each particular corporeal form. The body is a 'secret place', fully knowable to just one mind, and to God.

'The Unknown God' shows that what Mark Knight and Emma Mason describe as a distinctively Catholic view of a 'sacramental universe', which finds 'God's revelation in the natural world', might also locate the spiritual in the human body, and might be informed as much by physiology and psychology as by faith.[41] This is equally evident in the articles on science published in *Merry England* under the Meynells' editorship. A series of essays written by Catholic priest Joseph Adalbert Dewe in 1893–4, for instance, integrates the journal's Catholic perspective with some wide-ranging speculations about the rhythms of the material universe. Writing in November 1893, Dewe argues that

> The body of man, which is such as befits an instrument of thought to an intelligent being, exhibits a continual scene of movement. The palpitation of the heart, the expansion or contraction of the lungs, the

40 F. Elizabeth Gray, 'Making Christ: Alice Meynell, Poetry, and the Eucharist', *Christianity and Literature* 52.2 (2003): 159–79, 168 and 172.

41 Mark Knight and Emma Mason, *Nineteenth-Century Religion and Literature: An Introduction* (Oxford: Oxford University Press, 2006), p. 199.

> vibration of the nervous system, the processes of digestion and assimilation, are more continual and more rapid than we find in the body of any ordinary animal endowed with a less perfect organisation.

These movements demonstrate 'the dependence of the more perfect forms of life upon incessant motion and friction between the material atoms'.[42] But while Dewe is happy to claim 'that there is in every material atom a principle of motion', he explains this principle in dualist terms: 'a material substance, whatever it might be, is manifestly inert and cannot be in itself a cause of motion, though it may be capable of communicating it'. Motion's cause 'must, therefore, be of quite a different nature from the material substance through which it acts' (Dewe, 'Nature of Electricity', 25). This dualism does not stop Dewe from expanding the wave paradigm even further than most Victorian theorists. A month later, he speculates that 'the sense of smell', like those of hearing and sight, 'is produced by vibration caused in the nerve by external particles'. Odours are formed by 'the rapid vibrations of the particles received into the nostrils'.[43]

In these articles, a theory of material vibration is linked both to a comprehensive analogy between the senses and to a Catholic dualism. Meynell's openness to this mixing of perspectives is evident not just in her willingness to publish Dewe's speculations, but also in her elaboration of a comparable synthesis in another of her *Collected Poems*. 'To the Body', first published in 1906, is the most overtly physiological of Meynell's poems in its vocabulary:

> Thou inmost, ultimate
> Council of judgment, palace of decrees,
> Where the high senses hold their spiritual state,
> Sued by earth's embassies,
> And sign, approve, accept, conceive, create;
>
> Create—thy senses close
> With the world's pleas. The random odours reach
> Their sweetness in the place of thy repose,

42 J.A. Dewe, 'On the Nature of Electricity', *Merry England* 22 (1893): 22–35, 31.
43 Dewe, 'The Science and Harmony of Smell', *Merry England* 22 (1893): 123–8, 125.

> Upon thy tongue the peach,
> And in thy nostrils breathes the breathing rose. (*Collected Poems*, 55)

Although framed in different terms, these opening stanzas set out a view of the body comparable to that presented in 'The Unknown God', as a 'separate dwelling' which encloses the mind but which also, through windows and doors both physical and metaphysical, enables communication with others. The stanzas' vividly sensory language can be read in the context of several different Victorian models of the embodied mind. It aligns with what Nicholas Dames has termed a 'wave theory of physiological affect', which defined both 'consciousness in general' and 'aesthetic reception in particular' as the mind's processing of the periodic ebb and flow of sensory data.[44] In the work of writers such as Grant Allen, this theory was founded on the hypothesis of a structural equivalence between the motions of the universe and those of the body. The aesthetic pleasure afforded by sound and light, Allen argues, originates in 'sympathetic vibrations' stimulated in auditory and optical nerves by waves in the air and in the ether.[45] Meynell's poem, like Dewe's article, extends this model of universal and embodied motion to other senses, suggesting that 'tongue' and 'nostrils' also contribute to the body's aesthetic activity.

At the same time, 'To the Body' articulates a Catholic dualism in which matter is sanctified: the 'high senses' are 'spiritual', evaluating the earth's physical data and transforming it into the raw material of an intransitive creativity. And the poem also exalts the senses in a way that is comparable to the 1880 'speculation' in *Nature*, identifying them as preliminary steps in a diffusive exchange through which thought itself merges with its physical environment. The mind, from this perspective, is both endowed with and denied agency: it may be the 'ultimate' judge of the earth, but, as the poem's grammar indicates, the earth also acts on it. 'Odours' are positioned as the subject of the verb 'reach', purposively moving towards the body and attaining their 'sweet-

44 Nicholas Dames, *The Physiology of the Novel: Reading, Neural Science, and the Form of Victorian Fiction* (Oxford: Oxford University Press, 2007), pp. 53–4.

45 Grant Allen, *Physiological Aesthetics* (London: Henry S. King, 1877), pp. 104 and 139.

ness' through collaboration with subjective sensory and mental processes, and the rose actively 'breathes' with the nostrils.

The poem's closing stanzas demonstrate how, in Meynell's hands, poetic form acts as a fractal expression both of the rhythmic waves that organise the embodied mind and the physical universe, and of the reciprocal interaction between them:

> To thee, secluded one,
> The dark vibrations of the sightless skies,
> The lovely inexplicit colours run;
> The light gropes for those eyes.
> O thou august! thou dost command the sun.
>
> Music, all dumb, hath trod
> Into thine ear her one effectual way;
> And fire and cold approach to gain thy nod,
> Where thou call'st up the day,
> Where thou awaitest the appeal of God. (*Collected Poems*, 55)

Through the sole instance of the language of 'vibrations' in her poetry, Meynell here summarises the analogical argument on which much late-Victorian speculation in physics, psychology, parapsychology, and aesthetics depended: light and sound are transmitted through the air and across the universe in waves that resonate with the rhythms of physiology, of thought, and of poetic expression. The direct reference to the paradigm of vibratory motion suggests Meynell's confidence in its applicability not just to poetry in general but to her specific notion of poetic form as an irregular cycle of recurrences. As the uneven metrical tread of the trochee 'Music' reveals, the rhythmic waves of sense are not predictable, in part because of the immense distances they must traverse before manifesting themselves in the body, distances conveyed here in the delayed rhymes and halting rhythms through which the 'dark vibrations of the sightless skies' grope and run towards the eyes. The poem's depiction of sensory experience as an interlinked series of physical, physiological, and psychological vibrations also encapsulates Meynell's view of the mind's relation to external reality. She maintains that the mind is 'secluded' within the body, isolated from other minds and from matter by the interiority of its sensations. But she also asserts that the senses connect the embodied mind both to physical phenomena and to the divine.

The poem ends with God, but its final line shows how, despite her commitment to Catholic orthodoxy, Meynell's faith was inflected by theories of physiological psychology. The body is presented as the active agent rather than the passive object of communion with the divine: it 'commands' and God 'appeals', and the appeal of God is heard, like 'the world's pleas' and the rhythms of poetry, through the motions of the senses.

4

Walter Pater's Embodied Knowledge: In and Out of Psychophysiology

Bénédicte Coste

'Winckelmann's first years in Rome present all the elements of an intellectual situation of the highest interest': arriving in Rome after years spent in Germany steeped in 'alien traditions', Winckelmann was ready to embrace the 'broad horizons', and 'boundless intellectual promise'[1] of Italy. Walter Pater's attentive description might well describe his own situation as a budding British cultural historian and literary critic in the late 1860s. 'Developments in the sciences of the mind' with their major impact in the twentieth century, 'transformed our notions of what it is to be human', Suzy Anger convincingly argues, citing as examples the 'grounding of psychology in biology, theories on the relation between brain and mind, constructions of psychopathology, studies of altered mental states (dreaming, hallucination), theories of the unconscious, re-imaginings of the role of conscious volition in behavior, the study of comparative psychology (animal minds), the study of the criminal mind, and the relations between the supernatural and new understandings of the mind' developed during that seminal decade.[2] Indeed the transformation of the 1870s had been prepared by theories that renegotiated the old dualism between body and mind, such as Henry Maudsley's discussion of 'mental phenomena from a physiological rather than from a metaphysical point of view',[3] and Alexander Bain's emphasis on the parallel between the facts

1 Walter Pater, *The Renaissance: Studies in Art and Poetry* (1893) ed. Adam Phillips (Oxford: Oxford University Press, 1988), p. 122.

2 Suzy Anger, 'The Victorian Mental Sciences', *Victorian Literature and Culture* 46.1 (2018): 275–87.

3 Henry Maudsley, *The Physiology and Pathology of the Mind* (New York: Appleton, 1867), p. v.

of consciousness and those of the physical changes in the organism in his 'Systematic Exposition of the Human Mind'.[4] Those physiological approaches questioned the distinction between the mental and the physical, contributing to 'the naturalization of mind'.[5] Such conceptualisations were accompanied by the redistribution of scientific authority, the development of scientific education, the creation of numerous learned societies[6] and the professionalisation and disciplinarisation of the fields of investigation that were to form the sciences of the mind of the twentieth century, including psychology.[7] Historians of science agree that such features were significant in the last third of the century along with broader social and cultural transformations including the dissemination and diversification of the printed word. An efflorescence of periodicals – magazines, generalist or specialised, and scientific journals – enabled a wide array of discussions, including debates on identity, cognition, perception and emotion, led by 'intellectual groups, including freelance intellectuals who saw themselves as doing psychology (Bain, Spencer, Lewes), gentleman scientists who engaged in psychology (Darwin, Galton, Romanes), physiologists (Carpenter, D. Ferrier, Maudsley), Darwinian biologists (Huxley, Lloyd Morgan), and philosophers (Hamilton, J. S. Mill) or philosopher-psychologists (Sully, Ward, Stout)'.[8] Those very

4 In *The Senses and The Intellect* (London: John W. Parker and Son, 1855, 2nd ed. 1865), Alexander Bain defined 'Mind' by three attributes: 'Feeling', including emotion, passion, affection, sentiment, 'Volition' and 'Thought', including intellect or cognition. *The Emotions of the Will* (London: John W. Parker and Son, 1859) has a chapter on 'Æsthetic emotions', and Bain qualifies the 1859 version of the 'meanings of Consciousness' including 'all that regards the connexions of mind with physical processes', p. v. The volume was reviewed in the *Westminster Review* issue where Pater published 'Winckelmann'. Bain's views were recapitulated in *Mind and Body, the theories of their relations* (London: Henry S. King and Co, 1873).

5 L.S. Jacyna, 'The Physiology of Mind, the Unity of Nature, and the Moral Order in Victorian Thought', *The British Journal for the History of Science*, 47.14 (1981): 109–32, 111.

6 Along with the famous *Mind: A Quarterly Review of Psychology and Philosophy* created by Bain (1876), the Physiological Society was founded in 1876 and the *Journal of Physiology* first appeared in 1878. The first issue of *Brain*, a journal devoted to brain physiology, appeared in 1879.

7 Alan F. Collins, 'England', in David B. Baker, ed., *The Oxford Handbook of the History of Psychology: Global Perspectives* (Oxford: Oxford University Press, 2012).

8 Gary Hatfield, 'Psychology Old and New', in Thomas Baldwin, ed., *Cambridge*

debates opened 'boundless intellectual horizons' for Walter Pater.

As a young Oxford don, Pater began to contribute to intellectual discussions as early as 1866, publishing a sustained piece on Winckelmann[9] in the *Westminster Review*,[10] before switching to the *Fortnightly Review*, which hosted several contributions on fifteenth-century art that were later revised, completed, and collated in *Studies in the History of the Renaissance* (1873). The volume was controversial above all for its 'Preface' and its 'Conclusion', which revisit aesthetics using materialistic and evolutionary psychological theories. The 'Preface' defines aesthetic experience as an analysis by an 'aesthetic' critic of the sensations triggered by various objects[11] reduced to a series of 'elements', through a process similar to chemistry, to uncover their 'virtue' ('Preface' xxx). The 'Conclusion' characterises the subject of aesthetic analysis as an impressionable mind, whose identity resides in 'the passage and dissolution of impressions, images, sensations'.[12] Pater later enriched what appears here to be a theory of the perceiving and sensitive individual. In a time when fresh physiology-based psychological conceptions revised eighteenth-century associationist theories, in which the gradual accumulation of data in sensory experience is further organised in the mind through patterns of association, he 'sought to ground both aesthetic experience and critical practice in a conceptualization of sensations and impressions—of the material imprints that phenomena leave upon the sensorium, and which the mind seeks to organize into a kind of self.'[13]

History of Philosophy, 1870–1945 (Cambridge: Cambridge University Press, 2003), pp. 93–110.

9 Pater's substantial review supposedly discussed a biography of Winckelmann along with a translation of *The History of Ancient Arts among the Greeks.*

10 [Walter Pater], 'Winckelmann', *The Westminster Review* 87 (January 1867): 80–110.

11 '[P]owers or forces producing pleasurable sensations, each of a more or less peculiar or unique kind'. Walter Pater, *The Renaissance: Studies in Art and Poetry* (1893) ed. Adam Phillips (Oxford: Oxford UP, 1988), p. xxx.

12 Walter Pater, 'Conclusion', in *Studies in the History of the Renaissance* (1873) ed. Mathew Beaumont (Oxford: World's Classics, Oxford University Press, 2010), p. 119. Such an audacious statement was only marginally modified in subsequent editions of *The Renaissance* in 1877, 1888, and 1893.

13 Jeremy Melius, 'Pater, Impressionism, and the Undoing of Sense', in André Dombrowski, ed., *Wiley Blackwell Companion to Impressionism* (Hoboken, New Jersey: Wiley-Blackwell, 2021), p. 93.

What follows attempts to trace Pater's path at the turn of the 1860s among competing discourses that sought to revise the philosophical dualism between body and mind. Pater's early theorising of the subject appears remarkably coherent when contextualised in contemporary debates: confronted with a plurality of theories and conceptions of subjectivity emanating from different bodies of knowledge (psychophysiology, psychology, psychopathology, philosophy) that became increasingly specialised in the following decades, he did not rally to any of them but chose literary prose – 'the special and privileged artistic faculty of the present day'[14] – to formulate and express his conception of how the working of the psychic apparatus operates. In perception and knowledge of vessels of sensation, he boldly reduced 'all works of art, and the fairer forms of nature and human life' to objects (Pater 1988, xxx).

I situate Pater's conceptions within the intellectual ebullience from the late 1860s onwards, contending that his conception of the mind – or rather the psychic apparatus or psyche, informed by Maudsley and Herbert Spencer's definition[15] – was coherent although succinct. I then argue that he chose literary prose and developed his rigorous terminology. He made the wager that prose could adequately express his conceptions, arguably for wider reading constituencies than increasingly specialised investigators of the mind or brain. Therefore, Pater both disciplined literary prose and contributed to the disciplinarisation of literary criticism.

As Ian Small underlined in a seminal article, Pater adopted and adapted to his purpose the discourse and terminologies of British psychology in the 1860s and early 1870s.[16] Pater's ideas and 'set of appropriate terms' in the chapters of *The Renaissance* are borrowed from different discourses, including physiology and what eventually came to define itself as psychology, attempting to account for both cognition in general and the 'psychology of aesthetics' in particular (Small 82). The debate was led by contributors who envisaged their activity as a scientific explanation of the working of the psychical apparatus especially in its inter-

[14] Walter Pater, 'Style', in *Appreciations* (1890; London: Macmillan, 1931), p. 7.

[15] Both Maudsley and Spencer envisaged 'mind' in an evolutionary perspective as continuously 'evolving' out of 'life'.

[16] Ian Small, 'The Vocabulary of Pater's Criticism and the Psychology of Aesthetic', *The British Journal of Aesthetics*, 18.1 (Winter 1978): 81–7, 81.

actions with bodily actions. Their writings enabled psychology, among other disciplines, to progressively gain coherence and 'epistemic stability' (Hatfield). As a reviewer noted in the *Westminster Review*, 'the progress made by Psychology within the present generation is [. . .] greater than has been made since the foundation of science', before crediting Alexander Bain for '[t]he large acquisitions of new facts, the faithful description of phenomena, the reduction of them to law and the investigation of the physical "sides" of mental products'[17] and essayist Herbert Spencer for 'the application to mind of the revolutionary philosophy of evolution' (397). Both were changing 'not only the aspect but the constitution of Psychology' (397).

Huxley's epiphenomenalism,[18] which considered the brain as the seat of consciousness, physiological explanations superseding philosophical and psychological views, and W.K. Clifford, who argued that changes in the brain were invariably concomitant to sensation, thought, and emotion in his 'Mind and Body',[19] belonged to a proximate field of investigation according to the reviewer. Their conceptions echoed earlier hypotheses such as Thomas Laycock's work on reflex action and psychology[20] and W.B. Carpenter's 'Science of Human Nature'.[21] In those writings, physiologists treated psychological topics from a materialistic perspective, and the mind–body problem sometimes narrowed to an interpretation of cerebral localisation research.[22] Those

17 [Unsigned] 'The Development of Psychology', *The Westminster Review* 101 (1874): 396.

18 T.H. Huxley, 'On the hypothesis that animals are automata and its history', *Fortnightly Review* 16 (1874): 555–80.

19 W.K. Clifford, 'Mind and Body', *Fortnightly Review* 16 (1874): 714–30. Huxley's and Clifford's contributions were both published in the *Fortnightly Review*.

20 Thomas Laycock, 'Reflex, automatic, and unconscious cerebration', *Journal of Mental Science* 21 (1876): 477–98.

21 'I have especially applied myself to the elucidation of the share which the Mind has, not only in the *interpretation* of sense-impressions, but in the production of Sensorial states not less real to the Ego who experiences them than those called-forth by external objects', William Carpenter, 'Preface', in *Principles of mental physiology, with their applications to the training and discipline of the mind, and the study of its morbid conditions* (London: H. S. King, 1874), p. viii. William Carpenter developed and included 'psychological' chapters from his *Principles of Physiology* (1853).

22 In his *Functions of the Brain*, Ferrier presents to 'the student of physiology or psychology a systematic exposition' of his experiments on brain function

conceptions envisaged mental activities as a product of the organism in its relations with the world and in different degrees led to the hypothesis of a psychophysical parallelism.

Pater's indebtedness to writings discussing aesthetic cognition in influential periodicals has already been noted. 'Evolutionary theory and physiology provided tools for rescaling aesthetic response: for Herbert Spencer[23] and Grant Allen, the experience of beauty was a reflex that had evolved slowly in history; while for Alexander Bain, it was an immediate neurophysiological response to stimuli of form, color, or sound'.[24] In *The Emotions and The Will*, Bain defined consciousness in terms of its discontinuous impressions, themselves invested by language, which alone is capable of endowing them with a certain permanence, a view shared by Pater.[25] Like Bain, Pater also argued that the individual capacity to differentiate between impressions had to be cultivated. Aesthetic cognition depends on the continuous activity of the psychic apparatus: 'Our education becomes complete in proportion as our susceptibility to these impressions [of objects] increases in depth and variety'. (Pater 1988, xxx) He also echoed Spencer's evolutionary psychology where mental phenomena derive from physiological organisation and evolution and where aesthetic cognition, devoid of aim, provides a certain amount of pleasure expressed through sensations and emotions. Likewise, there is common ground between Pater's 'pleasurable sensations' and those of James Sully, following in Spencer's footsteps, defining art as 'the highest conceivable quality and quantity of human pleasure'[26] that could be provided to the subject, as well as his insistence on the individual character of aesthetic experience and his promotion of aesthetic education through multiplication and diversification of pleasurable sources.

(London: Smith Elder and Co, 1876), p. vii, including a chapter on 'the hemispheres considered psychologically', quoting from Bain and Spencer.

23 Herbert Spencer's *The Principles of Psychology* (London: Williams and Norgate, 1870–2) associates biological and mental functioning along evolutionary lines, in a more abstract and theoretical approach.

24 Benjamin Morgan, *The Outward Mind. Materialist Aesthetics in Victorian Science and Literature* (Chicago: University of Chicago Press, 2017), pp. 86–130.

25 '[O]bjects in the solidity with which language invests them', Pater, *The Renaissance*, p. 151.

26 James Sully, *Sensation and Intuition. Studies in Psychology and Aesthetics* (1874, London: Kegan Paul, 2nd ed. 1880), p. 349.

Indebted to those ideas, *The Renaissance* not only developed an account of aesthetic cognition which grounded British Aestheticism firmly in sensation. More importantly, it conceived of a psyche where all forms of cognition are possible, its aesthetic variant needing to be envisaged etymologically as deriving from the senses although not reducible to them. Terming it 'mind' (as opposed to 'brain', which would signal adhesion to theories localising some functions in specific brain areas), a term replete with different nuances but then anchoring discussions in a physiological field, Pater envisaged a psychic apparatus, the various functions of which he investigated – hence the choice of terming it 'psyche' in what follows. Grounding aesthetic cognition in the physio-psychological relationship between subject and objects, the 'Preface' defines it as a series of mental operations designed to 'discriminate' them by the impressions each elicits – 'to know one's own impression as it really is'. These impressions need to be 'strongly' experienced to be 'distinctly' realised (Pater 1988, xxix). Moreover, the aesthetic experience involves some psychic activity as the apparatus is confronted with 'a swarm of impressions' already situated in 'the inward world of thought and feeling' where 'each object is loosed into a group of impressions—colour, odour, texture—in the mind of the observer' (151). Decomposed into impressions, i.e. sensory qualities, the object is reduced to an evanescent series, 'unstable, flickering, inconsistent', that only our consciousness can make sensible in their characteristic intermittence: 'which burn and are extinguished with our consciousness of them' (151). The activity of those discrete 'flickering' sensory qualities, or what Pater terms 'data' (xxix), being therefore finite and divisible, constitutes a part of the psyche's activity.[27]

The psyche is characterised by its capacity to apprehend any object through the fragmentary and discontinuous sensory impressions it elicits, impressions that manifest themselves by the trace each one leaves: 'a single sharp impression, with a sense in it, a relic more or less fleeting, of such moments gone by' (151). Therefore, all reality, 'what is real in our life', is psychical: all aesthetic cognition is grounded in the apprehension of the trace of the impressions, i.e. both in a quantitative and qualitative process.

[27] '[T]hose impressions of the individual mind [. . .] are in perpetual flight; [. . .] each of them is limited by time, [. . .] each of them is infinitely divisible also'. Pater, *The Renaissance*, p. 151.

Perception and consciousness become mutually exclusive: 'all that is actual in it being a single moment, gone while we try to apprehend it, of which it may ever be more truly said that it has ceased to be than that it is' (151). The 'Conclusion' deploys a prototypical psychic apparatus subjected to a perpetual process of decomposition. All knowledge being individual and situated in 'the narrow chamber of the individual mind', any analysis carried out by the psyche only reveals an alternation between what is already a relic destined to be replaced by the next one. Paterian subjectivity becomes reduced to 'that strange, perpetual weaving and unweaving of ourselves'. (152)

In 1868, in a review of Morris's three volumes of poetry, some paragraphs of which were redeployed in the 'Conclusion', Pater was more radical, equating subjectivity with permanent loss: 'one washed out beyond the bar in a sea at ebb, losing even his personality, as the elements of which he is composed pass into new combinations. Struggling, as he must, to save himself, it is himself that he loses at every moment'.[28] His subdued 1873 expression led, however, to accusations of 'elegant materialism'[29] or 'Cyrenaicism'[30] as *The Renaissance* became a controversial volume.

Yet, apart from any moral issues that reviewers deemed debatable, such a Heraclitean model[31] of psychic activity raises serious issues; firstly, that of the reconstitution of the object necessary for its memorisation, and secondly, that of a locus where impressions can be preserved to return to consciousness as memories and weave individual history, providing one with a sense of history. Pater describes a prototypical individual subjected to a mere alternation between different traces, leaving memory undiscussed. He does not conceptualise or localise the site where impressions are stored to constitute individual memory and provide a sense of subjectivity. With its eloquent insistence on the psychic work done to each sensation, the radicalism of the 'Conclusion' seems to

28 [Walter Pater], 'Poems by William Morris', *The Westminster Review* 33 (October 1868): 300–12, 311.

29 [Mrs Oliphant], 'Review of *Studies in the History of the Renaissance*', *Blackwood's Magazine* 114 (November 1873): 604–6.

30 'Cyrenaicism['s] [. . .] moral philosophy bids us size the minute and make the most of it', Z, 'Modern Cyneraicism', *The Examiner* (12 April 1873), 381–2.

31 See Pater's epigraph: 'λέγει που Ἡράκλειτος ὅτι 'πάντα χωρεῖ καὶ οὐδὲν μένει': Pater, *The Renaissance*, p. 150.

miss (or elide) the structuring element that provides the individual with a sense of personal continuity. In a collection celebrating fifteenth-century Renaissance individualism (therefore privatising history) meant to sustain a sense of collective history, this question is central. There must be some memory and a place for memory, including an un- or non-conscious one, so that the flux of impressions can be discriminated, compared, and differentiated, thereby perfecting aesthetic education through psychic activity.

However, Pater resolves this aporia through his conception of the body and of historical transmission (which I discuss in what follows). The body appears as the repository of the sensorium (although Pater leaves almost undiscussed the inclusion of the individual within a given group, community and society), and transmission explicitly relies on the return of impressions through the experience of an individual renaissance. The body is conceived as a site of mental – here 'spiritual' – excitation: 'the human form, itself one entire medium of spiritual expression, trembling, blushing, melting into dew, with inward excitement'. (Pater 1988, 136) It reacts to impressions both from the external and the inner world, expressing inner quantitative processes, sometimes by what, concerning Oscar Wilde, M. Davis terms an 'unruly corporeality'.[32] Pater always carefully notes its excitation. The body stands as the interface between physiological and mental forms of excitation, transforming quantity into quality along lines that remain however undiscussed.

Pater's position as to the relation between mind and body is interesting as he opts neither for an all-bodily reaction nor for a strictly intellectual response. He relies on the phenomenon of enthusiasm as defined in Plato's *Phaedrus* (244 *c–d*): 'dependent as it is to a great degree on bodily temperament, [which] has a power of re-enforcing the purer emotions of the intellect with an almost physical excitement'. (Pater 1988, 122) If the body has the capacity to be variably excited by exterior impressions, some forms of inner excitation increase its animation and response. Physical and intellectual dimensions are intertwined, working together to make the subject fully cognisant, or, in Winckelmann's case, endowed with 'divinatory power over the Hellenic world' (122). Aesthetic cognition becomes '"enminded," attenuating distinctions between

[32] Michael Davis, 'Mind and Matter in *The Picture of Dorian Gray*', *Victorian Literature and Culture* 41 (2013): 547–60, 556.

inward self and outward world', as Morgan notes (Morgan, 133–73). Such 'enmindment' finds a privileged medium in Pater's body.

In a still unresolved (and unresolvable) debate, Pater subscribes neither to physiological accounts of the body's excitation nor to Grant Allen's theses in *Physiological Aesthetics* (1876) positing the possibility of aesthetic knowledge 'in purely physiological terms' (Small, 85). Rather, he shares Allen's later refusal to dissociate mental and physical aspects.[33] Such a careful position resonates with the prudence of various scientists of the mind in the 1870s who also conceived the phenomenal distinction between 'Mind' and 'Body' as ontologically relative, their epistemological dualism being susceptible to be replaced with some kind of superior 'monistic view'.[34] However, Pater is no proponent of such conciliation. He insists on envisaging a dialectic fuelled by variable intensities of excitation affecting body and mind. Traditional oppositions become subsumed into the notion, central to Pater's conceptualisation and later writings, of a 'personality', i.e., a being with specific qualities, including its susceptibility to various degrees of excitation, and itself susceptible to transmitting them according to a model exemplified by the relationship between Virgil and Dante or Winckelmann and Goethe. Such a relationship is understood as taking place through 'a passionate life or personality' (146) where body and mind are both subject to excitation. Those twin examples make it clear that transmission operates across history and existence, relying not so much on material occurrence but on a dimension exceeding it, one I would call the 'remainder' of the subject meant to 'importunate' other subjects by its 'passionate life'. That remainder appears as 'personality'.

Other remains or relics can act as vessels of aesthetic transmission: exciting texts and objects elicit specific experiences. Winckelmann begins with 'the words only of Greek poetry', 'divining beyond the words an unexpressed pulsation of sensuous life' foreshadowing other material fragments also endowed with the capacity to arouse his emotions when '[s]uddenly he is in contact with that life, still fervent in the relics of plastic art' (118). Such sensorial and sensual

33 Grant Allen, 'Pain and Death', *Mind: A Quarterly Review of Psychology and Philosophy* 18 (Apr. 1880): 201–16, 207.

34 Michael Clark, '"A plastic power ministering to organization": interpretations of the mind-body relation in late nineteenth-century British psychiatry', *Psychological Medicine* 13 (1983): 487–97, 492.

contact triggers a singular experience when the past comes back as a repressed memory replete with excitation:

> Filled as our culture is with the classical spirit, we can hardly imagine how deeply the human mind was moved, when, at the Renaissance, in the midst of a frozen world, the buried fire of ancient art rose up from under the soil. Winckelmann here reproduces for us the earlier sentiment of the Renaissance. On a sudden the imagination feels itself free.' (Pater 1988, 118).

His sensual contact with the relics liberates Winckelmann's imagination and Pater makes a parallel with collective recollection, understood as a 'sentiment' of the Renaissance. Experiencing that liberation, Winckelmann 'seems to realise that fancy of the reminiscence of a forgotten knowledge hidden for a time in the mind itself; as if the mind of one, lover and philosopher at once in some phase of pre-existence—πηιλοσοπηεσασ ποτε μετ ερετοσ—fallen into a new cycle, were beginning its intellectual culture over again, yet with a certain power of anticipating its results' (125). Winckelmann demonstrates the existence of 'a forgotten knowledge hidden for a time in the mind itself' susceptible both to be repressed and to return, transforming the subject by making him experience an authentic tridimensional temporality whereby past, present and future provide an individual sense of history. Winckelmann's experience shows Pater's conceptualisation of memory: memories are not sealed from the subject but return, lifting some mental repression in the individual experience of the Renaissance. Their return testifies to the existence of a site where impressions can be gathered and stored to be recollected, although Pater does not localise it or engage in any description, contenting himself with describing the liberating and temporalising effects it produces. Pater's psychical apparatus is therefore dynamically conceptualised, such a process also historicising the very notion of the subject.

On a collective level, transmission is accounted for by the paradigm of Greek antiquity: as the object ardently desired by Winckelmann, it can be characterised by its periodical absorption and resurfacing. History becomes a perpetual process where '[t]he spiritual forces of the past, which have prompted and informed the culture of a succeeding age, live, indeed, within that culture, but with an absorbed, underground life', the 'Hellenic element' being for its part characterised by its return in the course of history and as what structures history (127). Its return allows 'culture' to be 'drawn back to its sources to be clarified and corrected' (127–8). Transmission becomes predicated on that periodical return irrigating culture and shaping the future. Originating in ancient Greece, such a historical nucleus is passed down as 'a conscious tradition', i.e. a tradition unsystematically present to collective consciousness but susceptible to reappearing, therefore enacting some cultural renaissance. Pater's conception of both individual and historical 'renaissance' can be defined as an incessant return and revival of that repressed 'Hellenic element'. Its very repression is the means of its preservation, as shown by the historical relation between Hellenism and 'the medieval spirit':

> When the actual relics of the antique were restored to the world, [. . .] it was seen that the medieval spirit too had done something for the destiny of the antique. By hastening the decline of art, by withdrawing interest from it, and yet keeping unbroken the thread of its traditions, it had suffered the human mind to repose that it might awake when day came, with eyes refreshed, to those antique forms. (145)

The return of an ambiguous repressed compared to some 'ancient plague-pit' but also susceptible to revivify 'the life of nature and of the senses', frames Pater's collective history, as punctuated by continual irruptions. The renaissance is a collective process as well as an individual one. As a psychic process, it brings into play the dialectic of absorption and reappearance, repression and return. Such a process operating both on a collective and individual dimension characterises Pater's psychical apparatus as dynamic, also suggesting the existence of a site in the psyche where relics of impressions are repressed and recorded in the form of memories always susceptible to return. Winckelmann appears both as the ideal subject of embodied individual cognition and as a subject experiencing the return of some 'hidden knowledge', such subtle return constituting a genuine renaissance, which can be experimented collectively.

In 1867, Pater's second published review is indeed foundational on different counts, among which are his insistence on the place of bodily and mental excitation and his idea of an unconscious process structuring both individual and collective history. The R/renaissance is such an experience, correlating perhaps too strictly the relationship between the individual and collective dimensions.

From his earliest writings, Pater puts forward a theory of his own, certainly incomplete, but which can also be considered his response to the various contributions both on the issue of the structure of the 'mind' and of its relationship to the body.

Discussing Morris's medievalism in 1868, Pater returns to the subject's relationship with the historical past to reject any 'actual revival': 'We cannot conceive the age; we can conceive the element it has contributed to our culture; we can treat the subjects of the age bringing that into relief' (Pater 1868, 147). Any attempt to achieve a complete understanding or resuscitation of history being doomed, the individual has, however, the capacity to divide himself in the process of remembrance: 'to isolate such a phase, to throw it into relief, to be divided against ourselves in zeal for it, as we may hark back to some choice space of our own individual life' (147). Again, such inner division of the self points to a topical conceptualisation of the psyche, this time endowed with reflexivity. The site where impressions are stored is now depicted as 'some choice space of our own individual life' (147) to which we can return in the act of remembering.

Such a place morphed into a dwelling, the construction of which Pater details in 'The Child in the House' (1878), imaging more vividly 'the narrow chamber of the individual mind' enclosed behind 'that thick wall of personality' (Pater 1988, 151). In this short story, Pater engages in a much more ambitious task of narrativising the history of the psychical apparatus. He does so by dividing the narrative voice between a narrating 'I' and an inner focalisation on the character he evokes.[35] Insisting on the singularity of the (psychic) dwelling, he describes its construction as 'brain-building' through the recollection of one Florian Deleal (Pater 1878, 313). However, this construction is no mere physiological process, and the house is described as 'half-spiritualised',[36] the compound showing that in 1878, Pater still refuses to distinguish between a purely mental dwelling and a purely physiological one. The psychical apparatus progressively arises in the intermingling of the two, the material being 'homely' and the spiritual

[35] 'The child of whom I am writing', Walter H. Pater, 'Imaginary Portraits I. The Child in the House', *Macmillan's Magazine* 34 (1878): 313–21, 314; 'the sort of house I have described', 315.

[36] 'In that half-spiritualised house he could watch the better, over again, the gradual expansion of the soul which had come to be there': Pater, 'Imaginary Portraits I', 313.

being described by Pater as a 'soul-stuff' with an unknown origin: 'inward and outward being woven through and through each other into one inextricable texture—half, tint and trace and accident of homely colour and form, from the wood and the bricks; half, mere soul-stuff, floated thither from who knows how far' (313). In fact, the material origin is less important than the effects Florian's house has upon its owner, as it provides him with a sense of personal identity – 'a place "inclosed" and "sealed"' (316) – defining the subject first as an inhabitant, then demonstrating that all psychogenesis always appears a posteriori and only accounts for the subject's singularity. Florian, Pater's other typical subject after Winckelmann, also leads to the recognition of the subject's exile from the house that made him who he is, and to the 'agony of home-sickness' that will henceforth characterise him (321). Pater's early interest in literature may account for his development of ideal types to elaborate his minimal but efficient theory of the psychic apparatus, an interest that distinguishes his views from those of psychophysiologists. In 'The Child in the House' he further qualifies his ideal subject as a permanent exile, decentring one's sense of identity far more efficiently than simply conceiving of it as determined by (un)consciousness.

It is worth emphasising the precision of the terms used to explain what Pater describes as 'that mental journey' (313) to give a poetic history of the psyche. Such precision, coupled with his neological capacity, enables him to situate himself with marked originality at the heart of a debate between various theorists of psychogenetic development. Pater does not distinguish between the physical and the 'spiritual' and does not support a strict physiological localisation for cognitive and sensorial capacities. Every impression is described as having the capacity to elicit a physical, sensitive response from the subject that cannot be reduced to a simple reflex. The Paterian subject is neither an automaton nor the subject of unconscious cerebral activity but can be defined by a psyche with the capacity to conceptualise its own birth, narrativising it through the metaphorical construction of the dwelling: 'the noting, namely, of some things in the story of his spirit' (313). Pater poetises 'that process of brain-building by which we are, each one of us, what we are' (313).

Published in *Macmillan's Magazine*, Pater's publisher's magazine, the first 'Imaginary Portrait' is also a reminder that most of the debates about the definition of humanness first took place in periodicals including family magazines such as *Macmillan's*,[37] where fiction also contributed to an array of discourses and conceptualisations, a polylogue of overlapping, sometimes contradictory theories. As Sally Shuttleworth argued, '[l]iterary texts did not simply supply material for medical case studies, [but] also helped frame the questions and categories of an emerging scientific field';[38] Pater being notable for his definition of the subject as a permanent exile. Those questions usually echoed one another on the monthly basis of the main periodicals hosting them, periodicity contributing to structuring a lively multi-polar and multi-disciplinary debate whence modern psychology was forged.[39] It was also through this mode of publication, which was overwhelmingly his (*Marius* was the only one of Pater's longer writings not to appear in a periodical), that Pater chose to appear as a man of letters intervening in a general discussion.

Pater never embraced psychology (in the modern sense), psychophysiology or neurology, but appeared as what Matthew Beaumont terms a 'psychagogue',[40] relying on his own definition of a writer's task in *Plato and Platonism*.[41] The term, Beaumont comments, 'mediates usefully between psychology and rhetoric, thought and language, the inner and the outer' (Beaumont, 11), and helps describe Pater's position as a writer choosing logic and terminological rigour to elaborate the logic of the psychic apparatus and its workings, that of historical-artistic transmission, and that of the stages in the constitution of the psyche from the late 1860s onwards. His conceptions were enriched through an

[37] Gowan Dawson, 'Walter Pater's *Marius the Epicurean* and the Discourse of Science in *Macmillan's Magazine*: A Creature of the Nineteenth Century', *English Literature in Transition* 48.1 (2005): 38–54.

[38] Sally Shuttleworth, *The Mind of the Child: Child Development in Literature, Science, and Medicine, 1840–1900* (Oxford: Oxford University Press, 2010), p. 362.

[39] '[T]he strength of British psychology across the second half of the nineteenth century stems from the diversity of methods and approaches'. Hatfield, 'Psychology Old and New', 2003.

[40] Matthew Beaumont, 'Pater as Psychagogue: Psychology, Aesthetics, Rhetoric', *19: Interdisciplinary Studies in the Long Nineteenth Century* 12 (2011): 11.

[41] 'And as the special function of all speech as a fine art is the control of minds (*psychagogia*) it is in general with the soul of man – with a veritable psychology, with as much as possible as we can get of that – that the writer, the speaker, must be chiefly concerned, if he is to handle minds not by mere empiric routine [. . .] but by the power of veritable fine art.' Pater, *Appreciations*, p.121.

impressive series of publications, whether in fiction or in cultural and literary criticism in the following decades, but his epistemological positioning is worth stressing, as it situates him in literary criticism as a discipline itself in recomposition.[42] Such a position has long remained detrimental to his recognition as an educated contributor engaged in defining cognition.

'Style' also proposes another theorisation of the psyche through the polarity between 'soul' and 'mind' defined as qualities,[43] demonstrating Pater's constant additions and revisions of his conceptualisations when it comes to poetising the psyche. One of his first readers was attentive to such meticulousness when the article was included in *Appreciations* (1889), terming it 'a well-reasoned plea'.[44] Here Pater discusses 'the problem of style' envisaged as the appropriate use of words, i.e., the relationship between language and psyche, and language as it is processed by the psyche, with such a process involving the materialisation of language. Language is seen first and foremost as a musical instrument that the ideal man of letters or 'lover of words' plays 'scrupulously' (14), in particular by paying attention to 'the value of an atmosphere in which every term finds its utmost degree of expression', rejecting 'a constant tendency on the part of the majority of those who use them to efface the distinctions of language' (13). Through this attention, the man of letters ceases to be subjected to language and becomes its 'master'.[45]

Pater lists the qualities of his ideal word lover:[46] attentive to their materiality, their history, and therefore to the evolution of their use,[47] he develops 'a vocabulary faithful to the colouring of

42 Ian Small, 'Walter Pater', in *Conditions for Criticism. Authority, Knowledge, and Literature in the Late Nineteenth Century* (Oxford: Clarendon Press, 1991).

43 'By mind, the literary artist reaches us, through static and objective indications of design in his work, legible to all. By soul, he reaches us, somewhat capriciously perhaps, one and not another, through vagrant sympathy and a kind of immediate contact.' Pater, *Appreciations*, p. 25.

44 [C.L. Greaves], 'Review of Pater's *Appreciations*', *The Spectator* (21 December, 1889): 887–8.

45 '[H]e has the science of the instrument he plays on, perhaps, after all, with a freedom which in such case will be the freedom of a master.' Pater, *Appreciations*, p. 14.

46 'A lover of words for their own sake.' Pater, *Appreciations*, p. 20.

47 '[One] to whom nothing about them is unimportant, a minute and constant observer of their physiognomy.' Pater, *Appreciations*, p. 20.

his own spirit, and in the strictest sense original' (15). This time, the psyche is apprehended as metabolising words into sensory units, 'elementary particles of language [. . .] realised as colour and light and shade' (20), intended to reflect and mediate the mental image formed by the word lover. Their adequacy to the mental image must be strict to achieve not style defined as a general quality, but style as specific to each inner vision: 'the unique word, phrase, sentence, paragraph, essay, or song, absolutely proper to the single mental presentation or vision within' (29). In Pater's 'natural economy', words reflect thought and thought has language as its correlate,[48] the two being mutually adapted: 'some pre-existent adaptation, between a relative, somewhere in the world of thought and its correlative, somewhere in the world of language' (20) because each is here being materialised.

Pater traces the work of the psyche processing the diversity of the sensory and linguistic world to metabolise it and match it with an inner representation:

> Into the mind sensitive to 'form,' a flood of random sounds, colours, incidents, is ever penetrating from the world without, to become, by sympathetic selection, a part of its very structure, and, in turn, the visible vesture, and expression of that other world it sees so steadily within, nay, already with a partial conformity thereto, to be refined, enlarged, corrected, at a hundred points (31).[49]

Complicating contemporary understandings of 'mind', including its functional understanding, Pater gives the term a new meaning, turning it into a site for processing linguistic activity. The psyche remains characterised by the incessant renewal of what is now described as representations. Adaptation takes place between the diversity of both external representations and internal representations thanks to constant modifications or rectifications. Those adaptations transform linguistic impressions into a personal representation. Style intervenes as a 'tact or taste'[50] designed to refine

[48] 'From first to last our faculty of thinking is limited by our command of speech', Walter Pater, *Plato and Platonism* (London: Macmillan, 1893), p. 142.

[49] 'In Pater's writings, the material world and its sensations, however celebrated, are always thinning out into a kind of atmospheric texture and finally simply into text.' Melius, 'Pater, Impressionism, and the Undoing of Sense', p. 93. The nature of that text is precisely what Pater materialises.

[50] '[I]t is just there, just at those doubtful points that the function of style, as tact or taste, intervenes'. Pater, *Appreciations*, p. 31.

the suitability of the word to its purpose: 'precisely in that [exact proportion of the term to its purpose], is the absolute beauty of style, prose or verse' (34). Language becomes materialised to fit into Pater's material idea of the psyche as an interface between exterior and interior.

His (stubbornly masculine) proponent of style is defined as one who unifies theme and term, from word scale to the whole of the text: 'To give the phrase, the sentence, the structural member, the entire composition, song, or essay, a similar unity with its subject and with itself:—style is in the right way when it tends towards that' (22). Like Grant Allen,[51] Pater rejects or ignores David Ferrier's and others' theses on the localisation of language[52] privileging a material linguistic that reflects and expresses individual thought, style intervening to foster 'that absolute accordance of expression to idea' (34). Such material adaptation constitutes style as personal, individual and an expression of the subject. Pater's style should therefore be approached as the result of a process designed to bring expression into line with thought: 'the more perfect adaptation of words to their matter' (35). The fact that this adaptation or translation – in 'Style' translation appears as a perfect verbal transfer of mental representation[53] – was called into question in the twentieth century by Freudian psychoanalysis, among others, should in no way prevent us from considering that it is operative for Pater and that it undergirds his writings, including his defence of imaginative prose as the art of the modern world, the history of which he finely traces up to what he perceives as its chaotic condition. Pater relies on his conception of style to express not only his aesthetic judgements or his cultural and literary criticism, but also his constantly renewed conceptions of the psyche. Presenting his conceptions and contextualising them in

51 'It is the brain as a whole that thinks, and feels, and desires, and imagines, just as it is the body as a whole that walks, and swings, and digs, and dances. To locate the faculty of language, say, in a particular convolution of a particular hemisphere is almost as absurd, as it seems to me, as to locate, say, the faculty of writing in the last joint of the forefinger', Grant Allen, 'A Thinking Machine', *Gentleman's Magazine* 260 (January 1886): 41.

52 Paul Broca's 1861 studies on language, John Hughlings Jackson's on the localisation of speech, and David Ferrier's 1873 research on electrical stimulation of the cortex.

53 Pater defines 'all language' as involving 'translation from inward to outward'. Pater, *Appreciations*, p. 31.

contemporary debates by pointing out their specific character also reintegrates Pater within the fold of late-Victorian understandings of the psychical apparatus. Psychophysiological and evolutionary theories are the starting ground for Pater's elaboration of the subject, predicated on the embodied experience of the artists and writers portrayed in his writings. Steeped in overlapping theories, he embraces and defines literature as a discipline that can present his ideas on the workings of the psyche more accurately than other theories. Here Pater both disciplines prose and disciplinarises literary criticism.

Pater appears thus as a legitimate participant in *fin de siècle* ardour in theorising mind, body and their interactions. Approaching the question of 'what it means to be human' from a multidisciplinary background informed by competing ideas, theories and conceptualisations, he tailors language to his ends: imaginative prose, *le mot juste*. Such position enables him to occupy a specific place in late-nineteenth-century psychological conceptions. As the twenty-first century's ever-increasing specialisation and disciplinarisation undermine our capacity to ask that seminal question, Pater remains more relevant than ever.

5

Conversion-Crisis as a Marginal Experience in William James and Walter Pater

David Sweeney Coombs

Not quite synonyms, 'conversion' and 'crisis' were closely linked terms in the nineteenth century, shaping each other's meanings across a range of social and intellectual domains. William James's *Varieties of Religious Experience* (1902), a landmark text in psychology, philosophy and religious studies, affords an illustration of this conceptual overlap. James' naturalistic account of religion begins by dispensing with attention to orthodox observances, 'this second-hand religious life . . . this mass of suggested feeling and imitated conduct', in favour of the individual religious experiences he regards as their original source.[1] While he accounts for religious experiences in the scientific terms of psychology and physiology, James leaves open the question of their transcendent value and truthfulness, submitting them to the pragmatist principle that their truth is a function of whether they 'bring us good consequential fruits for life' (22). But both James's psychology and his pragmatism complicate his treatment of conversion. Notwithstanding his claim that religions originate in individual mystical experiences, James was deeply sceptical of the notions of 'instantaneous change and a unique and comprehensive alteration of character' in conventional conversion narratives.[2]

Shortly before he began working on the *Varieties of Religious Experience*, James expressed his scepticism about conversion in an 1897 letter to Henry Rankin:

[1] William James, 'Varieties of Religious Experience', in *William James: Writings 1902–1910* (New York: Library of America, 1987), p. 15. Hereafter cited parenthetically.

[2] Roger Ward, *Conversion in American Philosophy* (New York: Fordham, 2004), p. 110.

> In the matter of conversion I am quite willing to believe that a new truth may be supernaturally revealed to a subject when he really *asks*. But I am sure that in many cases of conversion it is less a new truth than a new power gained over life by a truth always known. It is a case of the conflict of two *self-systems* in a personality up to that time heterogeneously divided, but in which, after the conversion-crisis, the higher loves and powers come definitively to gain the upper-hand and expel the forces which up to that time had kept them down in the position of mere grumblers and protesters and agents of remorse and discontent.[3]

The remark that conversion reflects a new power in a truth always known suggests that James was already formulating one of the central claims in *Varieties*: that mystical experiences result when energies hitherto kept to margins of consciousness become its centre and focal point. Seen this way, conversion is an experience defined less by a radically new spiritual apprehension than by the return of the repressed. At the same time, James's letter shifts noticeably from the language of psychology to a register closer to history, describing conversion as a kind of revolution in personality, and the fulcrum of that rhetorical shift is 'conversion-crisis'.

This chapter explicates the philosophy of history implicit to James's account of conversion. In *The Varieties of Religious Experience*, James tries to explain conversion less as a punctual event than a gradual process. One of James's central motives in his preference for a gradualist explanation is the theory of truth he lays out in *Pragmatism* (1907), where he defines 'being true' as performing a 'marriage function' that assimilates a novel idea or experience to the body of our past understanding.[4] James's cumulative theory of truth here, I show, shares something with the epistemological theories of John Henry Newman, which took his own drawn-out conversion to Roman Catholicism as a model for a psychological account of how we come to believe in the truth of propositions. At the same time, both James and Newman retain the widespread conceptual linking of conversion to crisis, which opens out the individual experience of conversion to historical transformations as well as historical precedents.

[3] *The Letters of William James*, vol. II, ed. Henry James (Boston: Atlantic Monthly, 1920), p. 57.

[4] James, 'Pragmatism', in *William James: Writings 1902–1910*, p. 515. Hereafter cited parenthetically.

For James, conversion-crisis resolves a dilemma posed by the way his naturalistic account of religious experience in *The Varieties* risks finally transforming what the individual construes as an encounter with the transcendent force of the divine into a manifestation of psychological forces immanent to the self. Even James's position that the truth of religious experience must lie in the usefulness of its effects substitutes an immanent justification for a transcendent one.[5] This retreat to the immanent, individual self reflects James's historical moment, more than a century into the process of secularisation that redefined religious beliefs as matters of private judgement, with their socially sanctioned power to establish truth and belonging subsumed by the rationalised, liberal state. Historical secularisation unmoors individual experience from natural history no less than national history, and in James' account species history, planetary history, cosmological history – the former domains of natural theology – threaten to persist as an impersonal, transcendent background ironising any truth-claims for religious experience. One of the challenges James takes up is thus how to re-integrate individual experience with deep history and deep time, and the idea of conversion-crisis plays a key role in that effort.[6] To map out the conceptual history making that possible, I turn from James to the Victorian historical novel, a genre defined by the formal demand 'that certain crises in the personal destinies of a number of human beings coincide and interweave within the determining context of an historical crisis'.[7] My focus here is Walter Pater's *Marius the Epicurean* (1885), a novel centrally concerned with locating individual experience within historical time at larger scales. As it culminates in an ambiguous conversion that complements James's account in *The Varieties*, I suggest Pater's *Marius* explores the margins of indi-

[5] James's pragmatist truth criterion here is exemplary of a secular age in Charles Taylor's definition: a moment when 'the eclipse of all goals beyond human flourishing becomes [popularly] conceivable'. See Taylor, *A Secular Age* (Cambridge: Belknap 2007), p. 19.

[6] Here, I build on Gauri Viswanathan's account of conversion as a key nineteenth-century site for the contestation and re-negotiation of belonging, which she reads in a social and political register as an expression of dissent. See Viswanathan, *Outside the Fold: Conversion, Modernity, and Belief* (Princeton: Princeton University Press, 1998), esp. pp. 3–43.

[7] Georg Lukács, *The Historical Novel*, Hannah and Stanley Mitchell, trans., (Boston: Beacon, 1963), p. 141.

vidual experience and the historical novel and speculates about what might lie beyond them.

Conversion as a theory of the unconscious in James's *Varieties of Religious Experience*

Conversion plays a central but conflicted role in James's effort to give a psychological account of religious experience that is compatible with the possibility of its transcendent value. *The Varieties*' two chapters on conversion feature the book's most detailed engagement with psychology, where James theorises the dramatic transformation of beliefs in terms of the emerging scientific concept of an unconscious mind. His naturalistic account of conversion as a release of unconscious energies from the margins of consciousness to its focal point plays a crucial role in the concluding chapter as an argument against an exclusively scientific explication of religious experience. There, James presses the model of the mind that accounts for conversion into service as a demonstration that the margins of experience will always outstrip purportedly definitive and final explanation. As James tries to reconcile a naturalistic approach to religious phenomena with an openness to their potential truth as a mode of apprehension, conversion emerges as a key object of scientific explanation that simultaneously reveals the provisionality of scientific explanations.

James defines conversion as a transformation of the religious self 'especially if it be by crisis, or sudden' (183). But even as he largely retains the conceptual vocabulary of crisis used by Protestant Evangelicals in Britain and the United States to characterise conversions as a unique and instantaneous encounter with the divine, he reframes conversion-crisis as the abrupt surfacing of what was already present. James explains conversion-crisis as a manifestation of the unconscious, especially as the unconscious had come to be understood in new work by Sigmund Freud, Josef Breuer, Pierre Janet, Alfred Binet, and Morton Prince. Earlier nineteenth-century accounts of the unconscious primarily treated it either metaphysically as a substrate of the phenomenal world or naturalistically as a descriptor for reflex functions unavailable to introspection.[8] In

[8] For a survey of these theories, see Edward Reed, *From Soul to Mind: The Emergence of Psychology from Erasmus Darwin to William James* (New Haven: Yale, 1997), pp. 127–43.

The Varieties, though, James characterises the unconscious as a recent discovery, originating in the 1880s with work by Janet and the psychic researcher Frederic Myers, who were the first to posit the existence of an unconscious mind as a kind of distinct mental entity or 'secondary self'.[9] Janet and Myers are key interlocutors in James's account of conversion.[10] For Janet, unconscious secondary selves were primarily pathological; hence the therapeutic ring that crops into *The Varieties*' discussion of the 'sick soul', for whom conversion functions as a 'straightening out and unifying of the inner self' (158). Myers, in contrast, argued that in normal as well as pathological cases the self was multiform or many-sided, combining a supraliminal consciousness with a subliminal aggregate of different potential personalities, any of which might come to assume the focal point of consciousness. Citing Myers, James argues that conversions are a specific class of these '"uprushes" into the ordinary consciousness of energies originating in the subliminal parts of the mind' (216).

But James presses Myers's and Janet's ideas into the service of a very different model of experience and the mind. Both Myers and Janet stress the simultaneity of conscious and secondary selves, conceiving of them as comprising 'chains of memory' running in parallel.[11] The figure of memory as a chain tacitly relies on the associationist subdivision of experience into units – ideas, impressions or sensations – linked together in the mind through resemblance, contiguity, or contrast. By the time James wrote *The Varieties* he had already begun developing the alternative to associationism he called radical empiricism.[12] Rather than accept the associationist chain of memory, this approach conceives of the fundamental unit of experience as a central focal point of energy surrounded by an indeterminate margin. For James, the margin is the key feature of this reconceptualisation.

[9] Frederic Myers, 'Automatic Writing', in *Proceedings of the Society for Psychical Research*, vol. 3 (London: Trübner, 1885), p. 27.

[10] See Ann Taves, 'Religious Experience and the Divisible Self: William James (And Frederic Myers) as Theorist(s) of Religion', *Journal of the American Academy of Religion* 71.2 (2003): 303–26.

[11] Ibid. p. 311.

[12] For a timeline of James's development of his radical empiricism relative to his work on *The Varieties*, see David Lamberth, 'James' "Varieties" Reconsidered: Radical Empiricism, the Extra-Marginal, and Conversion', *American Journal of Theology and Philosophy* 15.3 (1994): 257–67.

> Inattentively realized as is the matter which the margin contains, it is nevertheless there, and helps both to guide our behavior and to determine the next movement of our attention. It lies around us like a 'magnetic field,' inside of which our centre of energy turns like a compass-needle, as the present phase of consciousness alters into its successor. Our whole past store of memories floats beyond this margin, ready at a touch to come in; and the entire mass of residual powers, impulses, and knowledges that constitute our empirical self stretches continuously beyond it. (214–5)

Instead of running in a parallel chain, the unconscious is a nebulous surround where 'our whole past store of memories' is located. Consciousness here occupies the focal point of the present, enveloped by an unconscious zone identified with the 'residue' of the past.

James' radical reconceptualisation of the basic unit of psychology as a field rather than a chain or even a stream (as in G.H. Lewes's famous metaphor) brings together turn-of-the-century ideas of the unconscious mind with the earlier naturalistic account of unconscious mental processes. Nineteenth-century empirical psychology had long characterised unconscious mental processes as the repository of past experiences. In these accounts, the 'unconscious' typically designates a sort of involuntary memory: the habits and reflexes acquired by experience that guide sensory-motor interactions without our awareness. The 'unconscious inference' of John Stuart Mill or Hermann von Helmholtz and the 'unconscious cerebration' of W.B. Carpenter are characteristic examples of these earlier models. James notes explicitly that his field theory follows the accepted psychological principle that 'the subliminal region . . . is a place . . . for the accumulation of vestiges of sensible experience' (218 n.1). *The Varieties* accounts for conversion by combining this long-standing principle with the late-nineteenth-century fascination for the abrupt surfacing of subconscious energies; its apparent instantaneity can thus be scientifically explained as the effect of 'the tension of subliminal memories reaching the bursting-point' (218 n.1).

But this scientific explanation raises problems for James, insofar as it seems to foreclose the possibility of a true religious account of conversion. For such an account to be true, the forces at work in a conversion must 'transcend the individual's personality', whereas Victorian conceptions of the unconscious, despite their agreement that those forces seem to impinge on the conscious individual from outside, nonetheless lodge them firmly in the self (196). In *The Varieties*, James wants to bridge the immanent and the transcendent, to give an account of religious experience that satisfies the criteria of naturalistic science and yet leaves an avenue open to forces beyond the human that are religiously construed as the divine. Without that avenue, the psychological explanation of those forces as a manifestation of the unconscious verges on what James, drawing from comparative anthropology, calls 'the survival theory': 'the notion that religion is probably only an anachronism, a case of "survival," an atavistic relapse into a mode of thought which humanity in its more enlightened examples has outgrown' (439). James initially dismisses survival theory, but as he does so a certain slipperiness appears in his argument around whether the human history embodied in survivals belongs to the realm of the immanent or the transcendent.

The open avenue to the transcendent which James seeks in *The Varieties* affords a glimpse of how he hopes we might locate ourselves in the deep time of species and planetary history, a need that had become urgent in the wake of natural theology. Where that earlier scientific paradigm assumed a fundamentally hospitable universe, nineteenth-century science envisioned a Heraclitean fire: 'It is impossible, in the present temper of the scientific imagination, to find in the driftings of the cosmic atoms . . . anything but a kind of aimless weather, doing and undoing, achieving no proper history, and leaving no result. Nature has no one distinguishable ultimate tendency with which it is possible to feel a sympathy. In the vast rhythm of her processes . . . she appears to cancel herself' (440). Survival theory, James suggests, is a corollary of this estranged universe. It too 'dwell[s] in universal and impersonal terms', dismissing individual religious experience as the primitive reflex of our universal species-being (446).[13] The upshot here is not just our irreparable divorce from the transcendent, but the dwindling of the immanent itself to utter insignificance. As James evocatively puts it, 'the bubbles on the foam which coats a stormy sea are floating episodes, made and unmade by the forces of the

[13] On the way anthropology's concept of survivals occludes personal psychology by grounding meaning in impersonal social codes, see Christopher Herbert, *Culture and Anomie: Ethnographic Imagination in the Nineteenth Century* (Chicago: University of Chicago, 1991), pp. 260–5.

wind and water. Our private selves are like those bubbles . . . their destinies weigh nothing and determine nothing in the world's irremediable current of events' (441–2).

James presents his radical empiricism as an escape hatch from the dwindling immanent. Radical empiricism takes it as axiomatic that experience itself is primary, and the analysis of experience into its ingredients (thought and thing) is the secondary result of subsequent experience. On this basis, James can contend that (1) the abstract scientific models of the universe are empty without the experience through which they are realised; and (2) that the field of consciousness's transmarginal zone is functionally equivalent to a transcendent '*MORE*' that can be plausibly, if not demonstrably, religiously construed (454). By identifying the unconscious with the 'more', James integrates the three major nineteenth-century theories of the unconscious: both the earlier reflexive and the emerging psychoanalytic concepts of the unconscious are here synthesised with the Romantic metaphysical school that took it for a kind of noumenal realm.

Deep history, survivals, and assent

In *The Varieties*, James struggles to coordinate history at three scales: the individual (or what Fernand Braudel called 'eventual history'), where the floating episodes of our lives toss in the fathomless current of events; the species, where impulses shaped over the course of 'deep history' endure as survivals; and the cosmic, where the vast rhythms of deep time defy history proper.[14] For this reason, if James dismisses the survival theory as reductive, he nonetheless ultimately can't do without a theory of survivals. As the anthropologist E.B. Tylor defined them, survivals are past practices and notions unreflectively continuing into social formations different from those in which they originated; as such, survivals constitute an 'unconscious record' potentially stretching back

[14] James's maritime metaphor finds a striking echo in Braudel's characterisation of eventual history as made up of 'surface disturbances, crests of foam that the tides of history carry on their backs'. See *The Mediterranean and the Mediterranean World in the Age of Philip II*, vol. 1, Siân Reynolds, trans. (New York: Harper & Row, 1972), p. 21. On the Victorian origins of 'deep history' as a concept and field, see Andrew Shyrock and Daniel Lord Smail, *Deep History: The Architecture of Past and Present* (Berkeley: University of California, 2011), pp. 17–23.

thousands of years.[15] Read rightly, survivals thus make human antiquity or even prehistory legible in the present. In that respect, they occupy what Noah Heringman describes as a 'middle ground of evolutionary time and antiquity' that, since the emergence of the idea of deep time in the eighteenth century, frequently serves as a 'threshold for contemplating human and prehuman [time] scales at once'.[16] For James as well, survivals perform something like that function. In *Pragmatism*, James embraces the idea of survivals he dismisses in *The Varieties* because survivals disclose the long-term history embedded within the individual mind's thoughts.

Pragmatism might seem an unlikely place for meditations on our entanglement in the deep past, since the pragmatic method's focus on the practical effects of ideas makes it above all, as James puts it, a program for indicating 'the ways in which existing realities may be *changed*' (509). But one of the changes James's lectures attempt to explain, on pragmatist lines, is how we come to accept a new idea as true. And here it turns out that a key practical value for any new idea is its capacity to assimilate new facts or experiences to the truths that we have previously accepted or admitted. This essentially conservative function entails a view of change as fundamentally gradual and additive: James compares changes in the 'ancient mass' of truths to the spreading of grease-spots or the growth of a new layer of cambium in a tree (559). Hence he observes, in an echo of his earlier remarks on conversion, that 'the most violent revolutions in an individual's beliefs leave most of his old order standing' (513).

In characterising that old order, James engages in the kind of speculations about the mind as a kind of historical record that became common among Victorian scientists after the publication of *On the Origin of Species* (1859). Tylor's theory of survivals was one such set of speculations. As Christopher Herbert observes, survivals afforded a way 'to delve below surfaces and to reveal deep patterns, deep trends, deep structures', and for this reason Tylor pointedly compared their study with 'excavations below the earth's surface to retrieve vestiges of paleolithic life'.[17] Despite James' reservations about survivals in *The Varieties*, the slow

[15] Edward Tylor, *Primitive Culture* (New York: Henry Holt, 1889), p. 104.

[16] Noah Heringman, 'Deep Time at the Dawn of the Anthropocene', *Representations* 129.1 (2015): 56–85, 58, 59.

[17] Herbert, *Culture and Anomie*, p. 256.

assimilation of new ideas he describes in *Pragmatism* leads him to a reassessment. If old truths endure so steadily for individual minds, he reasons, then our basic categories and concepts are themselves likely to be an unconscious record of potentially vast temporal extent: 'The most primitive ways of thinking may not be yet wholly expunged. Like our five fingers, our ear-bones, our rudimentary caudal appendage, or our other "vestigial" peculiarities, they may remain as indelible tokens of events in our race-history' (560). In this powerful analogy, our modes of thinking appear as living fossils, just as testimonial of our evolutionary history as our physical anatomy. And taking full licence from that prehistorical standing, James applies to the mind the same Uniformitarian methods of reasoning that led geologists to posit deep time as the correct scale for understanding changes to the earth's surface. To conclude that our common-sense categories are survivals inherited from remote ancestors is thus 'only follow[ing] the rule . . . of assuming the vast and remote to conform to the laws of formation that we can observe at work in the small and near' (566). A certain recursive, fractal logic becomes legible here, as a change in the present may model vaster processes of change at the levels of evolutionary and planetary time.

Although it developed independently, it is useful to compare James's pragmatism with John Henry Newman's notion of an 'illative sense'. In his *Essay in Aid of a Grammar of Assent* (1870), Newman proposes the illative sense as an explanation for how we transform the conditional acceptance of a proposition (which he calls an 'inference') into the unconditional acceptance that, for him, constitutes an 'assent'. Formal logic fails to capture this process, he claims, because its syllogisms cannot account for what really determines our judgments: a 'mass' or 'cumulation' of probabilities, independent of each other, but 'acting upon each other in correction and confirmation'.[18] Like James's ancient mass of truths, Newman's cumulation of probabilities limits our assent to new propositions. Moreover, Newman's illative sense participates in Victorian psychology's pervasive fascination with what Edward Reed has called 'a logical unconscious'.[19] Since in assenting 'the mind . . . is swayed and determined by a body of proof, which

[18] John Henry Newman, *An Essay in Aid of a Grammar of Assent* (South Bend, IN: Notre Dame, 1979), p. 233. Hereafter cited parenthetically.

[19] See Reed, *From Soul to Mind*, pp. 131–5.

it recognizes only as a body, and not in its constituent parts', the illative sense is in effect another unconscious mental process, similar to mid-century theories of perception as unconscious inference, as Newman's frequent analogies with perception suggest. Such unconsciousness in fact extends from the mental process of assenting to our assents themselves.

> A great many of our assents are merely expressions of our personal likings, tastes, principles, motives, and opinions . . . in other words, they are acts and manifestations of self: now what is more rare than self-knowledge? In proportion then to our ignorance of self, is our unconsciousness of those innumerable acts of assent, which we are incessantly making. (157)

This potential obliviousness to ourselves and our beliefs implied by the illative sense hints at the way Newman's notorious conversion to Roman Catholicism shaped his philosophical arguments about assent.

Newman's fictional and autobiographical accounts of his conversion leave no doubt that it involved a prolonged struggle to realise what was manifestly already the case. That experience left him with 'a great dislike of paper logic . . . It is the concrete being that reasons; pass a number of years, and I find my mind in a new place; how? the whole man moves; paper logic is but the record of it'.[20] His *Apologia Pro Vita Sua* (1864) suggests that there is an important doctrinal dimension to this delayed recognition of a belief already held. Newman himself had argued that Anglican doctrine was justified by its grounding in antiquity, insofar as it adhered to the precedents of early Christianity and eschewed the doctrinal developments Newman identified as 'Roman corruptions' (142). But in 1839 Newman's research into the fifth-century controversy over Monophysitism (the belief that Jesus had only a divine, not a divine and corporeal, nature) convinced him that to settle disputes, the Church can lawfully ratify a doctrinal position that hadn't previously been publicly recognised as having always already been part of its core revealed truths. In other words, the Church too can justifiably arrive at a belated awareness of its own unconscious assents. And although this realisation precedes his

[20] John Henry Newman, *Apologia Pro Vita Sua* (New York: Penguin, 1994), p. 158. Hereafter cited parenthetically.

formal conversion by six years, in the *Apologia* Newman recounts it as nothing less than a pivotal moment, a conversion-crisis triggered when 'the awful similitude . . . between the dead records of the past and the feverish chronicle of the present' reveals his own implication in the deep history of antiquity: 'Now here, in the middle of the fifth century, I found, as it seemed to me, Christendom of the sixteenth and nineteenth centuries reflected. I saw my face in that mirror, and I was a Monophysite' (114). For Newman individually, as for the Church historically, crisis demands a transformation that paradoxically affirms our identity with the past.[21]

"Winckelmann" and conversion as a non-experience

The parallel Newman draws between the mind's illative sense and the doctrinal development of the church reflects his own theological preoccupations, but similar homologies between the mind and the collective histories of antiquity and prehistory featured widely in Victorian culture after the 1860s. Take, for a well-known example, Walter Pater's account of the Renaissance as at once a historical event and a universal epistemological process. As Bénédicte Coste argues in her contribution to this volume, Pater's account of the Renaissance in 'Winckelmann' (1867) does double duty as a model of cultural as well as individual memory that serves as a necessary complement to his Epicurean reduction of the mind to 'a tremulous wisp constantly re-forming itself on the stream'.[22] So, Johann Winckelmann's individual encounter with antiquity in the eighteenth century 'reproduces' the earlier collective experience of the Renaissance (146). And as in James's discussion of survivals in *Pragmatism*, Pater's reasoning in 'Winckelmann' is self-consciously recursive: Winckelmann's intuitive grasp of the principles of classical sculpture allows him to see 'a whole sequence of laws in some hollowing the hand, or dividing of the hair'; in this extrapolation of the momentous from the minute he 'seems to realise that fancy of a forgotten knowledge

[21] Viswanathan similarly remarks that in Newman's work conversion is 'a form of change that is *not* real change', but rather a 'discovery of what is already present' that entails 'a return to origins'. *Outside the Fold*, pp. 68–9.

[22] Walter Pater, *The Renaissance: Studies in Art and Poetry*, ed. Donald Hill (Berkeley: University of California, 1980), p. 188. Hereafter cited parenthetically.

hidden for a time in the mind itself', and this act of anamnesis likewise reinscribes in miniature the re-emergence of 'the Hellenic element' from its 'absorbed, underground life' in medieval culture that constitutes the historical Renaissance (155, 158). As it lays out these nested homologies, 'Winckelmann' conceives of both historical and individual memory in terms of the abrupt surfacing of suppressed energies, as when 'in the midst of a frozen world, the buried fire of ancient art rose up from under the soil' (146).

Yet 'Winckelmann', strikingly, commences not with the genuine conversion we might expect from such resonance with Newman and James but rather with a disingenuous one, when Winckelmann formally but insincerely converts to Catholicism to secure the patronage necessary to travel to Rome. In exculpation, Pater cites Goethe's earlier biography, which pleaded for Winckelmann on the grounds that all Christian denominations were the same to him because he was at heart a pagan. This defence prepares the ground for the essay's later claim that 'a universal pagan sentiment', sanctifying the natural elements and conditions of human life, in fact makes up the 'broad foundation, in mere human nature, of all religions . . . ineradicable, like some persistent vegetable growth, because its seed is an element of the very soil out of which it springs' (160). Pater identifies paganism as itself a kind of survival, a set of enduring ritualistic impulses, and by following this line of reasoning he arrives at his ringing conclusion that 'Pagan and Christian art . . . are really continuous; and there is a sense in which it may be said that the Renaissance . . . was ever taking place' (180). Seen in these terms, there would be no insincerity in Winckelmann's conversion except insofar as this deeper identity of religious feeling renders conversion in general almost meaningless.

'Winckelmann' in this way expresses reservations about conversion that Pater would explore more fully in *Marius the Epicurean*. A historical conversion romance set in Antonine Rome, *Marius* is read by contemporary critics as adopting a subversive scepticism towards the genre's defining event. Like James in *The Varieties*, Pater in *Marius* seems to mistrust the genre's tendency to narrate conversion as a dramatic, instantaneous transformation. Maureen Moran thus notes that while the historical conversion romance tends to rely on 'a sudden, apocalyptic reversal of fortune or spiritual intervention' to motivate its protagonist's conversion, Marius's spiritual development is pointedly incremental, following the novel's broader 'tendency to synthesize rather than oppose contending systems of belief'.[23] Over the course of Marius's life, the mental impulses and dispositions animating Roman paganism as well as Epicureanism and Stoicism are shown to endure within the new dispensation of Christianity as well as the modernity of the nineteenth century. In his analysis of how Pater drew from Tylor's anthropology in conceiving of that syncretic approach, Sebastian Lecourt proposes that 'one might even say that the novel replaces conversion with survival as its preferred mode of religious change—one based on the transformation of the old rather than the irruption of the new'.[24] In *Marius*, we might say, Pater subsumes conversion within the Renaissance that is ever taking place.

But the apparent gradualism of that perpetual Renaissance in these critical accounts sits uneasily with his characterisation of it, in 'Winckelmann', as the volcanic eruption of antiquity into the present. The sudden violence of this metaphor for an incremental transformation points to the paradoxical status of Pater's Renaissance as both punctual historic event and constantly unfolding process. James Porter describes 'Renaissance' for Pater as 'the startling juxtaposition of the past with the future along a timeline that confounds the very idea of historical sequence, because it involves the literal contemporaneity of past, present, and future at any historical time. Renaissance is thus both an event in time and time's confounding'.[25] The resulting tension goes some way towards explaining the fact that, as several critics of *Marius* have noticed, 'progressive and cyclical views of history are both present in Pater's thought . . . in cavalier alternation, sometimes within the same page or argument'.[26] Nor is this merely a problem in Pater's philosophy of history in *Marius* itself. As Carolyn Williams suggests, the tension 'between "historical novelty" and mythic

23 Maureen Moran, 'Pater's "Great Change": *Marius the Epicurean* as Historical Conversion Romance', in Laurel Brake et al., eds, *Walter Pater: Transparencies of Desire* (Greensboro: ELT, 2002), pp. 177, 178.

24 Sebastian Lecourt, '"To surrender himself, in perfectly liberal inquiry": Walter Pater, Many-Sidedness, and the Conversion Novel', *Victorian Studies* 53.2 (2011): 231–53, 242.

25 James I. Porter, 'Reception, Receptivity, and Anachronism in *Marius the Epicurean*', in Charles Martindale et al., eds, *Pater the Classicist: Classical Scholarship, Reception, and Aestheticism* (Oxford: Oxford University, 2017), p. 151.

26 Avrom Fleishman, *The English Historical Novel: Walter Scott to Virginia Woolf* (Baltimore: Johns Hopkins, 1971), p. 172.

repetition' is crucial to Pater's poetics even in his earliest surviving essay, 'Diaphaneitè' (1864).[27]

A kind of proem for *The Renaissance* and *Marius* justifying their focus on an individual figure as exemplifying larger historical forces, 'Diaphaneitè' is, among other things, a theory of historical fiction. Williams reads the diaphanous hero as Pater's ethereal spin on Walter Scott's wavering hero, whose wavering sympathies provide the neutral ground for the meeting of opposed historical currents. And noting that Pater, like most Victorians, read Scott extensively, Lene Østermark-Johansen argues that Scott's novels shaped 'the historical interest in the evolutionary benefit of crises [that] runs as an undercurrent in [Pater's] writings'.[28] Hence Pater's diaphanous hero is possessed of a certain 'revolutionism'.[29]

The diaphanous hero's revolutionism is qualified, however, in two ways. Revolution is inescapably violent insofar as, Pater claims, all progress is inescapably violent, but the diaphanous hero submits to have that violence channelled inward: 'Poetry and poetical history have dreamed of a crisis, where it must needs be that some human victim be sent down into the grave. These are they whom in its profound emotion humanity might choose to send" (208–9). The otherworldly equipoise that makes the diaphanous hero an ideal human sacrifice also suffuses their revolutionism with the languor of long duration: 'in this nature revolutionism is softened, harmonized, subdued as by distance. It is the revolutionism of one who has slept a hundred years' (208). In *Marius*, Pater's only complete historical novel, the diaphanous hero's languorous revolutionism appears as a crisis of religious experience and belief.

Marius the Epicurean and conversion as a marginal experience

In the preface to *The Renaissance*, Pater famously claims that experience should be aesthetic criticism's fundamental object of inquiry. In *Marius*, Pater suggests that a similar rule obtains in theology and philosophy, proposing that abstract or metaphysical

[27] Carolyn Williams, *Transfigured World: Walter Pater's Aesthetic Historicism* (Ithaca: Cornell, 1989), p. 170.

[28] Lene Østermark-Johansen, *Walter Pater's European Imagination* (Oxford: Oxford University Press, 2022), p. 330.

[29] Walter Pater, *Imaginary Portraits* (New York: Allworth, 1997), p. 208. Hereafter cited parenthetically.

principles 'reveal their true significance . . . when translated into a precept as to how it were best to feel and act; in other words, under [their] sentimental or ethical equivalent'.[30] The novel itself proceeds accordingly, staging its depictions of Roman paganism, Hellenistic philosophy and early Christianity during the final years of the Antonine dynasty through Marius's lifelong preoccupation with how to value and attend to experience. The one abstract principle Marius consistently maintains throughout the novel, even in the midst of his second thoughts, is the 'skeptical apprehension that the little point of the present moment alone really is, between a past which has ceased to be and the future which may never come', which he translates as a precept to 'yield himself to the improvement of the present with an absolutely disengaged mind' (93). The crux of Marius's crisis of belief in the novel is thus temporal: how to reconcile the Epicurean attention to the concrete, unique experience of the present moment with either the collective past embodied in pagan tradition or the future he senses emerging in early Christianity.

It is one of the novel's ironies, however, that Marius' sceptical devotion to the present is itself a repetition of the historical past. As Pater repeatedly suggests, Marius retains the habit created by his early paganism of regarding the things of the world as full of presences with valid claims on him. Here, we find an instance of a survival in Tylor's terms: a habit that reflexively persists after the social context engendering it has changed. Survivals of this kind become the basis of Cornelius Fronto's Stoic justification of traditional morals. Fronto calls on Marius to recognise 'a remnant of right conduct . . . not so much through his own free election, as from a deference, an "assent," entire, habitual, unconscious, to custom' (164). As Pater signals by putting 'assent' in quotation marks, Fronto reconceives of Tylor's survivals by way of Newman's illative sense. As survivals become assents, however, their significance subtly changes. Assents, for both Newman and Pater, could be just as reflexive and unconscious as survivals, but they could also become conscious in ways that powerfully bind individuals to a larger social collective, what Fronto calls 'a universal commonwealth of minds—which yet becomes conscious . . . in a select body of just men made perfect' (165). Echoing this

30 Walter Pater, *Marius the Epicurean: His Sensations and Ideas* (Kansas City: Valancourt, 2008), p. 91. Hereafter cited parenthetically.

point, Pater suggests that 'a little more of reasonable "assent"' would have allowed Epicureans like Marius access to 'the complementary influence of some greater system, in which they may find their due place' (174, 170).

For Marius, too, that assent turns on a homology between his own experience and the history of the great system. Where Newman recognises his face in the glass of the Monophysitism controversy, Marius 'retraces in his intellectual pilgrimage the actual historic order of old philosophy' by embracing Heraclitus's sceptical account of the flow of experience while ignoring his metaphysical speculations, which comprised a 'bold, pantheistic flight ... from the fleeting object to that one universal life, in which the whole sphere of physical change might be reckoned but as a single pulsation' (90, 89). Noting that *Marius* is replete with such homologies, Fleishman attributes them to the widespread Victorian interest in Ernst Haeckel's embryological hypothesis that ontogeny recapitulates phylogeny.[31] But the novel applies this idea well beyond biology and the history of antiquity.

Marius takes individual recapitulations of historical developments as the basis for its own metaphysical speculations. Drawing an analogy with the way his body was both his own and determined by a vast network of material forces and conditions, Marius reflects that his mind might be part of an even greater system than human history.

> Might not the intellectual being also ... be but a moment, an impulse or series of impulses, belonging to an intellectual system without him, diffusing itself through all time and place—that great stream of spiritual energy, of which his own imperfect thoughts ... were the remote and therefore imperfect pulsations. It was the hypothesis ... which had dawned on the contemplations of ... Plato ... [and] Aristotle ... It was easier to conceive of the material fabric of the world around him as but an element in a world of thought ... than of mind as an element ... in a material order; because mind was really nearer to himself: it was an explanation of what was known less by what was known better. (203–4)

Marius here both continues his retracing of the history of thought – returning to and extending Heraclitus's metaphysical ideas and

[31] *The English Historical Novel*, p. 171.

thus following the same trajectory that Pater ascribes to the history of philosophy – while scaling that homology up to a speculative pantheistic history of cosmic time. And, as James would more explicitly do in *Pragmatism*, Pater suggests that drawing such a homology simply follows the accepted Uniformitarian method of explaining the vast and remote in terms of the small and the near.

In the novel, no less than in geology, one effect of this method is a profound gradualism, for its attunement to the patterns playing out across timescales suggests that, as Marcus Aurelius puts it, 'the wheel of the world hath ever the same motion, upward and downward, from generation to generation' (135). Marius's efforts to discover great systems within his own experience is thus a significant factor in the widespread critical judgement that the novel is committed 'to a gradualism so extreme that at any present moment change cannot even be perceived'.[32] However, that gradualism is haunted in the novel by three intertwined historical crises: the Antonine Plague, the Marcomannic Wars, and the Lyon Persecution. These crises bridge the past and present not through homology or scalar repetition but instead through a transformation so instantaneous that it verges on anachronism, as when Pater suggests that this second century plague so transforms the countryside that in just a few years it accomplishes 'a large part in the formation of the melancholy picturesque of modern Italy' (118).

Uneasily playing out in the background of much of the novel's discourse and introspection, these crises periodically burst into prominence, killing Flavian in his youth, interrupting Fronto's public address on the universal commonwealth of minds with a sudden troop mobilisation, and, ultimately, sweeping up Marius in the spasm of persecutory violence that concludes the novel. In this way, Pater interweaves these historical crises with the crises in the lives of the novel's characters, most centrally through the destiny he had earlier marked out for the diaphanous hero, with Marius as the 'human victim' demanded by a populace panicked by 'prophecies of the world's impending conflagration' (118).

In *Marius*, that interweaving of personal and historical crisis yields a mode of experience. Marius's Epicureanism is in fact born out of a sense of perpetual crisis in its medical sense: an awareness of every moment as a potentially decisive turning point between

[32] Williams, *Transfigured World*, p. 182.

life and death. Marius takes this lesson from Flavian's early death, and Pater suggests that a 'call upon men's attention of the crisis in which they find themselves' is core to the philosophy (91). This experience of individual crisis also generates a form of historical foresight. Marius's encounter with Flavian's poetry is the model here. Written feverishly in a race against his death from plague, Flavian's poetry uncannily approximates the tones and cadence of medieval Latin.

> The impression thus forced upon Marius [in reading it] connected itself with a feeling, the precise inverse of that . . . which seems to say—*You have been just here, just thus, before!*—a feeling in his case not reminiscent but prescient, which passed over him many times afterward . . . as if he detected . . . the process of actual change to a wholly undreamed of and renewed condition of human body and soul. (75)

Marius's experience here is attuned to the future even as Pater describes it insistently in terms of uncanny memories and déjà vu.

Inverse déjà vu confounds time in a way that invites comparison to the notion of a Renaissance that is perpetually taking place, but *Marius* goes on to pointedly distinguish between the two. Pater's Renaissance figures in the novel as the early Christian community Marius encounters through his friend Cornelius, which impresses him as preserving in a new form the elements of the classical culture it would supersede: 'As if in anticipation of the sixteenth century, the church was becoming *humanistic*, in a best and earliest *Renaissance*' (240). Pater directly cautions us not to identify this moment with the kind of prescience Marius experienced in reading Flavian's poetry. The narrator allows that 'the reader may think perhaps, that Marius, who . . . had his visionary aptitudes, by an inversion of one Plato's peculiarities with which he was of course familiar, must have descended, by *fore-sight*, upon a later age than his own', but the reader would be wrong here because 'it was indeed hardly an anticipation' (234). This earliest Renaissance is not an instance of inverse anamnesis. However anachronistic, it's real. But the novel stipulates that its condition of possibility is precisely the absence of crisis, because at this moment of relative peace 'the time had gone by when men became Christians under the influence of some sudden overpowering impression, and with all the untranquillising effects of such a crisis' (235).

These both are and are not the circumstances under which Marius becomes a Christian at the end of the novel. His conversion is an effect of crisis, precipitated by the abrupt resumption of Christian persecutions following an earthquake, but it isn't accompanied by a sudden overpowering impression. Of his turn as a Sidney Carton figure in allowing Cornelius to be mistaken for him as a non-Christian and released in his stead, Marius reflects that after long waiting for 'the great crisis which is to try what is in us . . . At last, the great act, the critical moment, comes, easily, almost unconsciously. Another motion of the clock, and our fatal line . . . has been passed, which changes ourselves or our lives' (293). His conversion follows the same pattern, transpiring when the country people he is left to die among anoint him and give him the Eucharist while he is physically helpless and only questionably aware of what is happening. Conversion and crisis, in James' terms, occur while remaining at the outskirts of consciousness rather than while bursting hence to its focal point.

If Marius' own culminating conversion-crisis doesn't vouchsafe to him a final experience of inverse déjà vu, it does afford him the anticipation of such an experience. That anticipation confirms the value of his Epicureanism as 'a self-preparation towards possible further revelation, some day—an ampler vision, which should take up into itself and explain the world's delightful shows, as the scattered fragments of a poetry, till then but half understood, might be taken up into the text of a lost epic, recovered at last' (297). Lukács argued that the historical novel could overcome the distance between the world of epic, defined by its organic, spontaneous totality, and the world of the novel, defined by modernity's fragmentation and anomie. By synthesising individual and collective life through the movement of a progressive national history, the classical historical novel, exemplified by *Waverley*, restores what Hegel called the epic's 'totality of objects' in the form of what Lukács in *The Historical Novel* called 'the totality of history'.[33] Pater's novel, however, lacks a progressive national history that could mediate between Marius's individual destiny and a collective or transcendent whole. His conversion-crisis affords him the glimpse of a possible restoration to epic totality, but it remains only a glimpse, prospective and fleeting. Marius remains within Lukács' world of the novel, 'a world abandoned by

[33] Lukács, *The Historical Novel*, p. 13.

God', in which 'a mere glimpse of meaning is the highest life has to offer . . . and . . . the only thing worth the commitment of an entire life'.[34] A modern, secularised world, in other words, still very much like our own. And that not least in the way that, by imagining a cosmological totality to be disclosed in a possible recovered epic to come, *Marius the Epicurean* anticipates contemporary efforts to imagine 'a historical novel of the future', whose adequacy to our moment of impending resource-exhaustion and ecological transformation demands nothing less than a 'planetary-scale grand narrative'.[35] Concluding on the cusp of an unrealised transformation that would also be a recovery of lost epic plenitude, Pater's historical conversion novel, like James in *The Varieties*, remains open to the possibility of a religious experience that has not yet been forthcoming but that remains, tantalisingly, just beyond the margins.

34 Lukács, *The Theory of the Novel*, Anna Bostock, trans. (Boston: MIT, 1971), pp. 88, 80.

35 Ian Duncan, 'History and the Novel after Lukács', *NOVEL: A Forum on Fiction* 50.3 (2017): 388–96, 393.

6

Self-Taste, Embodiment, and Language in Gerard Manley Hopkins

Amanda Paxton

The sense of taste held particular interest for the Jesuit priest and poet Gerard Manley Hopkins. In his notes on the *Spiritual Exercises*, a regimen of meditations and spiritual practices developed by the sixteenth-century priest Ignatius of Loyola, founder of the Jesuits, Hopkins imputes a metaphorical taste to intangible virtues: ‘each virtue to have its own sweetness—one rich, another ~~re~~freshi~~ng~~, a third cordial, like incense, violets, or sweet-herbs, or ~~like~~, for taste, like honey, fruit, or wine’.[1] Similarly, his reflections on the Ignatian Meditation on Hell posit a taste associated with sin: ‘taste <u>as with taste of tongue</u> all that is bitter there;, the tears ceaselessly and fruitlessly flowing; the grief over their hopeless loss; the worm of conscience, which is the mind gnawing and feeding on its own most miserable self. It is still the same story:; <u>they</u>, their sins are the bitterness, tasted sweet once, now taste most bitter; no worm but themselves gnaws them and gnaws no one but themselves’ (*CW* vol. 5, 529). Not only do these two extracts indicate his imputation of taste to abstractions like virtue and sin, but they also recall work he had begun in 1880 in which he developed a theory of ‘self-taste’, his idea that the particularity of selfhood can be formulated metaphorically as self-taste: ‘that taste of myself, of <u>I</u> and <u>me</u> above and in all things ^which is^ more distinctive than the taste of ale or alum, more distinctive than the smell of walnutleaf or camphor, and ^is^ incommunicable by any means to another man’ (*CW* vol. 5, 349). As Atti Viragh puts it, ‘While all

[1] *The Collected Works of Gerard Manley Hopkins*, vol. 5: *Sermons and Spiritual Writings*, Jude Nixon and Noel Barber, S.J., eds (Oxford: Oxford University Press, 2019), 446–7.

sensory things can have their own peculiar taste, [for Hopkins] the self has a uniqueness that is more distinctive than any—so distinctive, even God cannot share it'.[2]

In this chapter I argue that, through his theory of self-taste, Hopkins presents a model of consciousness as continuous, qualitative and irreducible, in contrast to the 'discontinuous' and quantitative models posited by materialist accounts of the mind that were becoming dominant in the later nineteenth century. In fact, Hopkins's approach to identity and language speaks to concerns shared by turn-of-the-century figures in process philosophy such as Henri Bergson and William James, who questioned prevailing associationist models of consciousness and struggled with the challenges of language as a means of conveying the continuity and plenitude of experience. I begin by tracing Hopkins's various mentions of the sense of taste throughout his writing and contextualising them in light of then-contemporary discourses around the sense of taste in nineteenth-century associationist psychology. From there, I move to the work of Bergson and James, who would challenge what they found to be the failure of associationist psychology and language itself: for these two thinkers, neither materialist psychology nor language reflects the fullness of human experience and its resistance to being reduced to individualised sensations and functions. Last, I show that Hopkins's poetic language serves as a tool for a more holistic and authentic mode of expressing this continuity of experience. The essay concludes with an analysis of what I argue constitutes Hopkins's use of the middle voice, a linguistic form rarely found in English, to address the fragmentation inherent in language and its consequent failure to represent experience fully. Well before the advent of process philosophy, Hopkins tackled questions of selfhood, experience, and expression that would preoccupy later thinkers.

'My taste was me'

Hopkins often used the word 'taste' throughout his letters and notes in ways that combined metaphorical and literal meanings. In his early writing, the term predominantly refers to aesthetic judge-

[2] Atti Viragh, 'The Grammar of Instress: Gerard Manley Hopkins and the Victorian Philosophers of *Mind*', *New Literary History* 51.3 (2020): 501–22, 512.

ment, as in his 1864 observation that ‘I am coming to think much of taste myself, good taste and moderation’.[3] Later, he integrates the aesthetic meaning of ‘taste’ with the alimentary one, as in an 1879 letter to his friend Robert Bridges (‘The Horatian humour of the fish is real humour. The vulgar ~~stan~~ verses about Anne leave a bad taste’ [*CW* vol. 1, 336]); an 1883 letter to Coventry Patmore (‘The passage about Golden-Tongue is ~~sower~~ sour and to my taste flavours the whole too much’[4]); and an 1885 letter to his mother, Kate (‘There is a kind of slobbery nice~~s~~ness and good humour all over it, very common in some books and very distasteful to me, ^when^ without the salt of humour’ [*CW* vol. 2, 709]). In his religious writings, such as his sermons and retreat notes, the usage is almost entirely gustatory, appearing in such places as sermons about Eve tasting the apple in Eden or the parables of the wedding feasts in the gospels of Matthew and Luke.

However, in his retreat notes from 1880 on the ‘First Principle and Foundation’ of the *Spiritual Exercises*, Hopkins introduces the metaphor of taste as a sense by which the self is known. The context for the notes – the Ignatian principle that humanity is created to praise and serve God – generates an epistemological discussion in Hopkins’s hands, leading to his claim that creation might be understood by considering either ‘the world without’ or ‘the world within’, of which he chooses the latter (*CW* vol. 5, 348). He identifies the particularities of his own selfhood as a starting point and notes that the outward-turned sense of sight holds no purchase for their investigation: ‘I find myself both as man and as myself something ~~to me~~ most determined and distinctive, at pitch, more distinctive and higher pitched than anything else I *see*’ (*CW* vol. 5, 348; emphasis added).[5] When trying to trace the origin of his own distinctiveness, he finds again that sight fails:

3 *The Collected Works of Gerard Manley Hopkins. Volume 1: Correspondence 1852–1881*, R.K.R. Thornton and Catherine Phillips, eds (Oxford: Oxford University Press, 2016), p. 72.

4 *The Collected Works of Gerard Manley Hopkins. Volume 2: Correspondence 1882–1889*, R.K.R. Thornton and Catherine Phillips, eds (Oxford: Oxford University Press, 2016), p. 622.

5 Julia Saville defines Hopkins’s use of the term ‘pitch’ to mean ‘the hidden singularity of the object’ (70), as indicated in a journal entry of his from 1871: ‘End of March and beginning of April—This is the time to study inscape in the spraying of trees, for the swelling buds carry them to a pitch which the eye could not else gather’ (*CW* 3, 505–6).

'when I ask, where does all this throng and stack of being, so rich, so distinctive, so important, come from / nothing I *see* can answer me' (*CW* vol. 5, 349; emphasis added). Where sight disappoints, taste emerges as the sense through which self is experienced 'at one tankard, that of my own being', disclosing 'that inmost self of mine which has been ^said^ to be and to be felt to be, to taste, more distinctive than ~~clove or alum~~, the taste of clove or alum, the smell of walnutleaf or hart'shorn' (*CW* vol. 5, 349, 351–2).[6]

Invoking the language of a sense perception – taste – as a source of empirical data about his own internal being, Hopkins troubles a fundamental distinction in Locke's understanding of how the mind acquires 'the materials of reason and knowledge'.[7] For Locke, there exist two sources of knowledge. The first, sensation, accounts for the majority of human ideas, and it arrives through the senses as they convey information about 'external material things' (52). The second, reflection, comes by way of an 'internal sense' through which the mind reflects on itself (51). In using the sense of taste to convey an internal reality utterly unique to himself – more distinctive than any other experience in creation – Hopkins posits a model of selfhood that seems to adopt the language of physiopsychology yet resists a full slide into materialism or Cartesian dualism.

The absolute inaccessibility of this sensory experience to any other being forms the logical crux connecting Hopkins's meditation on selfhood to the *Spiritual Exercises*. Returning to the Ignatian First Principle, concerning creation and createdness, Hopkins poses the question: 'From what then do I with all my being and ~~es~~ above all that taste of self, that selfbeing, come?' (*CW* vol. 5, 350). Any originary 'universal mind' must still exist outside the 'self-taste' experienced by individuals (*CW* vol. 5, 350), each of whom stands replete with her own 'knowledge and powers, pleasures, pains, merit, guilt, shame, dangers, ^fortunes,^ fates' (*CW* vol. 5, 352). Even a creator God cannot fully 'taste' each soul's most interior being. Here Hopkins introduces a further characteristic of 'self-taste': that of shame. He notes, 'these things and above all my shame, my guilt, my fate are the very things in

6 For a link between the notion of self-taste and the new proto-phenomenological theories appearing in Hopkins' time, see Viragh, 'The Grammar of Instress'.

7 John Locke, *An Essay Concerning Human Understanding* (1689) (London: Thomas Tegg, 1825), p. 51.

feeling, in tasting, which I most taste that selftaste which nothing in the world can match' (*CW* vol. 5, 352), an assertion that would return in the lines of his 1885 sonnet: 'I am gall, I am heartburn. God's most deep decree / Bitter would have me taste: my taste was me'.[8]

Hopkins's concept of self-taste has received various scholarly treatments, in which the motifs of isolation and Christian fallenness predominate. Joshua King traces the priest's use of the idea in the observation that, 'Hopkins's taste of self passes from undeniable evidence for God's creation of humanity and nature to a curse, the rank air and flavor of a solipsistic prison distinguishable from Hell only by an act of brute faith'.[9] Similarly, Jill Muller notes that 'Hopkins's erstwhile celebration of his distinctive "self-taste" has become a bitterly parodic communion' by the time of the Dublin sonnets, 'in which he consumes self-risen "dull dough" (12) and recognizes in his own flavor the "gall" (9) with which Christ was tormented by Calvary'.[10] Critical discussion has largely centred on the religious resonances in the Jesuit's references to taste.[11] Granted, Hopkins's use of the sense as a figuration of selfhood is imbued with spiritual significance, as is virtually all his thought. A further dimension of meaning, however, lies in his decision to use this sense perception as a tool for self-knowledge, particularly in the context of nineteenth-century philosophy and psychology.

8 *The Poetical Works of Gerard Manley Hopkins*, ed. Norman MacKenzie (Oxford: Oxford University Press, 1990), p. 181.

9 Joshua King, 'Patmore, Hopkins, and the Problem of the English Metrical Law', *Hopkins Quarterly* 38.1/2 (Winter–Spring, 2011): 31–49.

10 Jill Muller, *Gerard Manley Hopkins and Victorian Catholicism: A Heart in Hiding* (New York: Routledge, 2003), p. 80.

11 See also Daniel A. Harris, *Inspirations Unbidden: The 'Terrible Sonnets' of Gerard Manley Hopkins* (Berkeley: U of California P, 1982), pp. 65 and 68; René Gallet, '"No worst, there is none . . .": A Reassessment', *The Hopkins Quarterly* 15.1/4 (1988–1989): 73–82, 78; N.M.L. Nathan, 'Hopkins's Selfless Self of Self', *Journal of Literature & Theology* 7.4 (1993): 397–402. One exception to the focus on spirituality and shame is Mariaconcetta Costantini's cultural materialist examination of the cultural understandings of 'ale' and 'alum', two of the tastes that Hopkins mentions in his notes ('Food Metaphors in Gerard Manley Hopkins', *Victorian Poetry* 55.3 (2017): 259–85, 277).

Taste and holism

In this section, I demonstrate that Hopkins uses empirical sensory data to reject what he described as the materialist notion of experience as merely 'a string of broken existences' (*CW* vol. 5, 350). I argue that his use of the sense of taste as the most expedient means of understanding the self is best understood in relation to nineteenth-century psychology's understandings of taste as a sense perception: taste was considered unique because of its intrinsic qualities of continuity and complexity. Therefore, Hopkins's concept of 'self-taste' represents selfhood as something equally complex, continuous yet impossible to duplicate, mutable yet sustained. Last, I show that, through his model of self-taste, Hopkins moves beyond Cartesian dualism and instead sees embodiment as a central element of subjectivity.

By invoking the sense of taste as an epistemological means for apprehending selfhood, Hopkins may at first appear to be appealing to contemporary threads in psychology. Locke would use the phrase 'simple ideas' to describe senses such as 'the taste of sugar', which are 'uncompounded' and therefore irreducible into smaller forms (62). Similarly, David Hume would consider taste a 'simple perception', which cannot be separated into further components.[12] Taken together, the varieties of sense impressions and ideas – ranging in complexity – create selfhood and experience in Hume's theory of self as a bundle of sensations rather than a single, continuous phenomenon. In this schema, selfhood is an ever-changing amalgamation of perceptions at any given moment, all of which 'are different, and distinguishable, and separable from each other, and may be separately consider'd, and may exist separately, and have no need of anything to support their existence' (*Treatise* 300). The reducibility of sensations, emotions and ideas is therefore fundamental to the bundle conception of the self.

Associationist psychologies, originating in the empiricism of Hume and finding their expression in nineteenth-century figures such as John Stuart Mill and Alexander Bain, sought out materialist mechanisms to explain psychological phenomena, including learning and emotions. For thinkers like Bain, simple perceptions

[12] *A Treatise on Human Nature* (1739–40), ed. Ernest C. Mossner (London: Penguin, 1969), p. 50.

become the raw and atomised data for experience, attaching to specific sensory organs and thereby creating what we know as consciousness. Thus, Bain describes the ways in which 'mental states can become numerical' if one attends to the refined, individualised components from which they are constituted.[13] For Bain, the sense of experience as continuous, as a 'stream of thought', obscures the underlying truth that experience is but 'a series of distinct ideas, more or less rapid in their succession; the rapidity being measurable by the number that pass through the mind in a given time' (*Emotions* 29).

Hopkins, however, does not follow these associationist principles in his discussion of selfhood. Rather, his use of taste works against such claims, reflecting a lifelong scepticism of reductionist materialism. In an 1867 essay written for his Oxford 'coach' Walter Pater, he observes that '[m]aterial explanation cannot be refined into explaining thought and it is all to no purpose to ~~know~~ show an organ for each faculty and a nerve vibrating for each ~~thought~~ idea, because this only shows in the last detail what broadly no one doubted, to wit that the activities of the spirit are conveyed in those of the body as scent is conveyed in spirits of wine, remaining still inexplicably distinct'.[14] Around the same time, he comments in his notes on Plato, 'It does us good to read him—as e.g. agst. the atomism of Humery' (*CW* vol. 4, 250). Less than ten years later he would joke about Bain in a letter to Bridges, asking, 'Is that Mr. Peter Bain anything to (as the Irish say) Alexander Bain? A Bain and a Baynes are connected with the London University and its enemies call it a Baneful Institution' (*CW* vol. 1, 253). And in the same retreat notes of 1880 in which he introduces the concept of self-taste, he decries the suggestion that 'Being' might be constituted by 'the mental flush of a string

[13] *The Emotions and the Will*, 3rd edn (London: Longmans, Green, and Co., 1875), p. 29.

[14] *The Collected Works of Gerard Manley Hopkins. Volume 4, Oxford Essays and Notes*, ed. Lesley Higgins (Oxford: Oxford University Press, 2006), p. 287. Remarking on Hopkins's undergraduate claim that 'the activities of the spirit are conveyed in those of the body as scent is conveyed in spirits of wine', William Cohen notes that Hopkins 'opposes [materialism] philosophically, and yet the terms in which he does so are inescapably material. He gives voice to the immateriality of spirit by describing it with the simile of an olfactory sensation' (*Embodied: Victorian Literature and the Senses* (Minneapolis: University of Minnesota Press, 2009), p. 109).

of broken existences at very small average intervals', calling the concept itself 'incredible because monstrous' (*CW* vol. 5, 350).

The intervention Hopkins makes through his term 'self-taste' can best be understood by returning to the materialist school of thought to which he responded variously throughout his writings. Delineating Hopkins's position from the Cartesian *cogito*, J. Hillis Miller writes, 'I taste myself, therefore I am'.[15] As Miller's phrasing indicates, Hopkins does not reject the material world for a dualistic Cartesian model, despite his suspicion of materialism. Instead, he develops his own philosophy of the senses.

In his *Analysis of the Phenomena of the Human Mind* (1829), James Mill distinguishes taste for its inability to be separated fully from smell and touch. In the case of smell, he says, the two senses 'are so intimately blended as to seem but one'.[16] As concerns touch, '[t]he organ of taste has the sense of touch, and most objects of taste are objects of touch' (21). From this observation Mill conjures a near-surrealist fantasy of consciousness, inviting the reader to imagine an individual for whom all senses but taste have been rendered 'inactive' and who is consequently 'but a passive recipient of one taste after another' (21). In such a scenario, Mill contends, '[i]f [the individual] conceives a mere train of those sensations, perfectly unmixed with any other feeling, he will have the conception of a being made up of tastes; a thread of consciousness, which may be called mere taste; a life which is merely taste' (21). If the reader is prepared to accept Mill's challenge and imagine a being who, able to bracket out all other senses, becomes a 'thread of consciousness' that one might call 'mere taste', the effect comes quite close to Hopkins's own collapsing of selfhood into taste. Bearing in mind, however, that Mill's discussion of taste is largely predicated on taste's inextricability from the senses of smell and touch, it might be more rightly said, following his own premises, that a consciousness comprised of taste would either be an impossibility, or would by necessity exceed the singular sense itself and extend to a more continuous and holistic model. If '[i]t is not so easy', for Mill, 'in the case of [taste], . . . to conceive ourselves as having this class of feelings and no other', it becomes equally dif-

15 J. Hillis Miller, *The Disappearance of God: Five Nineteenth-Century Writers* (Cambridge, MA: Harvard University Press, 1963), p. 271.

16 James Mill, *Analysis of the Phenomena of the Human Mind* (London: Baldwin and Cradock, 1829), p. 20.

ficult to imagine a consciousness in which taste remains bounded to one sensation (20). Instead, a consciousness predicated on the sense of taste would itself by necessity be expansive, just as the sense of taste itself is defined by its inability to be limited to one single 'class of feelings' (20).

Taste was also singled out by Bain, whose *The Senses and the Intellect* (1855) granted it 'a complexity, which hardly belongs to any other sense' (*Senses* 152).[17] Within Bain's logic, the very quality that makes taste the least intellectual sense simultaneously renders it the most complex – namely, its irreducibility to the 'simple perception' of Hume or Locke. Although Bain notes that taste is the least intellectual of the senses (sight being the most), taste adopts a complexity because of its compound nature. Bain initially calls the tongue 'the seat of a twofold sensibility, taste and touch', but he soon adds a third, '*relish*, or a participation in the alimentary sensations' (*Senses* 152; original emphasis). If anything, the sense of taste acquires its own status – albeit one outside of the intellectual – by virtue of its inextricability from so many other bodily systems and perceptual apparatuses. Bain's language recalls that of Hopkins's retreat notes as he tries to parse the reduction of a sense organ in a field of what the psychologist himself calls 'continuity': 'there is an obvious continuity of structure in the tongue and alimentary canal, a common character of surface, as regards mucous membrane, glands, and papillæ, which would imply some community of action and feeling, in the midst of diversity' (*Senses* 152).

This 'community of action and feeling' does not raise the esteem of taste for Bain, who ascribes a hierarchy of sorts to the senses, largely predicated on their amenity to further reduction (*Senses* 152). The sense of touch, for instance, is granted a 'superiority' over the sense of smell because the sensations of the former are more easily distinguished from each other: 'the distinctness or separateness of the sensations [are] felt over the different parts of the skin. The sensations of the different parts of the surface of smell, would seem all to fuse into one stream of sensibility; it is not possible ever to refer a smell to any one portion of the membrane more than another' (*Senses* 172). Similarly, for Bain, sight holds a primary status among the senses because of his view that its sensations provide 'more than any other thing, . . . the material

[17] Alexander Bain, *The Senses and the Intellect* (London: John W. Parker and Son, 1855), p. 152.

of thought, memory, and imagination' (*Senses* 349). Taste, by contrast, cannot be summoned at will the way the memory of a visual image can. Its data are, perhaps, too holistic, too internal, to be conjured. Nevertheless, Bain identifies certain noteworthy tastes in his discussion, including one that Hopkins would highlight years later: the taste of alum, commercially manufactured in Britain from alum shale and used in the nineteenth century in medicine, cosmetics, and textile-dying. Like the elusive sense of taste itself – mercurial by virtue of its connections to the relish of the alimentary canal, to the sense of touch across the palate – alum too defies singular description. Bain terms alum 'sweet as well as astringent', and later remarks on astringency itself as 'a distinct form of the sensation of taste', giving the example of 'alum in the mouth' (*Senses* 157). The astringent quality of alum shifts 'farther and farther from the proper feeling of taste towards some grosser results of chemical and mechanical action. Astringent substances act on the skin and on the mucous membranes generally' (*Senses* 157). Like taste, alum breaches its restraints, shifting into various contiguous forms of sensation.

Hopkins's turn to the sense of taste and to the example of alum works against any attempt at material reductionism. Walter Ong, S.J. rightly notes, 'The self, the "me" or "I," that Hopkins "tastes" is not amenable to direct scientific analysis: it is experienced as immediately present, without parts, and as essentially nameless'.[18] Taste resists *analysis* in the etymological sense of separating an object into its constituent parts.

In drawing on taste to posit selfhood, and in concurrently rejecting sight as the appropriate sense for the task, Hopkins proffers complex responses to contemporary scientific conversations. For him, empiricist sensory perception not only provides information about the external world – as one might find in the sense of vision – but also the internal one. His attention to the sense of taste as a vehicle of identity exceeds Hume's atomistic bundle theory of the self. By contrast, Hopkins metaphorically figures selfhood as a sense perception that is stable yet continuous and irreducible, multifaceted yet holistic. Furthermore, he affirms many of Bain's descriptions of sight and taste while nonetheless challenging the associationist model.

18 Walter Ong, S.J., *Hopkins, the Self, and God* (Toronto: University of Toronto Press, 1993), p. 28.

Streams of thought

In 1889, the year of Hopkins's death, Henri Bergson published his doctoral dissertation, to be translated into English in 1910 as *Time and Free Will: An Essay on the Immediate Data of Consciousness*. Here, Bergson contends that Immanuel Kant erred in ascribing the same properties to time as to space. Whereas space is amenable to enumeration – lines can be cut into smaller lines of equal or varying sizes; area and volume can be calculated numerically – time is only artificially measurable and divisible. Rather than being a 'homogeneous medium' like space, time in Bergson's view is in continual flux, each moment inextricably changed and informed by the entirety of what has passed. The only means of comprehending this model of temporal experience, which Bergson famously termed *durée*, or duration, is qualitative rather than quantitative.

In his application of this position to consciousness, Bergson arrives at much the same ground Hopkins had been testing years earlier in his retreat notes. For Bergson, consciousness is subject to the cumulative, qualitative flux of temporality; therefore, like Hopkins, he views any gesture at atomistic reduction of psychical states as predicated on a fundamental misapprehension. The associationist errs, says Bergson, by 'reduc[ing] the self to an aggregate of conscious states: sensations, feelings, and ideas'.[19] Experience, however, is far more holistic, a space where 'states of consciousness, even when successive, permeate one another, and in the simplest of them the whole soul can be reflected' (98).

Whereas Bain would privilege senses according to the extent to which he discerned in their sense-data 'distinctness or separateness', Bergson rejects entirely the premise that such distinction is reflective of experience (Bain, *Senses* 172). In fact, Bergson invokes the senses to demonstrate a position quite opposed to that of associationism. Like Bain, Bergson attributes a continuous characteristic to the sense of taste, but he extends the same continuity to the sense of sight: 'Between flavours which are more or less bitter you will hardly distinguish anything but differences of quality; they are like different shades of one and the same colour' (39). Any imposition of *quantitative* analysis arises, he says, from the various reactions elicited by different gradations of flavour. According

[19] *Time and Free Will: An Essay on the Immediate Data of Consciousness*, F.L. Pogson, trans. (London: G. Allen, 1913), p. 165.

to what Bergson terms 'the English school' – which he identifies elsewhere as thinkers like Bain and Herbert Spencer – sensations are apprehended sequentially in time, as when 'we run our hands along a surface' (99). Since these apprehensions are successive, the associationist theory (according to Bergson) contends, their order can be reversed, as when one runs one's hand backwards along the same surface. Such a view, however, takes part in an inherent misconstrual of time as quantitative and divisible in the same way that space is. As an example of such an error, Bergson turns to another sense: that of hearing, when he compares the 'notes of a tune, melting . . . into one another', to 'a living being, whose parts, although distinct, permeate one another just because they are so closely connected' (100). Indeed, hearing the same musical notes played backwards generates an entirely distinct sensory and aesthetic experience, predicated in Bergson's model of the holistic nature of duration. Each note is imbued with the resonance and effect of the notes preceding it. Rather than consider each note in a tune to be a distinct sense-datum, Bergson proposes that we would more rightly consider such successions to be mutually penetrating, 'an interconnexion and organization of elements, each one of which represents the whole, and cannot be distinguished or isolated from it except by abstract thought' (101). Hopkins's choice of taste as the sense with which selfhood conveys itself *to* itself reflects a similar position, years in advance of Bergson's publication. The sense that had been singled out by Bain as the least intellectual yet most complex by virtue of its resistance to division and quantification provides a model of consciousness as continuous in ways that Bergson would elaborate in the late 1880s.

Bergson was not alone in positing this approach to consciousness. A year after *Time and Free Will* was first published, William James would proffer similar concepts in his *Principles of Psychology* (1890). James's chapter 'The Stream of Thought', developed from an article published in *Mind* in 1884, challenges the associationist tendency to 'formulate the mental facts in an atomistic sort of way, and to treat the higher states of consciousness as if they were all built out of unchanging simple ideas'.[20] Instead, James offers a theory of thought and experience as continuous rather than composed of discrete states or impressions. James is quick to disavow

[20] William James, 'The Stream of Thought', in *The Principles of Psychology*, vol. 1 (London: Henry Holt and Company, 1890), p. 236.

any metaphysical interventions in his analysis; he positions himself as providing observations on the 'brain-state[s]' of individuals, leaving metaphysical explanations to others ('Stream' 234). Like Hopkins, he traces experience through empirical data, and – also like Hopkins – he finds within this data evidence for a theory of selfhood that is *continuous*, a term James defines as 'without breach, crack, or division' ('Stream' 237). Describing this sense of continuity, James roots it in a coalescence of bodily and mental phenomena: 'as we think we feel our bodily selves as the seat of the thinking. If the thinking be our thinking, it must be suffused through all its parts with that peculiar warmth and intimacy that make it come as ours' ('Stream' 242). This appeal to 'warmth and intimacy' bears the same tones as Hopkins's description of self-taste as at once 'distinctive' and 'incommunicable': for both men, subjectivity itself is continuous, unbroken, and rooted in both body and mind.

Just as Hopkins relies on a sense that distinguishes itself for its lack of hard distinctions – particularly in contrast to touch and sight, as theorised by Bain – James enjoins the reader to consider all sense-data as inherently shifting. James insists that no sensation is ever experienced in an identical way by the percipient: 'however we might in ordinary conversation speak of getting the same sensation again, we never in strict theoretic accuracy could do so' ('Stream' 233). The explanation for this relativistic claim lies in what Bergson had termed *durée* – the premise that each experience is inexorably coloured by all the previous experiences of the individual. Bergson explains that within duration itself lies 'qualitative multiplicity', a 'pure heterogeneity within which there are no distinct qualities' (226). In describing this constant state of flux, James makes extensive use of the Heraclitean metaphor of a river, inviting the reader to use the metaphor of a 'stream of consciousness' to describe it.[21] Hopkins, too, would take Heraclitean

[21] Perhaps surprisingly, Bain would be the first to use the term 'stream of consciousness'. In his hands, the stream of consciousness is more akin to Humean bundle psychology than a Heraclitean model of flux. He observes, '[t]he concurrence of Sensations in one common stream of consciousness,—on the same cerebral highway,—enables those of different senses to be associated as readily as the sensations of the same sense' (*Senses* 359). In Bain's conception, the stream constitutes an amalgamation of separate sensations that are associated strongly enough to produce the semblance of continuity, a position James would later disparage in his remark that 'traditional psychology talks like one

mutability as a focus not only for his text 'That Nature Is A Heraclitean Fire', but also, as we will see, in his use of poetic language to convey the same continuity of experience he communicates in the model of self-taste.

Streams of language

In his 1908 Hibbert Lectures, James praises Bergson for his lucid prose style, 'a flexibility of verbal resource that follows the thought without a crease or wrinkle, as elastic silk underclothing follows the movements of one's body'.[22] The description could not be further from that which Hopkins's friend Bridges famously gives of the Jesuit's poetry in his Preface to the first publication of Hopkins's work, 29 years after his death. Bridges declares Hopkins's poems 'injured by a natural eccentricity, a love for subtlety and uncommonness'.[23] The gulf between these descriptions of the two writers notwithstanding, Hopkins's approach to language arguably achieves a solution to a central problem identified by Bergson years later: how to express the continuity of experience through the discontinuous medium of words.

In his Preface to *Time and Free Will*, Bergson articulates a fundamental difficulty with language in that it 'requires us to establish between our ideas the same sharp and precise distinctions, the same discontinuity, as between material objects' (xix). The incongruity is analogous to that which Bergson identifies at the heart of his argument: the misconception that time is divisible and measurable in the same way that space is. For Bergson, any attempt to frame the personal experience of consciousness in language invariably fails, since words by their nature separate and calcify that which they are intended to convey: 'the word with well-defined outlines, the rough and ready word, which stores up the stable, common, and consequently impersonal element in the impressions of mankind, overwhelms or at least covers over the delicate and fugitive impressions of our individual consciousness' (132). The more unique and deeply felt the experience, the more resistant it is

who should say a river consists of nothing but pailsful, spoonsful, quartpotsful, barrelsful, and other moulded forms of water' ('Stream' 255).

22 William James, *A Pluralistic Universe* (London: Longmans, Green, and Co., 1909), p. 227.

23 Robert Bridges, 'Preface to Notes', in *Gerard Manley Hopkins: The Critical Heritage*, ed. Gerald Roberts (London: Routledge, 1987), pp. 60–3, p. 61.

to linguistic transmission, whereas those experiences that are most easily conveyed by words are those to which associationism best applies (Bergson 136).

Even if he was unaware of Bergson's work, Bridges was attuned to a concern akin to Bergson's when he faults Hopkins's poems for 'aiming at an unattainable perfection of language (as if words—each with its twofold value in sense and in sound—could be arranged like so many separate gems to compose a whole expression of thought, in which the force of grammar and the beauty of rhythm absolutely correspond)' (63). Indeed, Hopkins's striving towards a means by which to express the inexpressible remains a critical chestnut among his readers. For instance, Miller attends to the ineffability inherent in the concept of self-taste: '[i]f it would be impossible to explain, to someone who had never tasted them, the taste of ale or alum or clove, so it is even more impossible to explain to another man how I taste to myself. My selftaste is, literally, "unspeakable." Words, those counters of shared experience, will not describe it' (*Disappearance* 271). The concept of self-taste, as we have seen, draws on Victorian psychophysiology to posit a model of self-experience that is continuous and irreducible – uncountable, as it were, by those 'counters' that we call words.

The impulse to convey the continuity of experience through the discordant medium of language resounds in Hopkins's poem 'That Nature is a Heraclitean Fire and of the comfort of the Resurrection' (1888), a meditation on Heraclitus's proposition that existence comprises the universal and ever-changing element of fire and is therefore fundamentally constituted by mutability. In a letter to Bridges, Hopkins jests about the text's inscrutability, remarking, 'I am going to preach tomorrow and put plainly to ~~the~~ ^a^ Highland congregation of MacDonalds, MacIntoshes, MacKillops, and the rest what I am ~~giving~~ putting not at all so plainly . . . in a sonnet in sprung rhythm with two codas' (*CW* vol. 2, 947). Behind its initial opacity, however, lies an effort towards more precise language that mirrors the complexity of experience.

Like his curtal sonnets, this one also exceeds the standard form, here taking the shape of a Caudate sonnet, a variation that normally includes a two-line coda, extending the typical 14 lines to 16.[24] Hopkins's Caudate sonnet, however, consists of twenty lines,

24 Around the same time, after penning 'Spelt from Sibyl's Leaves' (1886), which he called 'my long sonnet, the longest, I still say, ever made', Hopkins would

the last six of which constitute three codas (not, as he notes in his letter to Bridges, two). Beginning with a structure that already extends the standard sonnet, Hopkins adds further 'tails', echoing formally what Miller calls the 'ceaseless metamorphosis of one form into another' (*Disappearance* 327) and therefore pushing formally against the limitations of standardised language which 'cannot get hold of [its object] without arresting its mobility' (Bergson 129).

The poem represents peak Hopkins insofar as it strains against the confines of language, announcing in its opening lines a commitment to alliteration that carries through the text: 'Cloud -puffball, torn tufts, tossed pillows flaunt forth, then chevy on an air- / built throughfare' (*Poetical* 197). Each alliterative word is distinct while bearing the stamp (i.e. the first letter) of the preceding one, as if to exemplify the concept of duration as Bergson would later describe it, with each moment imbued with signification from those preceding it. Equally, the enjambment in the first lines signals another recurrent feature of the poem, in which only six of twenty lines close with end punctuation. The tumbling rush of text that bleeds unbroken from one line to another renders Heraclitean flux in the poetic form itself, and equally speaks to a model of experience based in continuity and transformation rather than associationist discreteness.

Similarly, Hopkins's famous neologisms reach a giddy abundance in a text brimming with 'shivelights and shadowtackle', 'yestertempest's creases', and 'manmarks', to name a few (*Poetical* 197). The pressing of old words into new pushes against the 'clean-cut distinctions' that Bergson would identify as symptomatic of both linguistic necessity and limitation (97). Reflecting on what he calls Hopkins's 'idiomatic neologisms',[25] Jacques Derrida lights on the term *inscape*, which Julia Saville defines as 'the species-specific pattern that becomes distinguishable to the viewer's eye when the features of a figure or object . . . become defined against the figure's unnoticed ground'.[26] Inscape, Derrida observes, stands alongside *self-taste* as an instance in which 'a singularity exceeds

experiment with codas in 'Tom's Garland' (1887) once Bridges sent him an explanation of their use in 1887 (*CW* vol. 2, 842).

[25] Jacques Derrida, 'Justices', *Critical Inquiry* 31.3 (2005): 689–721, 700.

[26] Julia Saville, 'Gerard Manley Hopkins', in David Scott Kastan, ed., *The Oxford Encyclopedia of British Literature*, vol. 1 (Oxford: Oxford University Press, 2006), pp. 70–4, p. 70.

the generality of the language. It thus overflows the language itself. The singular says itself, but it says itself as "unspeakable"' (700). Part of the fundamental unspeakability lies in the continuity of inscape and experience, resistant to the notion of distinct, self-contained words to convey its plenitude.

The middle voice

In 1890, William James would bemoan the failure of language to convey the essence of Being: 'If we could say in English "it thinks," as we say "it rains" or "it blows," we should be stating the fact most simply and with the minimum of assumption. As we cannot, we must simply say that *thought goes on*' ('Stream' 225). Herwig Friedl argues that 'it is *the middle voice* . . . whose absence in contemporary language is putting such a strain on pragmatist thinking' similar to that of James, 'once pragmatism begins to try and approach the problem of saying or, at least, of hinting at and of conveying the inner workings of Being as it unfolds'.[27] Rarely used in English but common in many languages, such as Ancient Greek, the middle voice is a verbal construction wherein the subject both performs and is affected by the verb.[28] As John Llewelyn explains, 'while in the active voice a verb refers to a procedure or event outside the subject (e.g. Greek *louein*, to wash something), in the middle voice the verb refers to a procedure or event to which the subject is interior (e.g. Greek *louesthai*, to wash oneself), so the standard middle-voiced verb is not simply reflexive'.[29] A key element to the middle voice, Friedl argues, is its ability to convey a subject that is transformed or determined by an event or action, without turning that subject into a 'mere recipient' of the action, as with the passive voice (480). In this final section, I argue that Hopkins's *selving*, *justicing*, and – if I may – *self-tasting* bring to language the 'inner workings of Being as it unfolds' through the

[27] Herwig Friedl, 'Thinking in Search of a Language: Pragmatism and the Muted Middle Voice', *Amerikastudien/American Studies* 47.4 (2002): 469–90, 478, emphasis added.

[28] John Lyons describes the middle voice as a construction in which 'the "action" or "state" affects the subject of the verb or his interests' (*Introduction to Theoretical Linguistics* (Cambridge: Cambridge University Press, 1968), p. 373).

[29] John Llewelyn, *Gerard Manley Hopkins and the Spell of John Duns Scotus* (Edinburgh: Edinburgh University Press, 2015), p. 5.

middle voice, transcending the grammar of standard English utterances in order to articulate consciousness in a way that conveys the fullness of continuity and process (Friedl 478).

In his 1868 notes on Parmenides, Hopkins reflects on classical approaches to Being and non-Being, crucially observing that, 'To be and to know or Being and thought are the same. The truth in thought is Being, stress, and each word is one way of acknowledging Being and each sentence by its copula is (or its equivalent) the utterance and assertion of it' (*CW* vol. 4, 315). Miller remarks that, for Hopkins, the 'true "stem of stress" between man and nature is the word itself. At the point of fusion, where subject meets object and coalesces with it, is born the word'.[30] There is for Hopkins what Miller terms a 'magic quality' ('Creation' 308) that brings the world into being through 'utterance and assertion' (*CW* vol. 4, 315). Crucially, Hopkins remarks that this coming-into-being through language hinges on the role of the *copula* in the sentence: in English, the verb 'to be', which binds the subject of a sentence to its subject complement. The centrality of the copula, of course, cannot help but reiterate the very problem of language in its separation of being from the subject of being: the subject of the sentence is by necessity separate from both the copula verb and from the subject complement, establishing the 'sharp and precise distinctions' of language that would so trouble Bergson (Bergson xix).

Nearly a decade after his notes on Parmenides, Hopkins would pen 'As kingfishers catch fire' (1877), a poem featuring two of the 'idiomatic neologisms' that would tantalize later readers like Derrida: *selves* and *justices* (700). Norman MacKenzie identifies the poem as a reflection on the Ignatian First Principle and Foundation, the same text that would inspire Hopkins's meditation on self-taste three years later.[31] Expanding on the concept that creation is a vehicle through which God makes himself known, the poem's famous lines exemplify the concept of 'selving' as a performance of one's innate essence:

> Each mortal thing does one thing and the same:
> Deals out that being indoors each one dwells;

[30] J. Hillis Miller, 'The Creation of the Self in Gerard Manley Hopkins', *ELH* 22.4 (1955): 293–319, 308.

[31] Norman MacKenzie, 'Commentary', in *The Poetical Works of Gerard Manley Hopkins*, pp. 213–513, p. 367.

Selves—goes itself; *myself* it speaks and spells,
Crying *What I do is me: for that I came*. (*Poetical* 141; original emphasis)

Importantly, the verb *selve* speaks directly to the 'utterance and assertion' of Being, yet it does so in a more immediate way than if it were to be broken into the copular clause 'I am myself'. Uncharacteristically providing a definition for a neologism in the text of his poem, Hopkins defaults to the reflexive phrases 'goes itself' and the strangely transitive construction, '*myself* it speaks and spells', yet these explanations are only secondary to the power of the verb that contains the essence of the copula in itself (*Poetical* 141). The sestet begins by introducing the verb *justice* to similar effect: 'the just man justices' (*Poetical* 141). As MacKenzie notes, the usage of *justice* as an intransitive verb meaning 'to act justly' does not appear in the *OED* (368). That said, the word is recorded as a transitive verb meaning 'To punish or reward appropriately, to treat justly' as early as 1300.[32] Given that the sestet continues, 'Keeps grace: that keeps all his goings graces', the verb might easily be read as a reflexive one: the just man performs justice on himself in such a way as to carry out God's design for him (*Poetical* 141). Transitive or intransitive, this new usage obviates the need for a copular clause ('the just man is just') or a reflexive one ('the just man performs justice on himself') in the same way that the verb *selve* obviates the reflexive copular clause ('I am myself'). The language becomes distilled, holistic, pressing into a single word the experience of Being, just as Hopkins's portmanteaux press language into continuity rather than discreteness.

The verb *selves* makes its second appearance in Hopkins's 1880 retreat notes when he develops his theory of self-taste: 'Nothing else in nature comes near this unspeakable stress of pitch, distinctiveness, and *selving*, this selfbeing of my own: nothing explains it or resembles it, except so far as this, that other men to themselves have the same feeling' (*CW*, vol. 5, 349; emphasis added). The appearance of self-taste alongside the second recorded mention of *selving* is noteworthy, since self-taste addresses a similar problem of language. As we have seen, the sense of taste is associated with complexity in the nineteenth-century discourse of sensation and

[32] See 'justice, v.' *OED Online*, Oxford University Press, March 2023, <www.oed.com/view/Entry/102199>.

epistemology, since taste bears so many ties to other senses and bodily processes. The notion of self-taste adds to this level of complexity by introducing the question of reflexivity: on a literal level, self-taste might denote the tongue, the organ of taste, tasting itself; on a metaphorical level, it denotes the individual perceiving her own interiority in a way that is inaccessible to any other being. Although Hopkins never uses the word 'self-taste' as a verb, it might readily serve as one; in such a form, moreover, it would take on a similar valence as *selves* and *justices* by conveying an action performed by a subject in which the subject is affected by the action of the verb, but which does *not* take on a grammatically reflexive form.

Such constructions are examples of the middle voice and speak to the usefulness of that grammatical structure in attempts to overcome the obstacles of expression posed by language as identified by thinkers like Bergson and James. As Charles E. Scott comments, the middle voice is 'the voice of something's taking place through its own enactment'.[33] Self-tasting, like selving and justicing, signals an action performed by a subject who, through performing that action, brings itself into being. On the level of language itself, that bringing into being is conveyed most robustly through the verb: the subject *selves*, *justices*, *self-tastes*.[34]

Philip Endean, S.J. observes that since the first appearance of the *Spiritual Exercises*, 'Ignatius's talk of *smelling* and *tasting* "the infinite gentleness and sweetness of the divinity of the soul and its virtues" . . . has been seen as a significant indication that Ignatius intended something more than the imaginative use of the everyday senses'.[35] In his reflections on the First Principle of the Ignatian *Spiritual Exercises*, Hopkins seems to agree. Indeed, his meditations on creation lead him to existential reflections on the nature of the self and the divine. Yet, at the same time, his apprehension of consciousness through 'self-taste' returns the metaphysical to the physical, finding in sensory embodiment a key to the mystery of the mind. When considering Hopkins's concept of self-taste as it relates to consciousness, sensory perception, and the con-

[33] Charles E. Scott, *The Question of Ethics: Nietzsche, Foucault, Heidegger* (Indianapolis: Indiana University Press, 1990), p. 24.

[34] Warm thanks to Tom Piliouris for sharing his linguistic expertise with me for this discussion.

[35] Philip Endean, S.J., 'The Ignatian Prayer of the Senses', *Heythrop Journal* 31 (1990): 391–418, 399, emphasis added.

cerns of later process philosophers, it may be most fitting to turn to his instructions to Bridges for reading his poem 'Spelt from Sibyl's Leaves', which he insisted be 'almost sung' rather than read silently (*CW* vol. 2, 842). Hopkins's aesthetic spiritual practice, rooted so deeply in poetry, rests in the body and in the quality of song, the notes of which, Bergson reminds us, melt 'into one another' like a 'living being, whose parts, although distinct, permeate one another' (*Time* 100). Like the temporal nature of selfhood and sense perception, poetry itself is a living presence, sung and embodied, that defies division and analysis, and that speaks, spells and, ultimately, selves.

7

Neuron Doctrine in Fiction by Marie Corelli and Oscar Wilde

Anne Stiles

This essay examines the ways in which laypeople understood neuroanatomical terminology in the late nineteenth and early twentieth centuries, a time of rapid professionalisation in the biosciences. Specifically, I look at the term 'neuron' or 'brain cell' and how it was understood by two literary authors whose careers peaked in the 1890s: Marie Corelli and Oscar Wilde. Both writers were relatively early adopters of the term around the same time that Spanish scientist Santiago Ramón y Cajal and his German colleagues, Albrecht von Kölliker and Heinrich Waldeyer-Hartz, first advanced what became known as neuron doctrine: that is, the idea that each nerve cell is an independent unit rather than part of an interconnected web or reticulum.[1]

For my literary examples, I have deliberately chosen two writers who, at first glance, seem as different as possible. Wilde is best known today as a gay icon, successful playwright, and consummate aesthete whose career ended in scandal when he was convicted of gross indecency with men in 1895. He was the son of a prominent Dublin eye and ear surgeon, Sir William Wilde, who founded a hospital and was knighted for his accomplishments in 1864.[2] Though Wilde studied classics at Oxford from 1874–8, he also took copious notes on scientific subjects during these years. Wilde's college notebooks suggest that was he particularly attentive to theories on the materiality of the mind by Thomas Henry

[1] Stanley Finger, *Minds Behind the Brain: A History of the Pioneers and Their Discoveries* (Oxford: Oxford University Press, 2000), p. 211.

[2] Anne Stiles, *Popular Fiction and Brain Science in the Late Nineteenth Century* (Cambridge: Cambridge University Press, 2012), p. 58.

Huxley, John Tyndall, and William Kingdon Clifford; evolutionary theories, including German naturalist Ernst Haeckel's work on cells and embryology; and the nature of microscopic particles more broadly.[3] The term 'brain cell' appears first in his poem 'Roses and Rue' (1884) and later in his essay 'The Critic as Artist' (1891) and his only novel, *The Picture of Dorian Gray* (1890, 1891; Cohn, "Oscar Wilde and the Brain Cell," 21). Because Wilde's views on science have been more thoroughly researched, they serve as a useful point of comparison for my discussion of Corelli, whose novels are still understudied despite her tremendous influence during her lifetime.

Corelli, who was the world's bestselling author during the 1890s and early years of the twentieth century, began her life under decidedly less auspicious circumstances. Recent research by Joanna Turner suggests that Corelli was born as Caroline Cody to Thomas and Harriet Cody, a labourer and charwoman residing in Marylebone, London. She was adopted at age five and renamed Mary by Mary Elizabeth Mills and her soon-to-be husband, Scottish journalist Charles Mackay.[4] Corelli allegedly retained a mild cockney accent into adulthood despite her middle-class upbringing in a literary family (Turner, 28). Her formal education consisted of a series of private governesses, free rein of her father's extensive library, and two years' residence at Gumley House, a French convent school in Isleworth (now part of West London) where she learned basic French and Italian (Turner, 30). Like most women of her era, Corelli's education emphasised music, modern languages, and polite literature rather than the latest scientific theories.[5]

In her fiction, Corelli staunchly opposed scientific materialism in favour of '*the knowledge of the love of God* as the true foundation of noble living', as she wrote in her 1896 novel *The Mighty*

[3] Elisha Cohn, 'Oscar Wilde and the Brain Cell', in Anne Stiles, Stanley Finger and François Boller, eds, *Literature, Neurology, and Neuroscience: Historical and Literary Connections* (Amsterdam: Elsevier, 2013), pp. 19–39, p. 21, p. 29.

[4] On Corelli's origins and the scholarly debate surrounding them, see Joanna Turner, '"The most accomplished liar in literature?" Uncovering Marie Corelli's Hidden Early Life', *Victorian Popular Fictions* 5.1 (2023): 21–36.

[5] Kirsten MacLeod, 'Introduction' to Marie Corelli, *Wormwood: A Drama of Paris* (Peterborough, Ontario: Broadview, 2004), pp. 9–55, pp. 13–14.

Atom.[6] Nonetheless, she used the term 'brain cell' in many of her works beginning in 1890 and continuing into the twentieth century. Both she and Wilde were fascinated by microscopic particles of all sorts (atoms, molecules and brain cells) but comprehended these entities in ways that might baffle modern readers.

This essay shows how each author invoked brain cells in idiosyncratic ways that drew on nineteenth-century philosophy, Spiritualism and other cultural movements in addition to mainstream science. In other words, neither author had a scientifically orthodox understanding of neuron doctrine. Instead, Wilde and Corelli's understandings of brain cells reflected their personal interests and preoccupations. Whereas Wilde wove the neuron into his aesthetic philosophy by viewing it as a beautiful object, Corelli imbued the brain cell with spiritual overtones befitting her fascination with new religious movements of the period. Each author also weighed in, at least implicitly, on the philosophical controversies raised by neuron doctrine and cerebral localisation more broadly. Wilde tended to view the neuron as an isolated, impermeable and unknowable entity, as mysterious as the soul itself.[7] He was less interested in the interactions between neurons and how they communicated. By contrast, Corelli focused on the permeability of brain cells and the connections between them in ways that suggested supernatural possibilities.

Neuron doctrine

For the greater part of the nineteenth century, scientific debate raged regarding the structure of the human nervous system. In 1839, German physiologist Theodor Schwann extended cell theory from plants to animals and argued that the human body was composed of distinct cells. Schwann stressed that 'each cell is an Individual, an independent whole' that nonetheless played a role in the workings of a larger organism.[8] This argument was widely accepted for all organs except the nervous system, which

[6] Marie Corelli, *The Mighty Atom* (Philadelphia: J.P. Lippincott, 1896), p. 3, emphasis in original.

[7] See Elisha Cohn, 'One Single Ivory Cell: Oscar Wilde and the Brain', *Journal of Victorian Culture* 17.2 (2012): 183–205.

[8] Theodor Schwann, *Microscopical Researches into the Accordance in the Structure and Growth of Animals and Plants*, trans. Henry Smith (New York: Kraus, 1969), p. 2.

seemed like a special case.[9] Scientists throughout Europe debated whether the brain and nerves made up a connected reticulum or network, or were composed of independent units or cells.

The philosophical stakes of this controversy were high. Cerebral localisationists, who believed that specific parts of the brain performed designated functions, squared off against those who took a more holistic approach to brain function. As I have argued elsewhere, neuron doctrine seemed to suggest the heretical possibility of multiple cells and selves.[10] Like other aspects of cerebral localisation theory, neuron doctrine apparently undermined revered religious concepts like the soul and free will by suggesting that humans are no more than the sum of our nerve impulses and anatomical functions. By contrast, holistic approaches to brain function seemingly left more room for these traditional religious viewpoints and for individual autonomy.[11] In the final decade of the nineteenth century, holistic approaches to brain function were increasingly seen as ideologically conservative in contrast to more progressive and popular cerebral localisation theories.[12]

These debates about the structure of the nervous system culminated in a series of groundbreaking discoveries in the last three decades of the nineteenth century. In 1873, Italian scientist Camillo Golgi invented a new silver staining technique that showed more clearly than ever before the structure of the whole nerve cell, including the cell body, axon, and branching dendrites (Finger, *Origins of Neuroscience*, 45). Based on his microscopic investigations and careful drawings of what he saw, Golgi favoured the holistic theory of the intertwining nerve reticulum. Spaniard Santiago Ramón y Cajal began using Golgi's silver staining technique in 1887 and improved upon it. But Cajal came to very different conclusions than

9 Stanley Finger, *Origins of Neuroscience: A History of Explorations into Brain Function* (Oxford: Oxford University Press, 1994), pp. 43–4.

10 Anne Stiles, 'Religion and Science in the 1890s', in Dustin Friedman and Kristin Mahoney, eds, *Nineteenth-Century Literature in Transition: the 1890s* (Cambridge: Cambridge University Press, 2023), pp. 285–304, p. 293. The present essay revisits some literary examples from this earlier piece, but uses a different theoretical framework (neuron doctrine as opposed to conflicts between religion and science).

11 For a closer look at the moral quandaries raised by cerebral localisation, see Stiles, *Popular Fiction and Brain Science*, pp. 1–24.

12 For a more nuanced account of holistic approaches brain function in the late nineteenth century and why they remained popular in some circles, see Chapter 4 of Finger, *Origins of Neuroscience*, pp. 51–62.

his Italian contemporary, arguing in an 1888 Spanish-language publication that each nerve cell should be regarded as 'an absolutely autonomous canton' and that neurons did not form reticula or nets (quoted in Finger, *Origins of Neuroscience*, 47).

Knowing that few European scientists read Spanish, Cajal headed to Berlin in 1889 in hopes of gaining wider recognition for his discoveries (Finger, *Minds Behind the Brain*, 210). There, he impressed Albrecht von Kölliker and Heinrich Waldeyer-Hartz, who promoted Cajal's findings within the European scientific community. Waldeyer-Hartz even coined the term 'neuron' in 1891 to denote the nerve cell as an independent unit (Finger, *Minds Behind the Brain*, 211). The term took off, and what became known as neuron doctrine increasingly gained acceptance among scientists.

But this was hardly the end of the debate. For instance, there remained the unresolved question of how impulses pass from one neuron to another. Cajal posited that impulses pass from one neuron to another unidirectionally across axons and dendrites, but the exact means of this communication was unclear. There were also respected scientists who still favoured the reticulum theory. In 1906, Cajal and Golgi were jointly awarded the Nobel Prize in Physiology or Medicine for their discoveries in neuroanatomy. In his acceptance speech, Golgi shocked his peers by hewing to the older reticulum theory, just as he had in the 1870s (Finger, *Minds Behind the Brain*, 215). The debate surrounding neuron doctrine would not be fully resolved until the 1950s, when electron microscopes finally enabled scientists to view the synaptic gap between nerve cells.[13] In the meantime, prominent laypeople as well as scientists discussed the significance of neuron doctrine, including two of the most influential literary figures of the age.

Brain cells in literature

Corelli and Wilde began writing about brain cells around the same time that neuron doctrine reached Britain.[14] According to

[13] Gordon Shepherd, *Foundations of the Neuron Doctrine* (Oxford: Oxford University Press, 1991), p. 275.

[14] According to the *Oxford English Dictionary*, the earliest known use of the term 'brain cell' was in a scientific journal in 1848. The term was initially quite rare, but usage climbed in the 1870s and 80s, peaking in the twenty-first century. See <https://www.oed.com/dictionary/brain-cell_n?tab=frequency#9915285022>.

the *Oxford English Dictionary,* the term 'neuron' was first used in English in 1891 in the scientific journal *Brain.* One cannot be sure whether either Corelli or Wilde knew about these scientific developments, though Wilde had an interest in cell theory more broadly.

Wilde was fascinated by microscopic particles (atoms, molecules, brain cells, etc.) both for their aesthetic beauty and their implications for human subjectivity, as Elisha Cohn suggests. In this regard, Wilde resembled his mentor at Oxford, the art critic John Ruskin, who gave lectures praising the beauties of microscopic particles to academic and lay audiences – including a talk at a girls' school where he waxed eloquent about the crystalline atomic structure of sugar candy (Cohn, 'Oscar Wilde and the Brain Cell', 21, 25). Ruskin was following a broader trend in which scientists appealed to lay audiences by rendering 'materialist concepts beautiful and scientific methods appealing' (Cohn, 'Oscar Wilde and the Brain Cell', 21). This strategy helped scientists like Tyndall, Clifford and Huxley make their theories of the materiality of the mind more palatable to lay audiences, who shuddered at the idea that the brain was no more than a finely tuned machine, as Huxley famously suggested in his 1874 lecture 'On the Hypothesis that Animals are Automata'.

This example suggests why cerebral localisation – including neuron doctrine – raised theological hackles. By mapping human brain function using animal experiments and clinical studies, localisationists blurred the boundaries between human, animal and machine. Their methods were sometimes gruesome (for instance, operating on live animals, with or without anaesthetic) and their conclusions seemingly left little place for human autonomy or the influence of a higher power (Stiles, *Popular Fiction and Brain Science*, 9).

Wilde's only novel engages with the controversial methods and materialist conclusions of cerebral localisation experiments, though this was not what initially arrested reviewers' attention. *The Picture of Dorian Gray* caused a sensation when a thirteen-chapter version first appeared in *Lippincott's Monthly Magazine* in June of 1890. Wilde's work was immediately attacked in the press as a 'poisonous book' that was 'spawned from the leprous literature of the French *décadents*' (quoted in MacLeod, 35). Reviewers were also incensed by the hedonistic, subtly homoerotic behaviour of the novel's three male protagonists. An edited and expanded twenty-chapter version of *The Picture of Dorian Gray* – with the homoerotic elements slightly toned down – was published by Ward, Lock, and Co. in 1891. Despite the controversy surrounding the novel, it was and remains 'the pre-eminent example of an English decadent *fin-de-siècle* novel' that introduced the British reading public to French poet Theophile Gautier's ideas about art for art's sake, a theme also championed by Walter Pater, Wilde's mentor at Oxford.[15]

Wilde also courted controversy by invoking debates surrounding scientific materialism, as recent critics such as Benjamin Morgan, Carolyn Lesjak, and Elisha Cohn have noted. In one provocative passage, Lord Henry, Dorian's friend and mentor, likens his unwholesome influence over his protégé to a scientific experiment:

> [Lord Henry] had been always enthralled by the methods of natural science, but the ordinary subject-matter of that science had seemed to him trivial and of no import. And so he had begun by vivisecting himself as he had ended by vivisecting others. Human life – that appeared to him the thing worth investigating.[16]

By suggesting that Lord Henry views his friend as an 'interesting study' and referring to vivisection, Wilde would have raised hackles of readers opposed to animal experimentation (Wilde, 50). This included a wide swath of the British reading public at the time, including celebrities like Lewis Carroll and Queen Victoria.[17]

Wilde and his contemporaries were acutely aware of antivivisection debates thanks in part to the well-publicised 1881 trial of Sir David Ferrier, who was hauled into court for allegedly violating the 1876 Anti-Vivisection Act. Ferrier was renowned for his paradigm-shifting cortical maps showing that specific areas of the brain controlled specific movements and functions, which he published in his landmark work *The Functions of the Brain* in 1876. Thanks to these maps, surgeons could conduct brain

[15] Frances Knight, *Victorian Christianity at the Fin de Siècle: The Culture of Religion in a Decadent Age* (London: I.B. Tauris, 2016), p. 45.

[16] Oscar Wilde, *The Picture of Dorian Gray*, ed. Joseph Bristow (Oxford: Oxford University Press, 2008), p. 50.

[17] Laura Otis, 'Howled Out of the Country: Wilkie Collins and H.G. Wells Retry David Ferrier', in Anne Stiles, ed., *Neurology and Literature, 1860–1920* (Basingstoke: Palgrave, 2007), pp. 27–51, p. 32.

surgery based solely on clinical symptoms even if no skull deformities were present. Many lives were saved as a result (Finger, *Minds Behind the Brain*, 172).

Antivivisectionists, however, opposed both Ferrier's methods and his materialistic conclusions. Ferrier had created his cortical maps by electrically stimulating the exposed brains of anaesthetised primates, cats, dogs and other mammals and seeing what behaviours resulted. He also performed experimental surgeries on monkeys in which he removed or damaged parts of the motor cortex and observed the resulting behavioural deficits. These surgeries proved controversial because Ferrier kept the monkeys alive following their operations and did not use anaesthetic in cases where it might have compromised his experimental results. Further, his studies powerfully supported Darwin's theory of natural selection by demonstrating correspondences between human and animal brains, especially primate brains (Otis, 29). They thus suggested that 'there was nothing sacred about the human will, not even human consciousness', as Laura Otis explains (31).

In some respects, Ferrier's widely publicised trial foreshadowed Wilde's own trials later in the century, which H.G. Wells memorably described as 'the graceless and pitiful downfall of a man of genius'.[18] While Ferrier was ultimately acquitted on a technicality, his trial lingered in public memory as a grisly exposé of science.[19] Thus, Lord Henry's mention of vivisection might easily suggest moral condemnation, whether of his own manipulation of Dorian, of scientific materialism, or both. But Wilde is careful to keep multiple possibilities at play: Lord Henry 'vivisects' himself as well as Dorian, and the result is a sense of fascination with 'human life' as 'worth investigating' (Wilde, 50). Indeed, in many cases where Wilde might easily condemn science and its materialist implications, he instead veers in the opposite direction, as Carolyn Lesjak notes. She reminds us of Wilde's use of epigrams that juxtapose opposites: 'the goal is to keep opposing terms in relation; it is never to collapse the distance between them nor opt for one

[18] H.G. Wells, *The Early Works of H.G. Wells, Atlantic Edition,* vol. 2 (London: T. Fischer Unwin, 1924), p. ix.

[19] Antivivisectionists alleged that Ferrier had neglected to apply for a Certificate B, which was required under the 1876 Anti-Vivisection Act in order to keep animals alive after they recovered from anaesthesia. But it turned out that Ferrier's associate, Gerald Francis Yeo, had applied for a Certificate B and had performed the surgery on the monkey's brain (Otis 35, 37).

pole over and against the other'.[20] Scientific materialism, in other words, is a pole that 'marks one side of the mind/matter divide', a contrasting term in the debates about poetry, beauty and magic that surface elsewhere in the novel (Lesjak, 13).

In a similar fashion, Dorian's musing about the brain cell, the latest discovery of cerebral localisation theory, ends with a contemplation of its aesthetic qualities. In a passage that appears in both the 1890 and 1891 versions of the novel, Dorian considers materialist conceptions of the mind following his cruel rejection of the actress Sybil Vane and her consequent suicide:

> For a season he inclined to the materialist doctrines of the *Darwinismus* movement in Germany, and found a curious pleasure in tracing the thoughts and passions of men to some pearly cell in the brain, or some white nerve in the body, delighting in the conception of the absolute dependence of the spirit on certain physical conditions, morbid or healthy, normal or diseased.[21]

Dorian's sudden interest in scientific materialism provides him with 'a convenient excuse for bad behavior', as Cohn observes ('One Single Ivory Cell', 197). At the same time, the passage aestheticises the bodily structures it renders visible: 'a pearly cell in the brain', 'some white nerve in the body', veering away from the moral condemnation one might otherwise expect. By viewing the brain cell as beautiful object, Wilde manages to sidestep the thorny issues raised by cerebral localisation, or at least put them on pause.

This passage appears in Chapter 11, where Dorian amasses collections of perfumes, jewels, musical instruments, tapestries and ecclesiastical vestments in emulation of the 'poisonous book' given to him by Lord Henry (Wilde, 107). This book is often assumed to be Joris-Karl Huysmans's *À Rebours* (1884), which Wilde's contemporary Arthur Symons called 'the breviary of the Decadence' (quoted in Knight, 107). This groundbreaking French novel concerns a 'bored, bisexual aesthete', Duc Jean Des Esseintes, who

[20] Carolyn Lesjak, 'Oscar Wilde and the Art/Work of Atoms', *Studies in the Literary Imagination* 43.1 (Spring 2010): 1–26, 12.

[21] Oscar Wilde, *The Picture of Dorian Gray*, ed. Joseph Bristow (Oxford: Oxford University Press, 2008), p. 113. In his explanatory notes to this edition, Bristow notes that the German term *Darwinismus* (Darwinism) suggests Haeckel as one source of Dorian's musings (214). This is consistent with Wilde's interest in Haeckel's writing as shown in his college notebooks.

engages in bizarre activities designed to absorb his senses, such as decorating a live tortoise with gemstones (Knight, 42). Like Des Esseintes, Dorian's sensory indulgences distract from his growing fear and *ennui*: 'these treasures . . . were to be to him means of forgetfulness, modes by which he could escape, for a season, from the fear that seemed to him at times to be almost too great to be borne' (Wilde, 119)

In the context of Chapter 11, the 'pearly cell in the brain' sounds like one of Dorian's aestheticised collectibles, a desirable object whose beauty decontextualises it from its materialist origins. The description of the cell as singular and isolated rather than plural or connected also sheds light on how Dorian views cells and selves. Wilde's depiction reflects the 'new understanding of the brain cell as a self-contained structure, its interior inaccessible, and its connection to other cells unexplained', as Cohn observes ('Oscar Wilde and the Brain Cell', 31). If one takes the cell as a metonym for the self, as both Corelli and Wilde tended to do, Dorian's view of the cell in isolation as opposed to part of a broader community or network suggests a larger problem with his thinking. Viewing himself in isolation allows Dorian to ignore the effects of his actions on others.

There are two subsequent references to brain cells in *Dorian Gray* following Dorian's (arguably) most heinous crime, his murder of painter Basil Hallward; these references also appear in both the 1890 and 1891 versions of the text. The first occurs as he makes his way to an opium den: '[f]rom cell to cell of his brain crept the one thought . . . the wild desire to live' (Wilde, 156). At the opium den, 'every cell of the brain, seems to be instinct with fearful impulses' (Wilde, 160). Notably, the first of these references implies the connectedness of brain cells, suggesting that Dorian finally begins to grasp the consequences of his actions on others. This quote is an exception to the rule in Wilde's literary works, which tend to view cells in isolation and emphasise their beauty and impenetrability to human understanding.

In contrast to Wilde, Marie Corelli was more interested in the interconnections between brain cells and the possibilities for communication between them. In several of her literary works, she imagined neural networks linking not just cells, but also other human brains, angels and spirits, and even God himself. She thus incorporated the brain cell into her personal religion, the so-called Electric Creed of Christianity, which she espoused in a series of works beginning with her debut novel, *The Romance of Two Worlds* (1886), and continuing into the twentieth century in works like *The Life Everlasting* (1911). In this creed, light, heat and electricity are equated with God's love and imbued with divine powers. Drawing an analogy between nerves and telegraph wires, Corelli argued that neural pathways could become direct routes between other human brains, extraterrestrials, and even to the Godhead itself, as one character suggests in *A Romance of Two Worlds*: 'Why should not a communication be established, like a sort of spiritual Atlantic cable, between man and the beings of other spheres and solar systems?'[22] (The Atlantic Cable, which was completed in 1866, allowed telegraphic messages to be sent between the United States and Europe). In *The Life Everlasting,* meanwhile, Corelli posited that 'the Soul's voice [is] carried through the radiant fibres connected with the nerves to the brain. The brain receives it, but cannot keep it – for it is transmitted by its own electric power to other brains'.[23] While most conservative Victorians feared cerebral localisation theories for their materialist implications, Corelli made nerves and nervous communication key to her personal faith, which was the basis of a small church in the United States.[24]

Corelli's unique fusion of science and spirituality was key to her enormous success. Though she is largely forgotten today, Corelli was one of the most famous women of her time. Her loyal fans included luminaries like Queen Victoria, Prime Minister William Gladstone, Lord Alfred Tennyson and even, for a time, Wilde, who said that Corelli 'wrote marvelous things in a marvelous way'.[25] Corelli met Wilde in 1887, shortly after her entrée into the literary scene (MacLeod, 56). He even asked her to write

[22] Marie Corelli, *A Romance of Two Worlds* (New York: A.L. Burt, 1887), p. 200.

[23] Marie Corelli, *The Life Everlasting* (New York: George H. Doran, 1911), p. 374.

[24] Brian Masters, *Now Barrabas Was a Rotter: The Extraordinary Life of Marie Corelli* (London: Hamish Hamilton, 1978), p. 94.

[25] Quoted in Julia Kuehn, 'Introduction' to Marie Corelli, *The Sorrows of Satan* (Kansas City, MO: Valancourt, 2008), pp. vii–xvii, p. x. Wilde evidently changed his initial view of Corelli, as suggested by an anecdote from his time in Reading Gaol. Asked if Corelli was a great writer, Wilde replied, 'Now don't think I've anything against her moral character . . . but from the way she writes she ought to be here' (quoted in Masters, 12).

for *The Woman's World*, which he edited between 1887 and 1889.[26]

Corelli's most loyal fan base, however, was the middle-class reading public. As biographer Annette Federico explains, Corelli's books broke all sales records at the time: 'on average, a Corelli novel sold 100,000 copies a year. At the turn of the century sales averaged 175,000 copies' (2). These numbers far surpassed those of Corelli's nearest competitors such as H.G. Wells, Mrs Humprey Ward, or Hall Caine (Masters, 6). Corelli suggested that her romances 'touched a chord somewhere in the great nerves of humanity', using neurological metaphors to explain her success.[27]

Corelli first adopted the term 'brain cell' in her fifth novel, *Wormwood* (1890), a potboiler about a young, upper-class Parisian who, after being betrayed by his fiancée, becomes addicted to absinthe and commits a series of escalating crimes. This novel bears a passing resemblance to *Dorian Gray* that may not be entirely coincidental. As Kirsten MacLeod notes, *Wormwood* is a satire of French naturalism and literary decadence, genres that Corelli saw as moral threats to the British reading public (35). Her targets included the largely male literary intelligentsia of her day who accorded prestige to naturalism and decadence and looked down on romances, Gothic melodramas, and other genres associated with women writers like Corelli (MacLeod, 31). The most famous naturalist at that time was Émile Zola, who is frequently mentioned in *Wormwood* and who employed aspects of the scientific method in his gritty portrayals of working-class life. As Zola writes in his 1880 treatise, 'The Experimental Novel', the author must 'dissect piece by piece' his characters to show how heredity and environment determine their actions.[28]

Literary decadence, meanwhile, concentrated on the eccentric, the bizarre, the perverse, and on the psychology of the artist. In France, decadence was closely associated with Huysmans as well as Charles Baudelaire, Paul Verlaine, and Arthur Rimbaud (MacLeod, 34–5). The premier example of English decadence was

[26] Annette Federico, *Idol of Suburbia: Marie Corelli and Late-Victorian Literary Culture* (Charlottesville: University Press of Virginia, 2000), p. 1.

[27] Marie Corelli to George Bentley, late March 1887, Corelli Collection (Cat. No. GEN MSS 332), Yale University, Beinecke Rare Book and Manuscript Library.

[28] Émile Zola, *The Experimental Novel and Other Essays*, trans. Belle Sherman (New York: Cassell Publishing, 1893), p. 25.

Wilde's *Dorian Gray,* which appeared in *Lippincott's Monthly* six months before the publication of *Wormwood. Dorian Gray* is thus unlikely to have escaped Corelli's attention, though she does not mention it in her letters of the period (MacLeod, 36). It is even possible that Corelli first learned of brain cells by reading Wilde's novel, though she understands their significance very differently.

Corelli's protagonist, Gaston Beauvais, resembles Dorian in his youth, wealth, manipulability and his steep moral decline in the middle and end of the novel. Though *Wormwood* is narrated by Gaston in the first person, he is not Corelli's mouthpiece, as she makes clear in her 'Introductory Note' to the novel. His is a type 'to be met with every day in Paris', Corelli writes, representative of 'the open atheism, heartlessness, flippancy, and flagrant immorality of the whole modern French school of thought' (*Wormwood*, 61). While Corelli is careful to distinguish her point of view from that of her protagonist, she nonetheless produces a novel that could easily be mistaken for a naturalist or decadent production, were it not for the occasional moral asides that remind the reader of her didactic purpose (MacLeod, 34, 36). She even requested that the cover of the novel be decorated in decadent motifs – 'an adder or serpent twisted through [a] big *W*' – against a background of pale green, the colour of absinthe as well as the colour Wilde popularised as the 'sign of a subtle artistic temperament' (quoted in Federico, 72). (Wilde himself was a noted *absintheur,* something Corelli may or may not have realised; MacLeod, 45.)

As a professed atheist and admirer of Zola, Gaston is given to scientific metaphors. Thus, after he learns of his fiancée's infidelity and begins drinking absinthe, Gaston dwells on its effects on the brain:

> When my brain was in its former condition before the *absinthe-furia* had penetrated to its every cell, it was like a group of sensitive fibres or cords which, when touched by memory, sentiment, affection, or any feeling whatsoever, would instantly respond in quick pulsations of eager and easy comprehension. Now, it seemed as if all those fibers had snapped" (*Wormwood*, 198).

In this passage, Corelli emphasises the neuron's permeability (to substances like absinthe, for instance) and interconnectivity with other cells by means of 'sensitive fibres or cords' that produce 'responsive vibrations' (*Wormwood*, 198). If Corelli intended the cell as a metonym for the self, as was the case with Wilde, then her protagonist seems to acknowledge the blurry boundaries of selfhood, especially in a chemically altered state of mind. Beauvais also implicitly recognises his interdependence with other characters in the novel and with human society more broadly, something Dorian typically refuses to acknowledge. From this passage alone, it is already clear that Corelli understood the brain cell quite differently from Wilde, who saw it as an isolated, unknowable – if beautiful – object.

Like Dorian, Gaston becomes increasingly unhinged as the narrative progresses and commits an escalating series of crimes. He murders his rival, Silvion Guidèl, the young priest-in-training who seduced his fiancée. He then drives his ex-fiancée, Pauline, to commit suicide by throwing herself into the Seine. Pauline's corpse ends up at the Paris morgue, where Gaston observes it for hours on end, justifying his actions in aesthetic terms: 'The girl, though dead, is beautiful! I am an artist – I have the soul of a poet!' (*Wormwood*, 339). These crimes are vaguely reminiscent of Dorian's, who murders artist Basil Hallward and whose cruel rejection of his actress fiancée, Sybil Vane, prompts her suicide.

While Dorian's drug of choice is opium, Gaston blames absinthe and its powerful action on the brain for his misdeeds. Gaston's second mention of brain cells occurs after Pauline's suicide, when he begins to hallucinate a green-eyed leopard that follows him through the streets of Paris: 'Let scientists explain this if they can, by learned dissertations on the nerve-connections between the spine and brain-cells, the fact remains that the impression created upon me of the actual palpable presence of the animal was distinct and terribly real' (*Wormwood*, 336). This offhand mention of brain cells once again emphasises connectivity; in this case the links between the brain, spine, and the motor and sensory neurons, a discovery of the early nineteenth century. Between 1811 and 1822, Sir Charles Bell and François Magendie independently discovered that the dorsal roots of the spinal cord transmit sensory information, whereas the ventral roots are motor, and that each connects to the brain, though whether the brain contained distinct sensory and motor areas was then uncertain (Finger, *Origins of Neuroscience*, 29). What eventually became known as the Bell-Magendie law demonstrates the interconnectedness of thought in the brain and motor action transmitted via nerves. Whereas Wilde underscores Dorian's detachment by viewing the brain cell in isolation, Corelli foregrounds the link between thought, action and (implicitly) responsibility for that action, even if Gaston denies culpability for his crimes.

The final mention of brain cells in *Wormwood* comes near the end of the novel, when Gaston becomes dangerously ill. His physician tells him that due to prolonged indulgence in absinthe, 'your brain cells are still heavily charged with poison, and a violent irritation has been set up in the nerve-tissues' (354). This irritation results in an 'irregular' and 'violently interrupted' flow of blood between the heart and brain that results in hallucinations and 'fits of delirium'. While one might question the doctor's medical logic, his remarks again underscore the permeability of the brain cell and the interconnectedness of different bodily systems. The physician also emphasises personal responsibility in the maintenance of bodily integrity, advising Gaston to abstain from his 'any sort of spiritous poison' – advice the protagonist predictably ignores (*Wormwood*, 355).

Critics have suggested that *Wormwood,* like George du Maurier's *Trilby* (1894) a few years later, is both a critique of decadence and a middle-class appropriation of this movement in which readers enjoy tantalising glimpses of a louche bohemian underworld (see Federico, 72–3 and MacLeod, 36–8). Yet Corelli emphatically refuses to follow Wilde's example of aestheticising or objectifying the brain cell. In *Wormwood,* the few mentions of brain cells gesture back to a traditional morality that is rooted in the body and compromised by sustained bodily damage, including decadent indulgence in mind-altering substances. Corelli uses neuroanatomical metaphors to remind us that bodies are fragile, permeable and connected to other bodies in ways that foreground personal responsibility. She thus holds true to her stated purpose of bringing together science (in this case, neuron doctrine), morality and religion in ways that consoled her world-weary readership, as described in the prologue to *A Romance of Two Worlds*: 'the light of Science must be brought to bear on the New Testament, in which its glorious pages will grow bright with hitherto unguessed mystical meanings' (10).

Corelli's understanding of the brain cell evolved in more occult and less orthodox directions in later works, including her most successful novel, *The Sorrows of Satan* (1895), often considered to be the first modern bestseller. The book was published six months after Wilde was convicted of gross indecency with other men; indeed, Corelli feared that the ongoing press surrounding the Wilde trials would interfere with her novel's sales.[29] Intriguingly, her work bears some resemblance to Wilde's; Federico describes *The Sorrows of Satan* as '*The Picture of Dorian Gray* meets *New Grub Street*' (83). Reviewer W.T. Stead, meanwhile, compared the novel to Milton's *Paradise Lost* (1667) because it makes a hero of Satan, who is more sympathetic than most of the human characters (Masters, 141).

The narrator is struggling novelist Geoffrey Tempest, an Oxford-educated classicist (like Wilde himself). Tempest suddenly inherits five million pounds on the same day that he meets mysterious Prince Lucio Rimânez, whose cynical *bon mots* recall Lord Henry but whose personal beauty rivals Dorian Gray. With Lucio's guidance, Tempest publishes his novel to glowing reviews and meets London's 'swagger' society. He embraces a hedonistic lifestyle, purchasing a landed estate, meeting the Prince of Wales, and marrying beautiful Lady Sybil Elton. The novel's climax occurs on Lucio's electric-powered yacht, where Rimânez reveals his true identity as Satan and forces Tempest to choose between himself and God. When Geoffrey chooses God, he is abandoned in the mid-Atlantic and rescued by a passing steamer. Tempest returns to England to find himself poor again, his fortune stolen by his bankers, while Lucio moves on to new targets.

Throughout the book, Corelli firmly positions herself against scientific materialism. Yet she includes a reference to cerebral localisation in Lucio's brief mention of brain cells and their occult significance. Lucio explains that bodily death is not the end of human existence, and that reincarnation is possible, due to 'the regeneration of atoms. The brain-cells are atoms, and within these, are other atoms called memories, curiously vital and marvellously prolific!' (Corelli, *The Sorrows of Satan*, 276). This passage misrepresents Cajal's neuron doctrine, which posited that nerve cells were separate entities, not that they possessed occult powers. But this example shows how Corelli creatively revised scientific ideas to bolster her Electric Creed. In *The Sorrows of Satan*, brain cells ensure the immortality of the soul by acting as storehouses of electricity, divine love and memories that somehow survive bodily death.

[29] Stephan Karschay, *Degeneration, Normativity, and the Gothic at the* Fin de Siècle (Basingstoke: Palgrave, 2015), p. 168.

A similar passage occurs in Corelli's 1892 novel *The Soul of Lilith*, the second instalment of the Heliobas trilogy in which she introduced her popular Electric Creed.[30] Middle Eastern scientist El-Râmi Zarânos explains to a doubting clergyman that 'the vibrations of the human brain, which like those emanation from the "brain of heaven" are full of light and fire . . . convey distinct impressions or patterns of thought'.[31] He speaks of the reality of 'thought-transference' or telepathy and adds that '*[a]ll* your past, every scene of it, is impressed in the curious little brain-particles that lie in their various cells' (Corelli, *The Soul of Lilith*, 34). Here, as in *The Sorrows of Satan*, Corelli imagines brain cells as containers of divine energies, memories and thoughts that may be transferred between cells or even between brains.

Corelli's references to brain cells in *The Sorrows of Satan* and *The Soul of Lilith* involve a mishmash of mainstream scientific theories, philosophy and occultism. The idea of the brain cell as storehouse of energy draws on mid-nineteenth-century neurasthenic logic in which conditions such as depression, insomnia, anxiety, migraines, etc. were attributed to a 'deficiency or lack of nerve force' in the body.[32] Physicians like George Beard, who invented the neurasthenia diagnosis in 1869, and Silas Weir Mitchell, who treated the condition with the infamous rest cure, applied electric charges to the body or head using a galvanic battery in the hopes of restoring the patient's depleted energies. These therapies, in turn, were based on neuroscientists' growing but imperfect awareness that nerve signals involved electricity in some form.[33] While the neurasthenia diagnosis and the rest cure were American inventions, both were brought to England in 1881 by gynaecologist

[30] Other works in this trilogy included *A Romance of Two Worlds* and *Ardath* (1889). All three feature a mystic sage named Heliobas as a major or minor character.

[31] Marie Corelli, *The Soul of Lilith* (New York: Lowell, Coryell and Co., 1892), p. 34.

[32] George Beard, *American Nervousness: Its Causes and Consequences* (New York: G.P. Putnam's Sons, 1881), p. vi.

[33] The electrophysiology of the neuron was not well understood until the mid-twentieth century, when the energy produced by neurons was found to be a byproduct of chemical reactions between ions of sodium, potassium, calcium, and chlorine (Shepherd 275–8). For further explanation of neurasthenic logic in Corelli's fiction, see also Stiles, *Popular Fiction and Brain Science*, 171–6.

William Smoult Playfair and used to treat Virginia Woolf, among others.[34]

Corelli's other sources may have included W.K. Clifford, a mathematician and philosopher who was 'one of the best advocates of scientific naturalism in the 1870s' before his career was cut short by tuberculosis in 1879.[35] Clifford's intellectually challenging theory of 'mind stuff' sparked the interest of Wilde, among others, and eventually trickled down to Spiritualist and occult circles. In his 1878 essay, 'On the Nature of Things-in-Themselves', Clifford proposed that our mental states are compounds of simpler states and feelings conjoined. He further argued that 'a moving molecule of inorganic matter does not possess mind, or consciousness, but it possesses a small piece of mind stuff . . . When matter takes the complex form of a living human brain, the corresponding mind-stuff takes the form of a human consciousness, having intelligence and volition'.[36] Other philosophers, including Herbert Spencer and Hippolyte Taine, argued along similar lines during the mid- to late-nineteenth century.

William James helpfully summarises these confusing arguments about 'mind stuff', 'mind atoms', or 'mind dust' in his 1890 text *Principles of Psychology*: 'each atom of the nebula . . . must have had an aboriginal atom of consciousness linked with it, and just as the material atoms have formed bodies and brains by massing themselves together, so the mental atoms, by an analogous process of aggregation, have fused into those larger consciousnesses which we know in ourselves and suppose to exist in our fellow animals.'[37] James was dubious of this theory, writing that it 'flies in the face of . . . logical intelligibility' (155). He felt that all mental phenomena could be explained using known facts about the brain, without recourse to so-called 'atoms of consciousness'. But proponents of the mind-stuff theory, especially philosophers

[34] Hilary Marland, '"Uterine Mischief": W.S. Playfair and his Neurasthenic Patients', in Marijke Gijsijt-Hoftstra and Roy Porter, eds, *Cultures of Neurasthenia from Beard to the First World War* (Amsterdam: Rodopi, 2001), pp. 117–39, p. 120.

[35] Roger Luckhurst, *The Invention of Telepathy, 1870–1901* (Oxford: Oxford University Press, 2002), p. 15.

[36] W.K. Clifford, 'On the Nature of Things-In-Themselves', *Mind* 3.9 (January 1878): 57–67, 65.

[37] William James, *The Principles of Psychology*, vol. 1 (New York: Henry Holt, 1890), p. 149.

and psychologists writing in the wake of Charles Darwin's *Origin of Species* (1859), found the concept helpful in explaining how the evolution of consciousness proceeded from single-celled organisms to higher animals such as human beings.

Theories of mind-stuff or mind atoms circulating in the mid-to-late nineteenth century also fascinated literary authors and unorthodox religious thinkers. For instance, Wilde and poet Constance Naden each wrote works in which atoms 'bear the kernels of consciousness' and are personified as thinking, feeling entities, as Benjamin Morgan explains.[38] Victorian Spiritualists and other heterodox believers, meanwhile, suggested that mind atoms could survive bodily death and facilitate telepathy, reincarnation or materialisation of spirit forms. Considering the 'theory of persistent mind-matter' in her 1893 book *The Philosophy of Individuality*, for instance, Unitarian minister Antoinette Brown Blackwell concluded that 'immortality for all conditioned being was the only logical conclusion'.[39] This roughly 500-page tome includes countless abstruse passages about atoms and atomic vibrations that allegedly prove that consciousness persists after death. Meanwhile, South-African-born mystic Laurence Oliphant argued in his book *Scientific Religion* (1887) that '[i]t is by this abnormal vibration of psychic atoms that most of the phenomena known as "telepathic" or psychic are produced – that wills are dominated, suggestions obeyed, trances induced, automatic writing and speaking are propelled through the medium, materialization ... displayed'.[40] (164) Blackwell and Oliphant are just two of many sources referencing mind atoms, psychic atoms or mind matter that surface in searches of the comprehensive online database, The International Association for the Preservation of Spiritualist and Occult Periodicals, which catalogues Spiritualist, Theosophical, and New Thought writing circulating in the late nineteenth and early twentieth centuries.

[38] Benjamin Morgan, *The Outward Mind: Materialist Aesthetics in Victorian Science and Literature* (Chicago: University of Chicago Press, 2017), pp. 146–7.

[39] Antoinette Brown Blackwell, *The Individuality of Consciousness* (New York: J.P. Putnam's Sons, 1893), p. iv.

[40] Laurence Oliphant, *Scientific Religion: or, Higher Possibilities of Life and Practice Through Operation of Natural Forces* (Edinburgh: William Blackwood and Sons, 1898), p. 164.

Corelli likely dabbled in these new religious movements, even if she sometimes presented herself to her reading public as an Orthodox Anglican.[41] This probably explains how she encountered occult discourses about mind atoms detectable in *The Soul of Lilith* and *The Sorrows of Satan*. Theories of mind-stuff, mind atoms, or mind dust appealed to Victorian spiritual seekers because they appeared scientific but were flexible enough to accommodate occult phenomena considered beyond the pale of science. Corelli took advantage of this flexibility to comfort world-weary readers distressed by the encroachment of science upon religious discourse.

The brain cell, much like the mind atom, was a poorly understood entity in the 1890s and thus open to a variety of interpretations and ideological uses. While Wilde saw brain cells as isolated objects of beauty consonant with his aesthetic world view, Corelli emphasised neurons' connectivity and, later, their occult potential as storehouses of energy and memory, including memories of past lives. Each author used this invisible particle to shore up his or her world view and imbue it with a veneer of scientific respectability. Each also used the brain cell – a very recent scientific discovery – to heighten contrast with the non-scientific elements of their belief systems (beauty, divinity, the immortality of the soul) and throw them into spectacular relief. In a few decades, better scientific understanding of brain cells would make such flights of fancy obsolete, but they live on in very different literary works of the 1890s and early twentieth century.[42]

[41] On whether Corelli should be considered primarily as an Anglican or as a proponent of new religious movements, see Mark Knight, 'The Limits of Orthodoxy in a Secular Age: The Strange Case of Marie Corelli', *Nineteenth-Century Literature* 73.3 (December 2018): 379–98.

[42] On early-twentieth-century mentions of brain cells in literature, see Chapter 5 of Stiles, *Popular Fiction and Brain Science*.

8

Vernon Lee: Empathy, Mnemic Engrams, and Satanic Aesthetics

Pamela K. Gilbert

This chapter will address Vernon Lee, born Violet Paget (1865–1935), as a theorist of physiological aesthetics, especially of the affects associated with aesthetic stimuli. It will then turn to her 1920 work, *Satan the Waster*. In this 'closet ballet', Lee both extends and reevaluates her earlier stance of the role of *Einfühlung*, most often translated as 'empathy', evaluating how positive affects can lead to immoral – indeed, 'Satanic' – results. This complex, nested ekphrasis includes Lee's mature ideas on aspects of affect, aesthetics and perception.[1]

Nineteenth-century theories of sympathy (different from, but related to later articulations of empathy) spring from a couple of sources.[2] In the eighteenth century, Scottish realists such as Thomas Reid theorised that people understand each other through 'sympathy', in which emotion is communicated through expressions made legible to all, by divine design: we feel, through imitation (or sometimes, contagion), what others feel when we see

[1] I would like to thank the Margaret Belcher Fellowship at the College of St. Hugh's, at the University of Oxford, for supporting this work and providing me with access to collections.

[2] Rae Greiner discusses the shift from sympathy to empathy in '1909: The Introduction of the Word "Empathy" into English', in Dino Franco Felluga, ed., *BRANCH: Britain, Representation and Nineteenth-Century History*, extension of *Romanticism and Victorianism on the Net* <https://branchcollective.org/?ps_articles=rae-greiner-1909-the-introduction-of-the-word-empathy-into-english>. See also Rae Greiner, *Sympathetic Realism in Nineteenth-Century British Fiction* (Baltimore: Johns Hopkins University Press, 2012), and Suzanne Keen, *Empathy and the Novel* (Oxford: Oxford University Press, 2007).

their emotional displays. This was retheorised, most famously by Adam Smith, to bring it firmly within the Enlightenment ideal of a sympathy that would be processed within an autonomous and reasonable individual. That individual would see another's emotion, imagine oneself in the place of the person expressing the emotion, and assess its appropriateness. This version of sympathy was imagined as profoundly pro-social: creating community bonds, regulating the emotions of outliers and promoting moral behaviour. By the mid- to late-nineteenth century, however, critiques of the moral value of such emotions as 'mere' sentimentalism were in the ascendant. Moreover, mid-Victorian evolutionary models of emotion accounted for some of these feelings in less benign ways. In art such as tragedy, psychological theorists such as Alexander Bain and Herbert Spencer suggested, readers or viewers atavistically exercise 'malevolence': 'any theory of the pleasure of tragedy that leaves out men's disinterested delight in the infliction of suffering is unequal to the explanation of the phenomenon', remarked Bain.[3]

By the 1880s and 1890s, psychologists were more interested in physiological versions of *Einfühlung*, such as Theodor Lipps's adaptation of Vischer's 1873 work to suggest that we experience art objects in our bodies, as muscular movement in imitation of their forms. He thus takes Hume's notion of sympathy as mirroring between humans and applies it to the aesthetic experience of inanimate objects, developing it this most fully in his 1903 *Äesthetik*.[4] Lee adopted and extended this definition in her work with Clementina Anstruther-Thomson in a formal aestheticism that suggested that the lines and heft of architecture, for example, were experienced physically in the observer's body, as Carolyn Burdett has detailed ('Subjective' np).[5] But in addition to aesthetics'

[3] Alexander Bain, *The Emotions and the Will*, 3rd edn (London: Longmans, Green and Co., 1875), p. 170.

[4] Theodor Lipps, 'Einfühlung, innere Nachahmung, und Organempfindungen', *Archiv für die gesammte Psychologie* 1 (1903): 185–204; *Äesthetik: Psycholgie des Schönen und der Kunst*, 2 vols (Hamburg and Leipzig: Voss, 1903, 1906).

[5] Carolyn Burdett, '"The subjective inside us can turn into the objective outside": Vernon Lee's Psychological Aesthetics', *19: Interdisciplinary Studies in the Long Nineteenth Century* 12 (2011) <www.19.bbk.ac.uk>. See Gustav Jahoda for full discussion of the German context of the move from Sympathy to Einfühlung, 'Theodor Lipps and the Shift from "Sympathy" to "Empathy"', *Journal of the History of the Behavioral Sciences* 41.2 (2005): 151–63, and

physiological moorings, an ethical element always interested Lee. In 'Anthropomorphic Aesthetics' Lee offers this initial discussion of *Einfühlung*: '"putting ourselves inside" the things to which we attribute modes of feeling and acting similar to ours . . . is . . . manifest throughout all poetry, where it borders on and overlaps moral and dramatic sympathy'.[6] Burdett writes of Lee's position in the latter decades of the nineteenth century, that Lee's concept of empathy opposed 'the trivialization and moral vacuity she feared characterized aestheticism. . . . Empathy . . . was a means of restoring a modern, scientifically validated moral role for art' (Burdett, 'Subjective', 3).[7] Most scholars agree, as Fraser Riddell says, that Lee's work from the mid-1880s onward connects aesthetic experiences directly to 'ethical capacities: our sense of duty to wider communities, our sensitivity to the feelings of others, our responsibility for careful reflection'.[8] This formal *Einfühlung*, then, had elements of what earlier theorists call sympathy, and Lee early on said it was analogous to, and later that it was a pre-condition for, sympathy. Still, the continuity of an ethical and a formal

Dan Zahavi, 'Empathy, Embodiment and Interpersonal Understanding: From Lipps to Schutz', *Inquiry* 53 (2010): 285–306, for the broader context of European thinking about empathy.

6 Lee and Clementina Anstruther-Thomson, *Beauty and Ugliness* (London: John Lane, 1912), p. 18. All citations here are from the reprint of the essay in the later collection, *Beauty and Ugliness* 1912.

7 Other critics have emphasised the ways in which Lee's ideas about empathy were important to her own relationships, especially with Anstruther-Thomson. Joseph Bristow, 'Vernon Lee's Art of Feeling', *Tulsa Studies in Women's Literature* 25.1 (Spring, 2006): 117–39, notes that Lee's writing 'suggests that the relation between art and feeling bears a strong (if not ineluctable) similarity to that of one friend entering into the emotional world of another' (134). See also Jill R. Ehnnen, 'On Art Objects and Women's Words: Ekphrasis in Vernon Lee (1887), Graham R. Tomson (1889), and Michael Field (1892)', *BRANCH: Britain, Representation, and Nineteenth-Century History* (2017), <www.branchcollective.org/?ps_articles=jill-r-ehnenn-on-art-objects-and-womens-words-ekphrasis-in-vernon-lee-1887-graham-r-tomson-1889-and-michael-field-1892>.

8 Fraser Riddell, '"Musical under the Touch of the Universe": Aesthetic Liberalism, Music, and Vernon Lee's Essayistic Art of Resonance', *Volupte: Interdisciplinary Journal of Decadence Studies* 5.2 (2023): 1–19, 3–4.

See also: Carolyn Burdett, 'Is Empathy the End of Sentimentality?' *Journal of Victorian Culture* 16. 2 (2011): 259–74; Jill R. Ehnnen, 'Haptic Ekphrasis', *Victorian Studies* 64.1 (2021): 88–114; and Kristin Mahoney, 'Ethics and Empathy in the Literary Criticism of Vernon Lee', *Nineteenth-Century Prose* 43.1–2 (2016): 193–210.

Einfühlung is never simple for Lee, as Rachel Baldacchino points out.[9] In 'Aesthetic Empathy' (1907), Lee clarifies that empathy is 'the beginning of sympathy'.[10] At first, however, 'attention is directed entirely to the feeling which one attributes to the other, and not at all to the imitation [in the self] of that . . . supposed feeling which is the act of sympathising (German *mitfühlen*)' (quoted in Baldacchino, p.55). Baldacchino also notes that this is the moment that Lee becomes dissatisfied with the German term and its English equivalent 'empathy'. By 1924, in *Art and Man*, Lee is even more insistent that aesthetic empathy primarily deals with the perceiver's mimicry and investment of the object with the perceiver's own memory and aims.[11]

Lee wanted to claim a moral value for aesthetic appreciation based not on sympathetic contact with another self through an artwork, but on current evolutionary ideas. Carolyn Burdett has traced Lee's use of Lipps to oppose both the aesthetes' rejection of moral value and the association of aesthetics with sexual selection or with Spencer's concept of play as a way of discharging nervous energy (Burdett, 'The Subjective' 8). Burdett shows that Lee wanted to attribute evolutionary benefits to the experience of beauty itself (1), and argues that Lee is influenced by Lipps's view of *Einfühlung* as enabling 'us [to] realize that we have selves and that other selves exist' (Burdett, 'The Subjective' 17).[12] The point of studying aesthetics, Lee suggests, is to discover the 'the evolutional reason' for pleasure in 'seemingly useless activities' (*Beauty and Ugliness* 73). But she also thought part of the evolutionary advantage of an aesthetic sense was due to the moral effect of art, rather than the amoral 'pleasure of Power, or Domination'

9 Rachel Baldacchino, 'Being in Borders: Empathy and Pacifism in the Essays of Vernon Lee (1900–1935)', PhD thesis (KU Leuven Faculty of Arts, 2018), pp. 55–6.

10 Vernon Lee, 'Aesthetic Empathy and its Organic Accompaniments', trans. R.L. Shields from the original French of Vernon Lee in the *Revue Philosophique*, lxiv (1907), in Vernon Lee and Clementina Anstruther-Thomson, *Beauty and Ugliness* (London: John Lane, 1912), pp. 45–76.

11 Lee (ed.), 'Introduction', in Clementina Anstruther-Thomson, *Art and Man: Essays & Fragments* (London: John Lane, 1924; Freeport, NY: Books for Libraries Press, 1924. Reprinted 1969).

12 See Susan Lanzoni, 'Practicing Psychology in the Art Gallery: Vernon Lee's Aesthetics of Empathy', *Journal of the History of the Behavioral Sciences* 45.4 (2009): 330–54, and Joseph Bristow for more on Lee's interest in evolution, and a discussion of Lee's productive combination of Lipps and Ribot.

(Bain 72), touted by mid-century evolutionary-psychological theorists as the aesthetic appeal of tragedy.

As Europe moved toward WWI, Lee was increasingly thinking about precisely this question. In 'Vicarious Tragedy' (1912), Lee responds to public conversation on the sinking of the Titanic, suggesting the 'dreadfully eighteenth-century' importance of sentimentality and sympathy as a corrective: 'Acute sensitiveness to the cruelty . . . of other men's fate . . . is . . . a powerful instrument for diminishing, however little, the world's mass of evil and ugliness'.[13] In addressing the less morally-savoury aspects of aesthetics, the taking of pleasure in representations of pain and violence, in her work on psychology, Lee turns to a different kind of formalism. Instead of the form of the perceived object in which her earlier work in *Beauty and Ugliness* had been most interested, these were the forms of feelings, emotional states encoded in individual bodies and memories that could be detached from a particular experience and activated later by different experiences, like empty moulds waiting to be filled. Lee's thinking about Memory-images, derived from Théodule Ribot, led her to a particular interpretation of this concept in Richard Semon's foundational *Mnemic Psychology*. In her wide-ranging 1923 introduction to this volume, Lee agrees that, for the transformation of sensations into perceptions, we rely on 'a nourishing matrix of engrams, left by previous sensations'.[14] Semon used the term 'engram' to describe a neural substrate for storing and regenerating memories; neurons that undergo persistent physical changes to become engrams. Engrams are activated after the initial formation of the memory by cues which might include, for example, smells, sounds, and so forth. These mnemic engrams give a form to affective memories, in the sense developed by Ribot as 'motor images' [*images motrices*] as opposed to sensory ones [*images sensibles*]. Lee accepts Ribot's claim that there can be a memory-image of past emotion, which new experiences can reactivate and through which they can be understood. These 'images', stored in the body's neuromuscular system, can have a formal structure related to 'motor sensations and their auditory representatives', as in music, but be relatively empty of

13 Lee, 'Vicarious Tragedy', *The Nation* XI (29 June 1912): 466–7, 467.

14 Lee, 'Introduction', in Richard Semon, *Mnemic Psychology*, trans. from the German by Bella Duffy (New York: Macmillan, 1923), pp. 11–53. (Rpt. London; Allen and Unwin, 1923), p. 20.

specific context for their emotional content (Lee, 'Introduction' to Semon, 29). That is, they are structured physically in changes to the body's neurological system, and they also structure the activation of emotion and memory in turn through neurological and muscular responses to new experience. Lee argues that music is able to evoke emotion because its 'emotional engram-complexes . . . have become so abstract' that they 'become identified with the musical pattern of notes' (29). She concludes that music's influence over emotion proves that 'emotional states can and do have mnemic images, free ideas of emotion, as reviviscible [sic] . . . as any other kind of schematic abstraction' (29). Lee suggests that emotional memory, in particular, tends to float free of specific events, becoming attached to other sense memories: anger might be induced, not by the specific memory of a particular action by a particular person, but by a random stimulus encoded at the same time, much as Semon's 'law of engraphy' suggested that stimuli simultaneous to the encoded event are encoded in the same engram-complex.[15] An engram, therefore, is roughly equivalent to a 'memory trace', encapsulating less a single detailed event than a series of connected sensations. Here, Lee also makes a key move in thinking about sympathy, attributing our understanding of others' emotions to 'mnemic storage and evocation of our own affective experience' (30). While she still acknowledges the eighteenth-century theory that sympathy is understood as emerging from our recognition of another's expression, here this is entirely based on the perceiver's own experiences, and may be detached from any actual recognition of another's feelings (30). Lee's thinking about music and memory engrams would become foundational for her later thinking on aesthetics and the moral role of emotions.

Throughout the 1890s and early twentieth century, Lee was continually thinking about the relationship of both music and writing to ethics, emotion and memory.[16] As time progresses, Lee gives increasing importance to the level of education and attention in the perceiver as central to the ethical potential of aesthesis.

15 R.W. Semon, *Mnemic Psychology* (London: G. Allen & Unwin, 1923) pp. 159–60.

16 Her work on music culminated in Lee and Clementina Anstruther-Thomson, *Music and Its Lovers: An Empirical Study of Emotional and Imaginative Responses to Music* (London: G. Allen & Unwin, 1932). See Martin for a discussion of how Henry Head's ideas about rhythm and 'schemata' influenced Lee's thinking about emotions.

By the time Lee is thinking through the activation of engrams in 1923, Lee distinguishes between 'unconscious sensory stimulation' and 'sensation', which is conscious, and refers the former to the 'mirroring function' Georges Sant-Paul discusses in the 1904 *Le Language Interieur et les Paraphasies* ('Introduction' *Mnemic Psychology* 43). It is these unconscious aspects of *Einfühlung*, specifically motor mirroring in the neuromuscular system of the perceiver, that structure engrams that can in turn be reactivated in quite different contexts. Increasingly, Lee becomes convinced this is what both music and literature can do. She also becomes more concerned about passive consumption of music, which might stir emotions and activate engrams in ways that the hearer does not fully understand.

Lee tends in her earlier writings to think of music as primarily emotional, but also, as many theorists of the time do, as more purely formal than representational art. In the 1890s, the figure of Wagner, who provoked polarised responses from critics everywhere, made Lee reflect on potentially problematic affective uses of music. Such music as Wagner's, she thought, by its difficulty, led to passive consumption or 'hearing' rather than active appreciation or 'listening'.[17] As Carlo Caballero puts it in his detailed study of Lee's response to Wagner, 'That Vernon Lee thought hearing inferior to listening is everywhere apparent'.[18] As with her judgement that sentimentalism has a moral role, she is drawn to the discipline and order associated with eighteenth-century 'classicism', such as Bach (Caballero 396). As this return to the eighteenth century suggests, by 1895, Lee was thinking of music and the social responsibility of the listener. Moreover, this is not simply a problem of individual morality or decadence: giving the example of Lee's 'Beauty and Sanity' (1895), Fraser Riddell shows

[17] For a detailed discussion of Lee's thinking about active and passive listening, evolution, physiology and music, especially with relation to Wundt, see Shafquat Towheed, '"Music is not Merely for Musicians": Vernon Lee's Musical Reading and Response', *The Yearbook of English Studies* 40.1/2 (2010): 273–94. See also Kristin Mahoney's 'Pacifism and Post-Victorian decadence: Vernon Lee at the Margins of the Twentieth Century', in *Literature and the Politics of Post-Victorian Decadence* (Cambridge: Cambridge University Press, 2015), pp. 57–84, for her changing ideas about music in the twentieth century.

[18] Carlo Caballero, '"A Wicked Voice": On Vernon Lee, Wagner, and the Effects of Music', *Victorian Studies* 35.4 (1992): 385–408, 395.

that Lee believes such music as Wagner's 'threatens the coherence of the social self' (Riddell 11).

Lee's critique of Wagner developed her own theories of attention and aesthetic expertise that still drew on modified eighteenth-century theories of sympathy as pro-social. Lee came to believe that the ethical benefits of aesthetics accrue when the perceiver is most actively engaged. But some forms of art discourage reasoned engagement. In Wagner's case, she distinguishes between the type of attention and appreciation a musician brings to bear and that of the average informed, but non-expert, listener. While Wagner's music is as complex as Bach's, it requires more expertise to appreciate it, and exhausts the inexpert hearer's ability to pay sustained attention.[19] Because Wagner frustrates the hearer's desire for forward movement and resolution, it obstructs 'constructive, . . . logical, activities demanding definite sequence and intelligible summing-up' (876). This hindrance of the logical process, combined with the continuous stimulation of nervous energy without discharge, leaves the hearer open to dangerous emotional suggestion.

Lee saw one element of Wagner as the most dangerous counter to his complexity; 'it contains extremely easy parts'. These are the 'leit motivs' which are easy to appreciate and recall: 'things which the least musical of mortals could not fail to grasp, and which acquire additional obviousness from their sudden emergence out of that welter of difficult music' (877). This drives the hearer to 'the inviolable stage of your own emotions, secretly haunted by the vague ghosts of your own past . . .' (877). The hearer has the flattering illusion of real engagement, when in fact the hearer is 'passive . . . safely imprisoned by the recurrence, the familiarity of those obvious and unforgetable little tunes, the Leitmotivs' (878–9). Though she does not discuss it in this review, her concern here with the leitmotif is clearly part of her consideration of engrams and emotional memory: the idea that a formal affective structure could be activated and amplified without any clear representational connection to a person, event or memory of anything beyond an emotion itself. The repetition of the leitmotif gives it a cumulative emotional force ingrained in the body itself, reactivated and strengthened with each repetition. Her concern with the potential of repetition to evade reason and revive (and pervert)

19 Lee, 'The Religious and Moral Status of Wagner', *The Fortnightly Review*, New Series, 89 (Jan–June 1911): 868–85, 875.

emotional structures would become increasingly important to her work on aesthetics in the period during and after WWII.

While still convinced in 1895 that, among the arts, music was the emotional manipulator par excellence ('Beauty' 137–8), Lee continued to explore the relation of words to music. Caballero notes that, in the same 1895 essay, Lee claims that lyric poetry differs from music, because words appeal to 'reason . . . We know the feeling, rather than feel it' (Lee, in Caballero 393). Here music is potentially more dangerous than poetry (Lee, in Caballero 393), but later Lee will increasingly emphasise the ethical dangers of words as having a more lasting impact than music, and subverting reason to the ends of emotion. Language, she argues in 1923, also can be understood through Ribot's elaboration of a term already in widespread use in the early 1890s, 'Images Motrices': words, she says, act as a 'skeleton . . . upon which the more unstable tissues of perceptions and their memory-images are held in place and articulated' ('Introduction' to Semon 38–39).[20] In short, she comes to believe that words, like music, can activate emotional memories in the same formal way, functioning as or provoking responses in engrams.

Lee thus came to believe that the author activates the reader's emotions in a process analogous in part to music. In *The Handling of Words* (1923), she writes, 'The Writer is really playing upon the contents of the Reader's mind, as the pianist, although his fingers touch only the keyboard, is really playing on the strings' which are 'the Reader's potential images and emotions'.[21] Though Lee emphasises that the ethical impact of literature depends at least in part on the qualities of readers' attentiveness, the desire to read is here intrinsically moral. It is a desire to revisit 'beneficent' emotions, which 'remake the soul's tissues' (Lee *Handling* 106). As a writer (and music lover), Lee wants to have it both ways; she worries about the dangers of aesthesis, and yet tries to find a way to save it. Kirsty Martin identifies the problem with Lee's idea of

[20] For a longer discussion of Lee's ideas about language, see Benjamin Morgan, 'Critical Empathy: Vernon Lee's Aesthetics and the Origins of Close Reading', *Victorian Studies* 55.1 (2012): 31–56, and a fuller discussion in Morgan, *The Outward Mind: Materialist Aesthetics in Victorian Science and Literature* (Chicago: University of Chicago Press, 2017); see also Mahoney, 'Ethics and Empathy'.

[21] Lee, *The Handling of Words and Other Studies in Literary Psychology* (London: John Lane, The Bodley Head, Ltd., 1923), p. 44.

intrinsic morality of reading, 'Lee implies that literature makes us think about life, and as such has moral value; on the other hand, she suggests that referring everything to our own life might make for a self-centred, appropriating attitude to art'.[22] I would add here that it is the quality and type of attention in the reader, as well as the nature of the writing that finally comes to determine the effect for Lee.

Given Lee's focus on art and form, it is unsurprising that, beyond her necessarily ekphrastic writings about art, ekphrasis was crucial within her fiction as well (as many have discussed: see, for example, Ehnnen and Burdett). And given her opinions on the particular ethical qualities inherent in fiction, it is unsurprising that a tension would arise between the uses of ekphrasis and the ethical intention of art. But this is perhaps most fully realised in her pacifist work, *The Ballet of the Nations* (1915), expanded and reissued as *Satan the Waster* (1920).[23] The first edition, which contained only the core of the piece, is already an extraordinary piece of ekphrasis: a closet ballet. The second iteration expands the treatment of the ballet, but also encapsulates it within an additional frame closet drama (the ballet remains as a ballet within a play) and finally wraps it in a great deal of essay commentary in the form of a 43-page introduction and a detailed section of 'notes' – essays written between 1916–19.[24] (The later 1930 reissue also

22 Kirsty Martin, *Modernism and the Rhythms of Sympathy: Vernon Lee, Virginia Woolf, D.H. Lawrence* (Oxford: Oxford University Press, 2013), pp. 64–5.

23 *The Ballet of the Nations: A Present-Day Morality Play* (New York: Putnam's Sons, 1915), unpaginated; *Satan the Waster: a Philosophic War Trilogy with Notes and Introduction*, (London: John Lane, 1920); reprinted with Preface added in 1930.

24 The work itself is hard to classify, as critics have noted, and *sui generis* among Lee's works (Beer 110). Patricia Pulham writes, 'The term "ballet" is no doubt intentionally ironic – Lee's ballet is a "dumb-show," a "danse macabre" that defies performance' ('Violence and the Pacifist Body in Vernon Lee's *The Ballet of Nations*. Conflict, Nationhood and Corporeality', in Petra Rau, ed., *Modern Literature: Bodies at War* (Palgrave Macmillan: 2010), pp. 46–63, p. 46). Drawing on Lee's own descriptions, Pulham compares it to both the medieval mystery play and the *auto-da-fé*, placing the body of Lee herself as an outspoken pacifist at the centre of the sacrificial structure (47). Lee calls her first ballet 'crude, emblematic' in the style of 'medieval masques' (*Satan* vii). She came to revise in part because she wanted to provide a more complex, 'prosaic human' explanation (vii), so she added the gramophone and cinematographic records of 'private realities' which show the multiple hidden

adds a short Preface by Lee in prescient dread of coming events.) The 'trilogy' redefines the central closet ballet as Part II, offering an opening Part with a conversation between theatre-manager Satan and Clio, Muse of History and Satan's 'sycophant', and a closing Part in which Satan shows Clio and the Ages-to-Come his collection of newsreels and recordings of the press coverage and statesmanship that led to the war – which they are unable to appreciate (66).

Sally Blackburn-Daniels has traced the provenance of the initial work, written at Whitsuntide in the first year of WWI, 'as an allegorical satire of the populistic and nationalistic attitudes pervading Europe at the time' and then performed by Lee as 'a spoken polemic' at Armfield's studio in Chelsea, and at the Margaret Morris theatre.[25] Lee was approached at the theatre by Chatto & Windus and G. P. Putnam and Sons, who asked to publish the text as a Christmas book with illustrations by Maxwell Armfield (Blackburn-Daniels). Lee disapproved of the prettified illustrations in the gift book, and *Satan the Waster: A trilogy* excises them, and adds the material detailed above. Most significantly for our purposes here, in the 1920 version, Lee begins to explicitly unpack the theme of how moral emotions and empathy become tools in the arsenal of Satan. In the 1920 introduction, Lee observes that the War has encouraged her to see certain things differently, specifically, emotions: 'I did not, in pre-war years, like thinking about Hatred, Self-Righteousness and Fear . . . least of all about the spuriousness and dangers of such fine things as Idealism, Pity and Indignation' (x). In this version, Lee both extends and reevaluates her earlier stance of the role of *Einfühlung* and ekphrasis, evaluating how positive affects can lead to 'Satanic' results.

In the ballet itself, 'Ballet-Master Death' supervises the dancers, who variously represent particular nations. The conceit of the work is as follows. Satan, who delights in wasting human virtue, regularly stages ballets, which are wars. The audience and orchestra consist of various emotions (the Widow Fear, for example) and other constituencies (science, for example), along with the Muse

origins of the war in the individual pursuits of various diplomats, journalists and so on. This is not tragic 'grandeur' (vii), but the tawdry human process of multiple individuals with their own aims contributing to an awful outcome.

[25] Sally Blackburn-Daniels, 'A Present-Day Morality for the Present Day', *19: Interdisciplinary Studies in the Long Nineteenth Century*, 30 (2020), <https://doi.org/10.16995/ntn.2931>.

of History and the Ages-to-Come. The orchestra is conducted by Death, the Miltonic son of Satan and Sin (although Satan specifies that his son is actually Horror, who has usurped Death's name). Satan begins the ballet by rousing the 'passions': each passion has its own instrument to play in the Orchestra of Patriotism.

In this nested ekphrasis, Lee meditates on aspects of affect, aesthetics and perception. The original *Ballet* was a closet production, to be read. The ekphrasis combines several elements: the staging of the frame drama, the appearance of the dancers, the ballet itself, and the music and musicians, as well as the media elements presented to the muse at the end. The muse, in conversation with Satan, describes the ballet. Regarding the expanded version, Lee emphasises in an initial note 'To the Reader', 'The whole of this drama is intended to be read, and especially read out loud, as *prose*; . . . And whatever rhythmical elements have been intentionally introduced, should be merely felt as . . . a timbre, of what is in other respects ordinary speech' (unpaginated frontispiece). Later, though the text offers several stage directions and set descriptions, Lee gives instructions in 'Author's Note for Stage Managers (Other Than Satan)', at the end of Part II:

> 'In the event of this play being performed, it is the author's imperative wish that no attempt be made at showing the Dancing of the Nations. The stage upon the stage must be turned in such a manner that nothing beyond the footlights, the Orchestra and auditorium shall be visible to the real spectators, only the changing illumination which accompanies the Ballet making its performance apparent. Similarly, in accordance with Satan's remarks . . ., none of the music must be audible, except the voice and drum of Heroism. Anything beyond this would necessarily be hideous, besides drowning or interrupting the dialogue' (57).

Her later remarks might suggest a softening on the staging of the frame drama, but reinscribe the unstageability of the ballet and unperformability of the music, and the importance of the words. And though those words are often ironic and polite, the Muse's description is occasionally vivid: nations 'dance upon stumps . . . a living jelly of blood and trampled flesh' on a stage covered with 'blood and mud and entrails' (51–2). Given Lee's insistence on physiological responses to art as not simply formal, but also ethical, what ethical response is possible under such mediated conditions? Lee suggests that such a response is perhaps more possible when our aesthetic perceptions are less directly engaged. In line with her later beliefs about emotional engrams, Lee suggests that even 'good' emotions can be activated in ways that have little to do with ethics – but which can *feel* as if they do. These are particularly susceptible of activation when responding to music or certain kinds of emotionally moving literature, or to visual beauty.

Lee's rejection of direct aesthetic perception of the 'ballet' is multifold. The first is her firm reiteration that this was a closet drama, not to be actually staged, the second is that it should be 'read out loud, as *prose*', not poetry. She avoids what might in the text itself seem musical. Though the musical instruments of the passions are identified, as are particular songs and composers, the music cannot be heard by the audience. Satan's framing reminds us that the words the Muse reads to us are a partial description. The audience is also denied all but a minimal description of some movements and the appearance of the characters.

In addition to the reader/audience's perceptual deficits, the text emphasises the inability of the players themselves to properly perceive what they are involved in. The Muse can only hear Heroism. We hear few of Heroism's words, though snatches of song are identified and narrated. The Muse tells us that his singing and drumming are monotonous. Heroism himself is blind, unable to see the drama of which he is a part. Through the mediation of the Muse, we can see described some of the dancers' actions, but not understand the music that motivates action. The stage prompter, Statecraft, is deaf. The musicians react to what is on the stage and the orchestral cues of Death/Horror. But at every level, ekphrasis is mediated not only by the fact of description rather than performance, but by Lee's emphasis on the unreliability and the imperfect sensoria of those who are relaying the description to us. The music, which is activating memory-engrams in the dancers and the audience of passions, remains unheard and undescribed.

As Gillian Beer puts it, Lee's 'satire chooses modes of representation that are "shallow", preoccupied with surface, that refuse the metaphors of profundity or "depth": masques, ballets'.[26] Lee denies us direct sensuous perception, offering instead an intellectual experience. The surface reflects back, leaving the reader to

26 Gillian Beer, 'The Dissidence of Vernon Lee: *Satan the Waster* and the Will to Believe', in Suzanne Raitt and Trudi Tate, eds, *Women's Fiction and the Great War* (Oxford: Clarendon Press, 1997), pp. 107–31, p. 124.

contemplate the role of their own emotions in the drama. Part of the intellectual experience is to consider the impact of the players' own inability to perceive properly. As Satan says, if Heroism could see his ballet master, or if the Muse could hear anything other than his singing and drumming, there would never be another ballet of nations (110). And, conversely, if the Muse and the Ages to Come were capable of properly understanding the sensory overload of the original, unedited gramophone and cinematographic materials showing the actual origins of the war, there would likewise be no tidy heroic narrative to continue enthusiasm for the hideous slaughter. Thus, audience-participants' proper perception of the war is impeded both by a tendency to aestheticise it based on faulty perceptual abilities (blindness, deafness), and an inability to understand its complexity without both aestheticizing and oversimplifying.[27] The dancer-nations themselves hear the music of the passions and fall into traditional patterns of patriotic feeling. Therefore, although they have sensory access to the music, they, too, are blinded by their own emotions.

Lee's remarks on Wagner are suggestive of her thinking about the orchestra of *Ballet*, and her choice to make the music of the cacophonous orchestra of patriotism largely unavailable to her audience. Lee invokes Wagner on at least four occasions: Satan describes the Muse as an 'ample-bosomed prima donna in a Wagner opera, but with the incomparable contralto, luscious but rolling, suitable to Handel', perhaps implying that the more measured qualities of Handel's music are put by Clio in the service of a narrative more appropriate to Wagner (5). He elaborates that his pleasure is in wasting human virtue to provide 'sublime effects', for 'one of . . . its Leit-Motivs, as Wagnerians say, is . . . the sweet and ardent loyalty of noble lads, ready to die themselves and kill other noble lads, lest dear comrades should have died in vain . . . And of such sacred, and much-needed virtue, I will make a vice' (11–12). An Ambassador persuades a king to go to war, 'by playing on the religious-romantic, the Wagner, stop' (87). Wagner thus comes to stand in for the unethical use of music to stir the passions to war, and the leitmotif is self-sacrifice, which Lee decries as the most dangerous of virtues. Lee also refers to the cacophonous

[27] Though elsewhere in her life and writing, Lee often rejects what we might today call ableism, in this text disability is used in its traditional allegorical form, with a negative valence.

Wagnerian dissidence of the music played by the passions. Satan instructs his players:

> As to the music, I need scarcely impress upon each of the Passions to keep strictly to his or her own part, and never be put out by the dissonances and conflicting rhythms produced by the contradictory parts of his fellow-performers: such incoherence conduces to the volume and impressiveness of the patriotic whole, and is rendered acceptable to the most fastidious ear by the perfection of the national unison and the constant recurrence of some favourite sentimental theme (42).

[– or leitmotif]. Here we see again reason lulled and the hearer returned upon emotions amplified by a combination of cacophony (or the sensory overload of 'Reality' shown in Act III), and the relief offered by deceptive, repetitive simplicity which gratifies the egotism of the hearer.

But Lee is not only suspicious of the emotional role of music here. While under the influence of the 'drum of unanimity' (280), the dancer-nations are influenced to do things they would not normally do. Yet Lee returns to her earlier reflections on Wagner to specify that real music only affects listeners while it plays: 'Once Wagner's insidious harmonies and diffluent melodies have died away, the audience returns to stock-broking, to chiffons and the practice of respectability' (*Satan* 135). Even if Wagner had some larger effect on listeners' behaviour, she points out, the narrative elements of story and scene, and 'above all, the words' may be at fault (136): 'The really dangerous part of literature is that, besides awakening passion, it justifies it' (136). Reading means that 'the justification, with its reasonable formulation, remains after the feeling has gone' (136). Literature, like music, may inspire heroic feelings – 'the longing to do and dare, to expand one's individuality, face danger, and incidentally, knock someone on the head, or wreck his furniture', but literature provides a pseudo-moral justification; music does not. Whereas before, Lee saw the writer's need to deal with ethics as a saving grace, now she worries that a writer uses 'ethical qualities for his aesthetic effects', and that morals, as part of 'Reality', should not be reduced to use for aesthetic purposes (136). Lee concludes that much literature does not seek 'restraint and lucidity' (137), because, in a telling musical comparison, these 'cannot compete with the facile, the brass-band or accordion, effects to be got out of heroism or the melting emotions' (137). Thus the final Wagner reference in *Satan* comes as Lee reflects upon the very different affordances of literature from music – yet conflates them. She writes that, whereas musicians are 'among mankind's greatest benefactors' because they both 'arouse and satisfy' emotions that are not connected to specific thoughts and therefore do not directly inspire actions, 'literature is a dual art . . . dealing in passion on the one hand and in reasons on the other; with the result, that . . . the reasons are the mere excuses for passion, and the means of giving passions a longer lease of life'. (135). Instead of seeing reason as the salutary mediator of emotions roused by literature, here literature is dangerous because it stirs emotions outlasting the aesthetic experience, and harnesses apparent reasonableness to its own aims. Lee acknowledges the change:

> This war, wherein words have played their part alongside high explosives and poison-gases—this war has made me think that since literature implies the readjustment (and consequent possible falsifying) of all emotional and imaginative values, it is a trade which can be decently plied only by people fully aware of these dangerous possibilities, and trained to recognize that, . . . it tends to turn us into the mouthpiece of our own and other folks' slovenly thought, inveterate prejudices and unrecognized semi-submerged passions (134).

The passions that provoke and continue the *Ballet* are not simply emotions of the moment, in the forms in which they are apparent in the play, but deep evolutionary structures, arising 'from obscure, changing yet undying, feelings, primordial and protean' (141). And these forms, these mnemic engrams that can be turned to multiple purposes, resist representation, as they have no easily recognisable traits, though they retain their evolutionary nature.

Satan the Waster is centrally concerned with emotions, and the actions they inspire. The 'passions' as they appear in the play are individually named and described, and it is their orchestral playing which fuels the dancer-nations. Once Fear and the other more primal passions are in place, Satan is able to attract the more elevated emotions, 'Lady Idealism and my young Prince Adventure . . . Idealism carried a silver trumpet and Adventure a woodland horn' (35). Such noble emotions are often mated with more negative ones: '"Here comes Hatred with Self-Righteousness", said Satan, nodding in the direction of a pair who pretended not to be acquainted, but were' (35). When the ballet seems likely to wind down, Satan turns to the resting virtues to bring fresh vigour to the dance:

> two . . . sat motionless . . .; their eyes fixed, their hearing intent, with horror so great it almost turned to pleasure. These two were called Pity and Indignation, sister and brother of divinest breed; she, wan like waters under moonlight and as gentle, murmurous and lovely, and also, like such waters, dangerous in her innocence. The other, golden and vivid as flame, and like flame, tipped with terrible scarlet, purifying but devastating (47).

This passage is worth parsing not only for its emphasis on the dangers of the 'virtuous' passions, especially indignation, which lies perilously close to self-righteous anger, rage and disgust, but for its emphasis on the way painful excitation of the virtuous emotions can become 'almost . . . pleasure'. Here, Lee's point is suggestive of earlier formulations by Bain and Spencer – formulations Lee had earlier decried – that the supposedly noble emotions roused by tragedy (or even earlier critiques of sentimentalism) might have more to do with the audience's self-gratulation and perhaps aggression than with true 'pity and terror', or sympathy for the principals. It is these siblings who revive the carnage. The Muse describes their 'horror almost pleasant in its excess' (55), Lee's second emphasis on how repulsion can be 'almost' enjoyed.

By framing the war as a dance both orchestrated and consumed by the passions as spectators *and* participants, Lee invokes a long tradition of writing about morality, emotion and aesthetics. Lee also asks the reader to consider how their most revered emotions may be turned to 'Satanic' purposes: pity is close to the morally-foundational emotional capacity for sympathy. But while close, it is not quite identical: as Lee insists in a note,

> It is her close kinship to Indignation which at times makes Pity dangerous. But for that flaming twin dragging her along on devastating pinions, Pity might transform into the very thing which Indignation dislikes most, namely Sympathy, itself in turn metamorphosing into Comprehension, and thence into True Justice . . . [which] sees, scrutinizes, and discriminates. Most often, as already hinted, Indignation drags Pity along, prevents that beneficent double transformation, and makes Pity pitiless' (*Satan* 287).

Satan praises the Justice's blindfold (39); Lee clarifies that real justice requires her full faculties to arrive at deep knowledge. Sympathy, she suggests, begins to combine feeling with the scrutiny of information and the exercise of reason to direct attention away from the emotion of the observer and toward the complex situation of the other. Formal empathy and its initial activation of engrams might begin to put the perceiver on the path to sympathy, but it is not in itself moral, and is easily led astray by a self-gratulatory pleasure in horror. Here we see the mature formulation of Lee's understanding of sympathy as something different from empathy, although depending on the same formal activation of memory-engrams as other emotional states.

The advent of the war and what seemed to many to be inexplicable forms of affective tribalism inspired a good deal of discussion of group psychology, returning to themes that had been less interesting to psychologists since the flurry of discussions of mob psychology that followed upon the French Revolution.[28] In *Satan*, Lee writes, 'I can see nothing better than myth-mongering and verbal confusion in current talk about a collective consciousness as if consciousness existed except in the individual' (281). Martin writes that Lee 'hints at an understanding of emotions and sympathy which might show how our feelings are shaped communally, [suggesting] . . . that our most individual feelings yet bear traces of our sympathetic involvement with others' (76), but that she stops short of seeing emotion 'as anything other than individualistic' (76). Martin notes this as a contradiction, but I read it as Lee arguing that the social element to our behaviours and feelings in groups does not negate the reliance of feelings on individual experience and engrams. Lee is at pains to distinguish between 'unanimity' (represented by the drum) and group psychology. For her, there is no merging of the individual with the group, what she

[28] Before the most well-known late nineteenth century works by Gustave Le Bon, (1895). *The Crowd: A Study of The Popular Mind* (New Jersey: Transaction Publishers, 1995), or Gabriel Tarde, (1890) *The Laws of Imitation* (London: General Books LLC, 2009), Charles Mackay wrote a less scientific treatment, *Extraordinary Popular Delusions and the Madness of Crowds* (London: Richard Bentley, 1841), and Carlyle explored the concept of the mob in *The French Revolution, A History* (London: James Fraser, 1837). For discussion of even earlier theories, see also Mary Fairclough *The Romantic Crowd: Sympathy, Controversy and Print Culture* (Cambridge: Cambridge University Press, 2013.

prefers to call the 'multitude' of individuals (*Satan* 282). However, the *psychology* of the multitude does differ from that of lone individuals: 'The multitude . . . has the intensity, the passion of the individual Ego, but instead of being subjected to vivifying criticism, . . . it is set apart in safe and enormous isolation' (284). She explains that this is why her drum of unanimity 'possesses only one note without overtones. Unanimity is not harmony, it is unison' (283). Heroism's drum offers a pleasurable feeling of being part of something larger that can lull the critical facility. Satan says, 'No other [music] has such imperious power over the nerves and muscles, and so little to say to the mind. For the drum knows neither intervals nor modes nor modulation, things requisite alike for music and rational existence' (49). One doesn't need some mystical fusing of individuals in a mass, when individuals' wishes to belong drive them to act in unison.

Many scholars, following Burdett's work, have detailed Lee's relationship to aestheticism: her sympathies with Pater combined with her determined rejection of art for art's sake. But Lee also desired to save the idea of the beautiful as intrinsically good, a holdover from much earlier periods of aesthetic reasoning, while embracing newer physiological understandings of the purposes and mechanisms of aesthetic perception. Under the pressure of the war, Lee is forced to confront the social and ethical role of aesthetics in a new way, one that attends to the moral limits of aesthetics. Martin sees Lee as conflicted in *The Ballet of the Nations*, which 'aims to repel sympathetic involvement on the part of the reader. . . . and . . . discourages sustained involvement' (Martin 69). Thus, Martin argues that 'Lee's literary practice never does truly do justice to her idea of empathy' (69). But I see Lee as coming here to a final understanding of both the dangers and the opportunities of empathy and sympathy – carefully distinguished – as she discusses in the note on Pity. Lee chooses a highly mediated ekphrastic form, and emphasises the characters' sensory limitations, to make the reader engage her words primarily through reason. She points to the dangers of 'feeling-in' without careful attention, both to the object, and to the emotions within the perceiver's self. She wants the perceiver to consider the emotional role of aesthesis through the mediation of analysis and of allegory. The dancers are not individuals to be sympathised with, but imaginary abstractions, stand-ins for the real individuals whose flesh and blood lies scattered over the stage. The allegorical frame of the morality play asks the reader to consider the abstractions in that light. In the closet drama, she eliminates the aesthesis of looking at individual dancers or the *mise en scène*, directing attention instead to the aesthesis of interpretation, the engagement of reason through words. Adding both the opening and closing with Satan and the Muse, and its modern equipment of the cinematograph, she directs our attention at narration and the dangers of words potentially misrepresenting reality. Clio is the verbal equivalent of Wagner, relieving the monotony of the drumming of unanimity with the leitmotif of self-sacrifice. Her narration lulls the hearer into returning to their own emotions, the appeals of nationalism, patriotism and belonging, instead of the sterner and more complex pleasures of analysis, contextualisation, and, yes, 'true sympathy'. Lee rejects her earlier faith in beauty as intrinsically moral, in favour of a wary conviction that aesthetics can be used to dark purposes.

Vernon Lee's long-term interest in physiological aesthetics led her from earlier, discredited notions of Smithian sympathy to a more formal understanding of Vischer's empathy, which challenged her desire to see beauty as intrinsically good, and aesthesis as inherently pro-social. But through her nuancing of sympathy, as Joseph Bristow notes, with Karl Groos's discussions of 'inner mimicry' as a physiological process and Titchener's focus on attention (133–4), she had already moved away from a concept of a natural or automatic aesthetic *Einfühlung* to the belief that different perceivers processed sensory information differently and that the quality of attention mattered to this process. This had already weakened the connection of aesthesis with morality, of the beautiful with the good, and Lee had replaced it with a notion of the adaptive value of beauty to the species. The war forced a reckoning that this concept could not survive undamaged. It was not enough for something to be aesthetically appealing for it to be morally good or pro-social; it had to be met with an educated level of attention and discernment. Moreover, the aesthetic, so far from being neutral, was actively dangerous in the hands of the wrong artist – or audience. This, too, gave the lie to the Victorian aesthetic movement's claim that art had no moral investments; good art, for Lee, had to be morally invested, lest it be used for ill.

Lee bridges the divide between Victorian – indeed, even classical conceptions of mind and body relationships – and modern ones. If she resisted both the amoralism of the aesthetes and the anti-ethical perspective on evolutionary science advanced by Bain and Spencer, she did so by appealing to the latest experimental science in psychology. Victorian literature taught readers to inhabit a particular psychology, to read the world through the lens of a particular theory of mind. The disruption posed by WWI was cataclysmic. Whereas earlier notions of evolutionary psychology suggested that 'dark' emotions might be engaged by the beauty of, say, stage tragedy, without incurring any moral burden, the war convinced Lee that aesthetic emotional appeals could inspire killing directly. Writers and visual artists disagreed strongly about whether the role of art was to seek beauty in opposition to wartime experiences, or conversely, whether art that failed to grapple with those horrors was illegitimate. In 1918, Tristan Tzara's 'Dada Manifesto' famously announced that 'beauty is dead', linking it to the subordination of the human individual to the mass in the war. Whereas her own predilections never departed significantly from classical ideals of visual beauty and the representation of form (versus post-war rejections of the beautiful by such post-expressionist artists as Otto Dix or Dadaists such as Marcel Duchamp or surrealists such as André Breton), her literary works suggest a move toward complexity and aesthetic distance to achieve the intellectual engagement she saw as essential to moral aesthesis. In her work with memory and emotion, she bridges the late-nineteenth-century interest in memory engrams and the 1920s interest in the activation of unconscious memories, and its inevitable connection to war trauma. Yet Lee never gives up on her desire to link aesthetics with a moral focus beyond the self. In *Proteus, or The Future of Intelligence* (1925), Lee praises the emergence of new understanding that reality that others do 'not exist merely to suit our likings' as a sign of intelligence and progress.[29] Gesturing to the dangers of past notions of immutable values, she argues that the present should do without 'Moral Beauty' in favour of 'decency', a morality based on duty to others and 'human usefulness' (39). In this way, she returns to the eighteenth-century notions of the pro-social roles of sympathy and beauty, while finally, reluctantly, relinquishing the grounding of sensuous beauty as eternal or innately good.

[29] Lee, *Proteus, or The Future of Intelligence* (London: Kegan Paul, Trench, Trubner and Co., 1925), pp. 14, 16.

Index

EU Authorised Representative:
Easy Access System Europe Mustamäe tee 50, 10621 Tallinn, Estonia
gpsr.requests@easproject.com

Printed and bound by CPI Group (UK) Ltd, Croydon, CR0 4YY
29/09/2026
02224981-0001